News Division

When more became less:
my experience in the 24-hour news world

News Division

When more became less: my experience in the 24-hour news world

Incorgnito
publishing press

Incorgnito Publishing Press
A division of Market Management Group, LLC
1651 Devonshire Lan
Sarasota, FL 34236
888-859-0792
Contact@incorgnitobooks.com

FIRST EDITION
Printed in the United States of America
ISBN: 978-1-944589-68-4
10 9 8 7 6 5 4 3 2 1

This book is dedicated to disciplined journalists everywhere. Those dutiful men and women whose enduring search for truth, without fear or favor, often in perilous situations, stirs awareness and contemplation.

News coverage by journalists, past and present, generates passionate debate and civil discourse. It elevates our societal consciousness. The deepening and interwoven complexities of an elaborate world demand that same ongoing coverage be fine-tuned, diligent, and omnipresent.

In the face of intense and often misguided skepticism and even cynicism, the courage to provide honest examination and determined reporting is increasingly valuable. Those entrusted with such a vital responsibility must know that their words, voices, endeavors, mettle, and their very presence are needed now more than ever.

Contents

FOREWORD

It's safe to say I am a confessed news junkie. That healthy affliction is the result of working in the business of news gathering for most of my adult life. "The News" is important to me. The information it regularly supplies me with is fundamental to the kind of up-to-date life I wish to live. I like knowing of the world around me; the world in which I live and the news fulfills that yearning.

The late TV executive Chet Collier enjoyed an illustrious career covering five decades in television entertainment and news, becoming a vice president at both CNBC and FOX News. He once said of the news business, "Viewers don't want to be informed; they want to feel informed."[1]

I want to BE informed. I want to know the information I receive is factual and reliable, and that the sources of the information are trustworthy and free from bias. But what was once a journalistic guarantee from our news providers has increasingly come into question. Our news world has been divided into

---

1   Chet Collier quoted in "Trust and the Competition Delusion." *Griffith Review*. Retrieved May 19, 2020 from https://www.griffithreview.com/articles/trust-competition-delusion-gruen/

segments and niches. The truth that was once a given is now anything but.

I wrote about my early years in network news in my first book, **NEWSREAL: A View Through the Lens When**. It's a memoir of the seven illuminating and gripping years during which I lived and worked abroad for NBC News. Over that time, I came of age in the golden age of international network news coverage when three powerful and trusted TV networks dominated the world of broadcast news. **NEWSREAL** concludes with the fall of Communism in Eastern Europe, a story which I covered. It was the last story I covered while based overseas, marking the end of my time as an ex-patriot.

Finality is not always just an end. The completion of that chapter in my life allowed for the beginning of another. This book is about the next chapter. The one undeniable theme that runs through both books, though, is my appetite for information, my need for news.

"The News" I grew up with and became a part of has undergone a great deal of change. Change in an advanced society like the one in which we live is inevitable and mostly the result of progress. For the news business, that progression has left an indelible mark on the way we receive, consume, interpret, and even believe our news.

I witnessed that change from within. The observations contained on these pages are drawn from stories that I covered. As the aforementioned news junkie, I felt fortunate to be working for "The News." To each news story I was assigned, I tried to bring with me experience, enthusiasm, and a sense of awareness—awareness of how both the individual story and the overall industry were developing. Some stories delivered a crushing sadness, and others, a feeling of exhilarating pride. There were some changes to my beloved news business that I questioned as alarming and others that I praised as inspiring.

During this time of change, a major shift came underway as each of the big-three networks was sold. CBS, NBC, and ABC were all acquired by new owners who had a new agenda for their news divisions. This new corporate ownership was accompanied by a greater corporate scrutiny of the bottom-line. The three broadcast news giants had always viewed the public's trust as their single biggest and most valuable investment; it was a trust forged and earned over decades. That old-school thinking became out of step with the new owners' focus on higher profits. To them, the news was simply a line item on a budget to be manipulated in the name of increasing profitability. News budgets tightened, jobs disappeared, and offices closed as financial accountability increased. From this viewpoint, long-established standards of broadcast journalism could be viewed as laborious, costly, or even competing with profitability.

The fast-paced news business sped up. The 24-hour news cycle was introduced, then emulated... and then found everywhere. A business already driven by deadlines became obsessed with hourly updates. In this constant and expedited war against time, "The News" suffered casualties. In our hurried-up world, accuracy was accompanied with inaccuracies, lead stories sometimes became misleading, and the unbiased became boring. With so much airtime to fill, the job of reporting eased and allowed for analysis. The once clear and impenetrable separation between fact-based journalism and opinion was demolished like the Berlin Wall. Now, educated opinions can be helpful, entertaining, and worthwhile. But it's a dangerous development when opinion is dressed up like "The News" and masquerades as the truth.

News is now everywhere. We need to look no further than the phone in our hand for the latest breaking story. Yet, I hesitate to place my undying trust in a source of information that is so unregulated, anonymous, and at times misinformed as the internet.

My zeal for the news does not make me a zealot. I recognize that my heightened interest in "The News" is the result of a news career that spanned four decades and covered five continents. I was fortunate (or perhaps cursed) in this, and have never expected others to share my level of interest in "The News." But it's because of that enriched perspective that I felt compelled to write this book and share my experiences. And, especially now. "The News" is under attack. Some of that is well deserved, and some of it self-inflicted. But look closer, beyond the generalizations about fake news and the news media.

Today, the search for truth through information is very much alive and every bit as important as it has always been. It's important that we ARE informed. For, if we are the most powerful nation on Earth, we owe it to each other and the rest of the world to be the most well-informed nation on Earth.

1

HOMELAND RETURN

I could not have felt more alien. I was a foreigner in my own county. A stranger at home. After seven years of living and working abroad, I was finally back in Chicago... and lost.

Where I had previously felt most at home would feel foreign to most people. Prior to Chicago, I had circled the globe for seven years while covering news for NBC. In the process, I'd acquired experience and collected war stories of my own. I'd seen first-hand the power and impact of journalism, and the many ways society benefits when a free press is combined with a strong and responsible platform like NBC News. I'd made lasting friend-ships with people of many nationalities, and I'd cultivated my contemplative perspective of the world in which we live. While living abroad, I had also made numerous business trips, visits, and vacations back to the states. Now, I wanted to bring my in-ternational work experience home with me and apply it to the domestic network market. And, finally, I was back on U.S. soil as an official U.S. resident once again.

It was a brave new world to me—a clean slate, and different from the life I had lived for most of the previous decade. As I contemplated my future, the anticipation was exciting. But, deep down, the uncertainty of it all was far more frightening than exciting. To compound my dilemma, I was the sole architect of my current situation. My return was not the result of my being fired or the closing of the Rome bureau (that would occur five years later). My bosses, from New York to London to Rome, had been pleased with my work and would have been happy for me to stay put. My homecoming was all my own doing. It had been entirely my choice to relocate to Chicago, the place where I had last resided before my European promotion.

I had lived a whirlwind of international news coverage. To say I needed a change would be like saying America needs to go on a diet. I had convinced myself and my bosses at NBC News that my bucket list of news coverage and life experiences had overflowed. I'd traveled to over 40 countries on four continents. Travel was part of the job and it had been a labor of love, but then again, too much of a good thing—even love—can be exhausting. My labor of love had become laborious, and I'd long since begun to quietly long for Americana, things like baseball games and 4th of July fireworks.

My determination to return stateside was not a frivolous whim. When I voiced my intentions, my immediate bosses back in New York were initially surprised. Eventually, they processed that, well, seven years was a long time to be gone, but they were hesitant to guarantee me staff employment in Chicago. They asked how I'd feel about living in Los Angeles, New York, or Miami, where openings were more likely at the time.

What I'd failed to share with them was that I had a master plan, and a change in scenery was only a portion of that plan.

There were major career implications that had weighed on my decision. Up to this point, I had worked as a staff cameraman for NBC News. As a staffer, I'd received a salary every week. If I worked "eight days a week" (Lennon/McCartney), I was paid the same as if I worked zero days a week (which was rare, as international news was a priority back then). Additionally, I received insurance benefits, retirement contributions, a housing allowance, expense account reimbursements, and other perks. It was an enviable and coveted job.

But while working as a staffer in the foreign press corps, I had also met and worked alongside "freelancers" in the same foreign press corps. This was a discovery for me; a previously unheard-of job title.

In today's "gig economy" where the independent contractor is the norm, freelancing is commonplace. But back in the 1980s, it was a relatively new concept. The norm was to work for a single company throughout your entire life. After which you'd revive a gold watch and a nice pension, and ride off into the sunset of retirement. A number of my NBC friends did just that, too, and when I was first hired, that seemed like a dream trajectory. But I am sometimes easily distracted.

From the outset, I was quietly intrigued by the concept of freelancing. To be certain, the freelancers with whom I worked envied me and the prestige and security that accompanied a staff position with a company like NBC News. Freelance cameramen (I should say "camera people" since there were a handful of female cameramen) were paid a wage similar to mine... when they worked, but if it was a "slow news day" with nothing to cover or report, freelancers weren't earning an income while I was still paid my staff salary. And, many of my freelancing colleagues chose that path out of necessity, as there simply weren't enough staff positions like the one I occupied for everyone.

As I began to better understand the concept, though, I realized freelancing wasn't just a career that only offered less.

It was a job where diversity, flexibility, growth, and expansion could be realized—IF you could handle the uncertainty of the next gig.

While I'd been overseas, most of the European freelancer crews (consisting of a cameraman and a soundman) I'd encountered had been London-based, where both American and English networks had massive bureaus. The smart and successful crews had cultivated relationships with all of the news networks, regardless of nationality. To cover news on a daily basis, those networks would always use a staff team of correspondent, producer, and crew. Frequently, the demands of news coverage were greater than the supply of staff people available. It was rare for networks to employ a freelance reporter, as that was the face seen on TV, the face of the network, and the face reporting and responsible for the facts. Freelance producers were occasionally employed, but freelance crew were more commonly employed, and for a simple reason. Television is a visual medium, with the most basic elements, the foundation, being pictures and sound. Devoid of a correspondent and producer, a crew can still get pictures and sound. The converse is impossible.

Me being a former cameraman, it might sound biased for me to say crews are the most valuable component. A more accurate and objective observation would be to say that crews are more necessary than any other component. As a result, as news coverage overseas expanded during the 80s, so did the use of freelancer crews.

This growing need afforded crews professional diversity. For instance, while on assignment for NBC covering the war in Lebanon, I saw a familiar freelance crew working for CBS. A few months later, while covering the West German elections in

Bonn, I bumped into the same crew working for the BBC. After that, I ran into them covering a Papal visit through Africa and they were in the employ of ABC. The smart ones with numerous clients seemed to be omnipresent. While I was dedicated to NBC, they were dedicated to all of network news—and, of course, to themselves.

Their interactions with many different networks allowed them, or more accurately *forced* them, to grow professionally. I had one boss, whereas freelancers had many bosses and knew many decision-makers. I understood the structure of my network. They understood the structure and nuances of many networks, which provided them a better overall image of the big picture of network news coverage.

Beyond the broader understanding that networking among the many networks could provide, I also realized there was a financial reward being reaped by successful freelancer cameramen.

As a staff cameraman, I was paid a wage by NBC. Freelancers were paid a similar wage. That network daily or weekly rate was pretty much set by the networks and it was comparable for both permanent and part-time employees. As mentioned, though, my salary was paid 365 days a year, and theirs was not. However, the camera equipment I operated as part of my staff job was purchased and owned by NBC, not me.

In the entrepreneurial freelance world, freelance cameramen purchased their state-of-the-art, tailor-made camera and sound equipment. Sophisticated professional video cameras are expensive electronic devices, and by 1990 they cost in the vicinity of $50,000 - $60,000. Combined with all of the support equipment required, such as lenses, monitors, tripods, lighting equipment, etc., the total outlay for a freelance cameraman could easily exceed $100,000. This represented a significant start-up investment and was vastly different from, say, a freelance writer buying a $1,000 laptop or a freelance photographer buying a $2,000 still camera.

No small businessman in his right mind would make that sort of investment without some means of compensation. The networks realized this and justified compensating the freelancers through budgetary maneuvering; it's like leasing your car versus buying it. Every freelance crew (complete with gear) that they hired was one less $100,000 investment they, the network, had to make in expensive equipment. It was a budgetary shell game. That $100,000 purchase could be shifted and spread out over time as a lease expense... on some other budget.

For each day a freelancer was hired by a network, the network or "client" would pay the freelancer to rent or lease their gear. A busy crew could recoup their initial capital investment in equipment within four to five months, with the remainder of the year being pure profit... year after year.

As an "envied" staff cameraman, I had one income stream—my salary. Freelancers had two income streams, their salaries as cameramen AND the income generated by the rental of their camera and audio gear. So, the freelancer was getting paid twice, double-dipping... on those days they were hired. The more they worked, the more they earned.

While the networks owned most of the equipment they needed to broadcast television news from around the world, this equipment rental niche was quietly growing and expanding into other areas. Entrepreneurial freelancers with the right connections and wherewithal were leasing portable editing equipment and mobile satellite uplink facilities, sending them into war-torn or remote locations. They assumed both the headaches and the risk. In return, the networks were only too happy to handsomely compensate the risk-takers and, in the process, open the door for further freelance expansion.

In today's world, where everything from server farms to supply chains is outsourced, this business approach seems pretty normal. But, at that time, it was reshaping the broadcast news business and very eye-opening.

And there were still other appealing aspects of freelancing that didn't appear in any financial equation.

The relationship with NBC that I'd chosen to dissolve had been cultivated over a decade, making that decision even more tormenting. In Dayton, Ohio, I had worked for an NBC affiliate, WKEF-TV, straight out of college. I had then moved to Chicago to work for WMAQ-TV, one of seven stations owned by NBC. It had been NBC News that later hired me and moved me to Europe. What I'd had with NBC had always been a fruitful, nurturing environment that allowed me to grow. It had been a monogamous relationship in that I had known no other network.

The freelancers I'd encountered overseas "whored" themselves out to anyone who would hire them. Compared to my valued and singular NBC relationship, that kind of temporary connection should've looked devalued or even cheap. But it didn't. Instead, it intrigued me. I secretly envied them for the relationships they'd built with ABC, CBS, CNN, the BBC, and others. I had competed with and worked alongside colleagues from the other networks, oftentimes socializing with them after the story. We all did the same job covering the news. But the inner workings, the idiosyncrasies of each network, were different, guardedly shrouded from each other. My intellectual curiosity wanted to know what it was like to work for ABC, CBS, CNN, etc.

The networks were beginning to see the wisdom of paying freelancers for the added expense of equipment rental because it saved them the upfront costs of buying extra cameras. They liked paying for labor only when they needed it. And, they liked saving on expenses like employee insurance benefits and pension contributions, especially for foreign-based workers. This freelance phenomenon was a growing market in Europe, and I was hoping it would eventually repeat itself in the U.S.

But I had been gone for so long, it had been difficult to gauge the support (or lack thereof) for freelancing in America... all from my vantage point in Europe. That was something I would learn, perhaps the hard way, once I was home.

And, there was one more career element that added to both the excitement and anxiety I felt about my return. I surreptitiously desired to do more storytelling beyond the camera. On each assignment I had as an NBC cameraman, my network job was finished once I handed over the videocassette to the producer, correspondent, and/or editor. They were responsible for combining our pictures and sounds with the written word to create an accurate, cohesive, and hopefully compelling story. I knew it was a quantum leap to go from photojournalist to storyteller, but that didn't stop me from fantasizing. In that dreamscape world, I romanticized about perhaps, someday, writing, producing... and storytelling.

Full disclosure here: In today's budget-conscience, do-more-with-less news environment, cameramen are urged to simultaneously take on multiple roles in the field. It is not uncommon for a cameraman to shoot the story, transfer the material to a laptop and then edit the story, after which he or she will finally transmit the story back to the bureau via wi-fi. Technology has partially allowed for the blending of these roles. But a focus on the bottom line is the true driver of this amalgamation of jobs. Something gets lost in saddling a single person with so many duties, regardless of what the current technology might allow for.

In the cosmos of news in 1990, however, a cameraman specialized in shooting, an editor specialized in editing, and a producer and correspondent specialized in writing. I may have harbored a desire to transition between the three roles, but it was an expedition rarely undertaken inside of a network. I just wondered if freelancing might be the vehicle to take me there.

My master plan was to, first and foremost, bring home my foreign network news understanding and travel knowledge, and apply it to domestic stories at home. I knew, or at least hoped, that the tenants of journalism I'd learned while working overseas would serve me well wherever I was based. At the same time, I wanted to expand my news horizons and experience the diversity of working for other networks. I wanted to invest in myself through the purchase of my expensive camera equipment. And I wanted to take on more challenging roles beyond the camera—roles that could compliment my cameraman's eye by developing my storytelling ability. Yet....

As I stood on the ground in Chicago as a newly arrived expat, reality set in. There was so much to do. I needed to set up a company. Incorporate that company. Insure that company. Capitalize that company by ordering and purchasing equipment. Secure office space for the company and equipment. Purchase and insure transportation. Design logos and print letterhead and stationery. It all seemed like lofty aspirations for a guy without a camera, client, or even a business card. Any thrill I may have felt before was overcome by angst. I didn't know what I didn't know. I couldn't have foreseen the hurdles in my path until I was back home and staring down that career path, that unknown and unfamiliar path. As I re-examined my master plan, words like *premature*, *ill-advised*, and *doomed* crept into my vocabulary. What if I set up my company... and the phone never rang?

For directional guidance, I called my NBC New York colleagues on the foreign desk, the people with whom I'd worked when I'd been part of the foreign press corps. I had consulted them when I'd just been beginning to toy with a move back home. They had assured me that, for a cameraman with my resume, the move from Rome to Chicago, from staff to freelancer, would not pose a problem. In other words, they had told me what I wanted to hear, and I had listened.

I was no longer toying with the move, though. The move had been completed. I was anxious to get busy again, but they were already busy covering the foreign news because, well, that was their job. It HAD been mine, too, before I'd chosen to leave the network. Which made me a FORMER colleague. And, because their expertise specialized in everything outside of the U.S., they were at a loss as to how they could guide a former international staff cameraman through a domestic freelance maze. Their advice that my move "would not pose a problem" was still very supportive, just a lot less useful.

This was a dilemma I'd only seen from a foreign perspective or from the outside looking in. I was now on the inside, or at least inside America. At all networks, there was and is a clear division between international news and domestic news. Before I could attempt to bridge that gap, I'd need to better understand the structure of my own... correction, my *former* network. And within that structure, because of the separation between the foreign and domestic news divisions, one could be a rockstar on the international scene and an unknown nobody domestically.

As for the other networks, I didn't even know who answered the phones at ABC, CBS, and CNN. Overcoming those obstacles loomed like Mt. Everest. I'd been a cameraman for over a decade, most of it spent at a network news organization. I'd honed my craft and circled the globe in building an impressive resume. And now, like every other unknown nobody, I'd be cold-calling potential clients and knocking on doors in the hopes of obtaining an introductory interview.

"Hi, my name is Tim Ortman. I've just returned from Europe after seven years of international network news coverage. I was wondering if I could schedule a time to introduce myself to your bureau chief and discuss any freelance cameraman opportunities at your network."

"Who?"

Connecting the dots of my master plan looked more like solving a Rubik's Cube.

The good news was that I had a place to live. I owned a beautiful condo on Lincoln Park with a view of Lake Michigan. It was ready and waiting for me. The bad news was that it was empty. Uninhabitable.

Instead of using "air freight," NBC choose to ship my personal belongings via "surface freight," meaning on a slow boat from Italy. This was a corporate decision that could only be described as penny-wise and pound-foolish. It was all about the dollars and cents, except this decision made no sense. What the NBC accountants had failed to calculate was the inefficiency of the Italian moving and shipping industry. My furniture, along with everything else I owned, was somewhere between my apartment in Rome and who knows where. And some of those belongings were pretty valuable, as far as I was concerned. Part of the "everything else I owned" was a small but budding wine collection I'd started while living in Europe. Based on winery visits in Germany, France, and Italy, I was just beginning to make sense of the confounding wine world and had set aside a few cases of things I liked. It was an enlightening start to a growing passion, and I did not appreciate being kept in the dark regarding the whereabouts of those bottles along with everything else I had to my name. I could not get a straight answer.

But, thanks to NBC's relocation services, until my belongings arrived, my temporary home would be the brand new and opulent Four Seasons Hotel situated on the "Magnificent Mile"—or, North Michigan Avenue. It was the ritziest, glitziest, most expensive real estate in Chicago, smack-dab in the heart of everything. As an added plus, all my living expenses (like per diem, laundry, and telephone charges) were covered by expense account. Whatever amount NBC saved by shipping my things "surface" versus "air" was spent ten-fold on my five-star relocation package.

Governmental ineptitude in Italy dates back to the emperors. After weeks of administrative delays, my belongings were finally identified and cleared by Italian customs for export to the U.S. It would then take a second eternity for them to go bobbing up and down across the Atlantic before eventually coming to rest on a New York dock and then being trucked to Chicago. By that time, I'd be on a first-name basis with most of the hotel staff who graciously assisted me with my every expensive need.

Through my FORMER network salary, I had saved up a nice sum to more than cover the equipment purchases and start-up costs associated with my new venture. Soon, the camera, lenses, lights, microphones, tripods, batteries, and extended ancillary equipment I had ordered would begin to arrive and I would have my very own camera package, making me officially available for hire. The Four Seasons was a wonderful place to call home, but it would not make for a wonderful office for equipment storage. Because of size limitations, my one-bedroom condo on the park wasn't a perfect fit, either. I needed to officially set up shop.

But where? I didn't know the various Chicago neighborhoods, and the downtown area where I lived was rapidly redeveloping. Real estate prices and rents were skyrocketing. I could ill-afford signing a bad lease, but I needed office space in a hurry. For advice, I turned to an old NBC friend.

Randy Birch had been a famous fixture on the NBC News scene for decades. To many, he was known simply as Birch, like the tree. His exact age was a mystery to all, and while it was never directly discussed or known for certain, I had always guessed he was about 20 years my senior. He was renowned for his camera skills, appearance, and wardrobe, which were all equally impeccable. It was debatable (and frequently debated) which one was his most impressive attribute. His 6-foot-2 frame, square jaw, and model-like looks were the perfect canvas for his permanently perfect tan, which in Chicago was no small feat. There was never a perfectly coifed blonde hair out of place, his stylish attire was always changing while remaining in vogue.

He was known to have covered Kansas tornados and Iowa floods dressed entirely in soft pastel colors, with a white Ralph Lauren cashmere sweater draped over his shoulders and tied loosely around his neck. After hours of shooting in the aftermath of natural disasters, he'd emerge from the debris and muck just as creased and clean as when he'd begun the day.

Randy was a second-generation cameraman, having inherited his talent from his famous father, Bill Birch. Bill had made his name as a news cameraman in the 50s and 60s before becoming a Chicago-based cinematographer for Hollywood films.

I met Bill shortly after my initial move to Chicago. I had studied cinematography in college and was always intrigued by film's more artistic allure, over the immediacy of video. At 23 and new to Chicago, I sheepishly approached Bill and asked if I might "walk in his shadow" to continue to learn and understand the film business. While not promising me employment, he graciously agreed to "show me the ropes" of the Chicago film and movie business. Soon after that, though, the sudden offer to join NBC News as a staff network cameraman and relocate to Europe was too good to pass up, so I very graciously said goodbye to both Bill and my dream of ever working in the film industry.

But now I was back, and my return brought with it numerous questions.

I had heard from folks in New York that Randy, like me, had left the network to pursue the path of a freelance cameraman. Having always worked domestically, he'd had a built-in client in NBC News Chicago. I was hoping to someday achieve the same, but the more pressing issue was office space. I called him to pick his brain. He was glad to hear I was back in Chicago and happy to discuss the freelance news market. He suggested we meet at his favorite Thai restaurant for lunch to get caught up.

I arrived early and he was 45 minutes late, looking like an aging male model who'd just walked off the runway.

"Sorry I'm late. A morning production meeting ran late. This whole freelance thing is exploding. I'm used to having only one client—NBC. And now everybody's calling me, and... anyway, when did you get back in town... or, I mean, back in the country?

"Good to see you. I've been back a couple of weeks, just getting my feet on the ground really. You're looking good. And it's good to hear that freelancing is working out for you. I can't wait to hear more." My competitive spirit and total lack of clients caused a growing envy within me. But I didn't want my insecurity to dominate and control our conversation, so I pressed ahead with my questions. "So, now that you're not working out of the NBC Bureau, are you working out of your home?"

"No, I live way north of the city. It's not too far from O'Hare (International Airport), so it works when we have to fly out to cover stories. But, for day to day work, it's just too far from the city. I wanted to be closer to the network bureaus and offices of my clients. So, I'm leasing out some of my dad's space. He has an enormous loft in a great location and only uses a portion of it. What were you thinking of doing? Where are you living?"

"I'm staying at the Four Seasons—thank you very much, NBC. But once my personal belongings arrive from Rome, and who knows when that'll be... I'll move into my condo on Lincoln Park. It's a great location, but it doesn't work as an office space. So, I'm looking."

"Let me talk to my dad. When I say it's an enormous space, I really mean it. There's plenty of room for you. We wouldn't even know you're there."

"Where is it?"

"Navy Pier. The city has changed a lot since you left. If you remember, Navy Pier used to be an old abandoned and dilapidated waterfront. And now the whole place is undergoing a total redevelopment. Everything north and east of downtown is on fire. It's all either being rehabbed or has already undergone a rehab. My dad bought into an old five-story loft building a block off Lake Michigan; totally redone. It has everything—new elevators, high ceilings, a great loading dock which is perfect for loading and unloading our gear. It even has a doorman. It's not that he needs the money, but I'm sure my dad would welcome the added income. And, it's not like he doesn't know who you are. You guys hit it off before your move to Europe."

I was dumbfounded. I'd been hoping to maybe get a recommendation for an affordable part of town to explore or an introduction to a reputable realtor. I'd never envisioned leaving this lunch with an actual space, already up and running. We continued to talk about the possibility of being co-tenants as we slurped up Panang Curry and noshed on Pad Thai.

Once consulted, Randy's father Bill thought it was a good idea, too, and with a handshake deal, I had a desk to call my own. It was a huge space, complete with 100-year-old iron support columns throughout the floorplan. One entire wall was made up of floor to ceiling windows that looked out onto the lake. A majority of space was dedicated to Bill's film and television "museum"; this entailed a vast collection of film cameras and equipment with which he had worked for over 50 years. The walls were adorned with movie posters, vintage photographs, and political campaign ads. We each had our workspace, and there was a series of large metal storage cabinets where all of our pricey equipment could be securely stored. And, as advertised, the doorman was a perfect finishing touch. Michel was the quintessential cheery, polite, and ever-present Irish doorman. From his gold-braided blue cap to his spit-shined black shoes to his thick brogue, he was something straight out of central casting.

Piece by piece, cable by cable, all the pricey equipment that I had ordered began to arrive. Such a camera package is the centerpiece of any freelance cameraman's endeavor. Certainly, one needed an accompanying "eye" or talent, but every self-respect-ing cameraman took pride in his gear. Since this was a personal investment, this pride was even greater within the freelance ranks. At the time, this was almost exclusively a men's club, so it also became a game of penis envy—who had the latest greatest camera with the longest widest lens. Finally, my package was complete and I was a complete freelance cameraman.

The accompanying bills for this expensive camera equipment were... expensive. The checks were flying out with nothing coming in. I continued to make the rounds to all of the network news bureaus in Chicago, officially hanging out my OPEN FOR BUSINESS sign. NBC News Chicago was receptive and assured me I would be assimilated into the established rotation of trusted vendors (like Randy). The other networks were less assuring.

What I was soon grasping was, unlike Europe, freelancing was a relatively new staffing method in the U.S. It existed, but only in its infancy. My learning curve was similar to playing a game of musical chairs, except when the music stopped and the freelance assignments were handed out, most of the chairs were already occupied by a Chicago cameraman NOT from across the Atlantic.

While living in Europe, I had thoroughly researched freelancing... in Europe. Like many things European, the translation isn't always exact. I felt like the network square peg in a round hole. I'd also failed to forecast my popularity, or rather, my lack thereof.

I figured my miscalculations were due to a lack of preparation or perhaps insufficient research, but not a lack of experience. I had an impressive international resume that dwarfed most domestic ones. Yet, I soon learned not to use these experiences or lessons as bragging rights. I rarely mentioned the assignments I'd covered while overseas. It became apparent that the decision-makers I was courting (who hired freelancers) felt either ambivalent, bored, or bullied by a resume that was so rich with global news coverage. Thus, what had before seemed like my strongest asset became irrelevant. Knowing it was unlikely that I'd be covering famines, revolutions, Communist regimes, or outright war from Chicago, talking about old war stories and yesterday's headlines was counterproductive. Instead, I focused on learning a more domestic network news agenda and the kinds of stories I *might* someday cover.

2

EMOTIONAL REUNION

There was a great deal of uncertainty swirling around my professional life. My personal life was being dominated by a similar level of uncertainty, too, but different kind. For a time, I had fashioned a distant hope for a rekindled dialogue or even relationship with my ex-wife. But as I'd arrived back in Chicago, that hope had faded into a disappointing ambiguity at best. And aside from my ex-wife, I simply did not know many women... I didn't know ANY women in the greater Chicagoland area.

To be more accurate, my being single was the result of a divorce I'd suffered while living overseas. A divorce which I'd caused.

Amy Powers was my high school sweetheart and my first love. We married out of college and she lovingly and dutifully followed me from promotion to promotion; from Dayton, Ohio to Chicago, Illinois and on to Bonn, West Germany. While I have detailed that marriage and subsequent break-up in my first book, some previously undisclosed elements had a profound impact on my return to the States and which therefore merit a mention here.

I never truly recovered from the demise of my marriage, though I assumed total responsibility for it. Soon after moving to Europe with Amy, I'd become almost intoxicated with my newfound success, which distracted me from the importance of my relationship with Amy. While off covering the war in Lebanon and building my career, I had an affair with a beautiful and famous photographer, Francoise Demulder, who was lovingly known by all simply as Fifi. She was older, connected, and far more experienced in war and life. At one point, I got myself in a dangerous situation with some fighters of the Palestinian Liberation Organization (PLO); she intervened and saved my ass from certain harm and possible death. That event forged a close bond between us and became the impetus for the affair and subsequent loving friendship. It was also the impetus for Amy's departure from Europe... and the end of our marriage.

I could not escape the guilt brought on by my infidelity and failure. I still loved my wife... I mean, my ex-wife. That indecision and schizophrenic love made a relationship with Fifi unsustainable. We parted ways and each returned to immersing ourselves in our work. Later on, in 2008, the world would lose an extraordinarily gifted photojournalist and wonderful human being when Francoise "Fifi" Demulder, at age 61, suffered a heart attack and lost her long battle with cancer.

Throughout our separation and divorce, however, Amy and I kept speaking. At first, the long-distance conversations were mostly updates... *"How are you doing? What are you up to?"* Over time, they became more open, serious, and on my part, apologetic, which helped defrost her understandably chilly mood towards me. On business trips back to New York, I would add a side trip to Chicago, which allowed for some personal face-to-face time. At one point, she flew to Rome and we spent a week together in Italy. We'd met as teenage kids and had known each other for 16 years. The attraction, while bruised, was still undeniable and mutual—and, over time, the intimacy returned.

She shared with me her desire to attend law school, which could be expensive. Back then, I was in a position to assist her financially and happy I could help out. I had purchased the condo on Lincoln Park, intending to use it as a rental property. Having a law student whom I loved to stay there rent-free was an even better use of it since I wasn't desperate for the rental income. At the same time, it was a sincere gesture to begin to repair the damage I'd done. I also shared with Amy my desire to someday return to the States. At first, it was in the abstract with no definite timetable. As I started to look down the road at calendars, the inevitable topic of a possible reunion began to surface. It was all very nebulous. *What if, one of these years way down the road, if I returned home? Do you think that, someday... maybe we might... at some point... you know...?"* Time had helped to heal her wounds and, in the process, a new love reemerged. My hope to reunite seemed to be a shared one.

Our divorce and reconciliation had occurred over a busy seven-year stretch. I had made multiple trips to Beirut to cover the out-of-control war engulfing most of Lebanon. I had witnessed a horrible famine of biblical proportions that claimed hundreds of thousands of victims as it spread like an incurable disease through Ethiopia and Chad. I had watched a "people-powered" revolution in the Philippines, where a widowed housewife assumed power from a totalitarian dictator. I'd been there when nuclear cruise missiles rolled into Western Europe, heightening the Cold War, and I'd observed the diplomatic negotiations that had helped thaw the same Cold War. I'd been present for presidential visits and G7 Summits. And, finally, I'd experienced the collapse of Communism in Eastern Europe.

It was an eventful time, and the events of my last foreign assignment would take a lasting toll on me.

In the Summer of 1989, I had officially submitted my request to return to America and embark on a freelance career. There was no steadfast date for my return, but the request started the machinations for my imminent departure. I've described the many professional considerations that led to that decision, but my reconciliation with Amy very much weighed on the decision. She had flourished while at law school, making the Law Review and graduating with honors. My conversations with Amy continued to point towards a reunion. Our on-again-and-off-again relationship was very much on again.

In October of 1989, Communism in Eastern Europe was on shaky ground. We just didn't know exactly how unstable it was at the time. Just below the surface, cracks were beginning to appear in the Communist foundations of Czechoslovakia, Hungary, Bulgaria, Romania, Albania, and... East Germany.

Three weeks before the eventual collapse of the Berlin Wall, I was assigned to cover the increasing unrest in Prague, Czechoslovakia. Historians and politicians from the time generally agree that the "fall of the Berlin Wall" actually began with a trickle of East German refugees who found a "loophole" in the strict Communist travel restrictions. Motivated by despair, a few hundred East Germans used what little travel freedom they had to drive from Communist East Germany to Communist Czechoslovakia. After arriving in Prague, they went straight to the embassy of West Germany, which, as a model of European Democracy, offered the kind of freedom the East Germans so desired.

Once there, they desperately climbed the wall surrounding the compound, landing on sovereign West Germany soil to claim political asylum. As word spread of this "great escape" from the east to the west, from Communism to Democracy, the trickle of a few hundred East Germans grew to a torrent of thousands. Something had to be done about the swelling numbers of political refugees inside the embassy. Negotiations between West Germany, East Germany, and Czechoslovakia produced a solution. The formerly East German refugees would board a train for West Germany, becoming free citizens in a completely different Germany than the one they had previously known.

It is difficult today to imagine the kind of oppressive life lived by those under communist rule in Eastern Europe. But that train ride was a life-altering journey for its passengers. Those East Germans had been starving for the kind of "Western" freedom so many Americans take for granted. For residents living behind the Iron Curtain, Democracy had previously only been discussed via rumors and hushed whispers. Then, suddenly, a three-hour trip could deliver them to West Germany, where they would feast upon the forbidden fruit they'd only dreamt of.

Amid all this very real human drama, I suddenly encountered some personal drama of my own.

Shortly after arriving in Prague, sitting in my hotel room, I phoned Amy in Chicago. We talked regularly, especially when I traveled to questionable locations… like behind the Iron Curtain. I immediately noticed that the warmth we'd painstakingly rekindled over the years was absent from her voice. So, too, were the caring greetings that usually began our calls. She spoke in a matter-of-fact cadence and cut to the chase.

"I'm not so certain your return to Chicago makes sense."

"Well, it makes perfect sense to me. I've been an ex-pat for seven years. I'm dizzy from all the travel and international news I've covered. I'm ready for a change. I'm... tired. I'm ready to come home."

"I'm not referring to your career, and by the way, YOU made the decision to move to Europe. I'm talking about us. I'm not sure WE make sense."

This was a radical departure from any of our previous conversations.

"Why do you say that?" I asked. "I mean, we're not engaged. Never even discussed marriage... again. I don't want you to feel trapped or forced into anything. You are certainly free to do what you want. But this is coming out of the blue. Did I miss something? What changed?"

There was a ten-second pause that felt like an hour while she mustered the courage to say what I'd feared.

"I've met someone."

That one jolted me like a body punch to the solar plexus and knocked the wind out of my lungs. But I gathered my breath, pretending like it was a minor revelation. I wanted to give her all of the space in the world to sort out the dilemma posed to her by this new *someone*. What I feared was that freedom more than space was the thing for which she was looking. "Okay, look, given my track record, I'm the last guy that could or would insist on monogamy (even though I had been monogamous during my 'comeback'), especially at this point in our relationship... or whatever this is we have."

"We don't have a relationship. It's just a bunch of broken pieces that we'll never be able to glue back together. I have a chance to start something new... with someone new."

"Who?"

"That's not important."

"You can tell me to get lost, but you can't tell me what's important to me. I get to decide that. I'm a little curious who you've decided to start your new life with. We've been through a lot together. You're just going to end it with one phone call—5,000 miles away. That's it?"

"Does it matter?"

In the big picture, it did not. But at that moment, I felt completely defeated, and in some morose way, I needed to know by whom I'd been vanquished.

"It does to me."

"I met a medical student. He's actually completing his residency. He's just starting his medical career and I'm just starting my law career. We're good together."

In my negative and increasingly depressed state, I thought a relationship between a lawyer and doctor could only play out like a Greek tragedy. Were there any two other professions that despised each other more? I did not go to the dark side, though, and instead tried to take the high road. "Well, it sounds like the perfect pair... at least on paper. Look, if this is some kind of tortured payback for Fifi, you don't have to do this. There are other ways we can work through this."

All she had left to say was, "I have to go."

"Okay. Well, at some point, we should address your living accommodations. Don't you think that makes sense?"

"I do. I've already begun looking for my own apartment. I'll be signing a lease shortly. Look, this is not... easy. Goodbye."

The "living accommodations" to which I had referred was my Lincoln Park condo, in which she resided. It would have been awkward for us to be living together in that condo while she was dating her med student. Clearly, she had given the living arrangements plenty of thought and was well on her way to moving out... and on. She was right. This was not easy.

It was raining and already late that evening in Prague. After I hung up with Amy, the walls of my hotel room began to close in on me. I pulled on my raincoat and grabbed my Walkman (a portable music device made popular by the pre-iPod generation). My only destination was anywhere but my hotel room. I put on my headphones, cinched up my hood against the constant nighttime drizzle, and hit play, hoping the rock-and-roll would numb my thoughts. It did not. I felt like a weight was on my shoulders and an anchor was tied around my neck. Staring at the ground, I wandered aimlessly through the quiet and empty old streets, seeing only my exhaled breath in front of me and the wet worn cobblestones at my feet.

Hours passed. I was lost somewhere in the streets of Prague and didn't give a damn. All the thinking and rethinking, trying to rationalize her call, did nothing to ease my distress. Was this some tortured payback for my affair with Fifi years before? I had admitted my guilt, served my time, paid restitution, and together we had moved on. I came to the painful conclusion that my pain would linger. And yes, my pain was very likely the result of Amy's pain, too.

I was devastated, but also cognizant of the fact that I wasn't in the streets of Prague to wallow in self-pity and depression. Amy's announcement put me in a negative state of mind, but NBC had put me in Czechoslovakia with a job to do—a fairly big one, too. My personal life appeared to be going through a tumultuous change, but the world around me was experiencing a far greater tumult.

The refugee crisis in Prague, and more specifically inside the West German embassy, was reaching crisis mode. As more and more East Germans flooded the embassy to claim political asylum, more and more international journalists were applying for visas to cover the story.

One morning, our NBC News team was sitting in the lobby discussing the rapidly developing story. My camera equipment was sitting next to my chair, a sure sign that we were with the news media. One of my canvas accessory bags carried a luggage tag emblazoned with a small peacock. A tall woman cautiously approached our small group and addressed no one in particular, "I'm sorry to interrupt. Are you guys with NBC News and is one of you David?" She spoke English fluently, as if it was her native language. She wasn't Eastern European, but I couldn't quite place her accent.

David Page, our producer, was flattered by the attention and responded, "We are and I'm David. Who might you be?"

"My name is Jennifer. I'm stringing for the CBC and the London Bureau Chief suggested I reach out to you guys."

Aha! The CBC, or Canadian Broadcasting Corporation. That explained the accent. Now, NBC and CBC shared resources. We weren't competitors, but more like allies. The term "stringer" is interchangeable with freelancer, although "stringer" was and is used more frequently with editorial types like reporters and producers. Jennifer was new to Prague and, like most enterprising stringers, she was eager to get invested in the story, to understand the facts behind it. Unlike most stringers, she was striking.

Tall and poised, she wore her straight blonde hair parted on the side in a natural, no-fuss fashion. She was dressed in the uniform worn by many a reporter; beige khakis and a blue denim long-sleeve shirt. It's unusual that a simple pair of khakis can be so flattering, but hers accentuated her fit long legs. And her standard shirt was smartly tucked into her pants, which smartly revealed her voluptuousness. She was difficult not to notice.

But she wasn't before us as a fashion model to be ogled. She was a journalist and wanted the truth. David briefed her on the big picture as well as the process for feeding or transmitting videotape back to London and New York. The heart of the story was the West German embassy and the refugees inside.

David offered, "Tim's spent more time in and around there than anyone, but you should go see it for yourself."

"I've seen video of people trying to get inside. You can feel their... desperation."

I offered, "We're going to check on it and get some fresh video in a little bit. You're welcome to jump in our car and join us."

"That would be great. Let me go up to my room and grab my gear. When are you guys leaving?"

"Why don't you meet us down here in 30 minutes and we'll head over to the embassy?"

She returned with her gear—a single bag. I learned she was filing radio reports for the CBC, which explained why her gear, consisting of a microphone and a cassette recorder, was considerably smaller than our television gear. I was happy to share with her what I'd learned while covering the story for the previous few weeks.

She looked up to us as the big American news organization, but I admired her, as well. She possessed a driving journalistic curiosity and no small amount of courage. Our team consisted of a producer, reporter, cameraman, and soundman. We were four dudes supported by a small local staff and a much larger one back in New York. She was by herself in a foreign country behind the Iron Curtain.

That said, although I was part of a much larger news team,

after Amy's rejection, I was emotionally alone. And, so was Jennifer. The more time Jennifer and I spent together, the stronger the bond grew. The mutual admiration became mutual attraction.

Our four-man NBC team frequently asked the one-woman CBC team to join us for dinner. Because of the time difference, Prague being six hours ahead of New York, it was often late in the evening before we finished work and sat down for dinner. On the occasion of one such late meal in the hotel restaurant, after the check had been paid and everyone had finished eating, everyone but us feeling tired and heading to their respective rooms, Jennifer and I lingered for just a moment and continued to chat. The others were already in the elevator, so no one noticed that we were the last to get up from the table and the last to leave the now empty restaurant. No one noticed when she nonchalantly and delicately slid her arm inside mine at the elbow. And when we exited the restaurant into the dimly lit hallway that led to the hotel, no one noticed when I stopped and turned to her. I grabbed her hands, rested my forehead on hers, and slowly raised my eyes to meet hers. Just as slowly, our eyes closed as I kissed her soft, welcoming lips.

We turned and continued down the dark hallway, arm in arm, until we reached the elevator.

I whispered, "I'm ready for bed.

She agreed, "Me, too."

When the doors opened, we walked into an empty elevator and, without further conversation, I pressed only one button—the one for my floor. She tightened her grip on my arm and snuggled closer to me. The unspoken bond between us had grown undeniable. I was excited by the thought of physical intimacy with a beautiful woman, and after the rejection I'd recently experienced, the emotional acceptance was every bit as exciting.

Inside my hotel room, the sex that evening was soft, loving, and unhurried. When we awoke the next morning, there was no regret, no remorse; just a deeper friendship for both of us.

Our growing friendship and intimacy were not things we flaunted in front of my NBC colleagues. Jennifer and I kept it to ourselves while enjoying each other's companionship. There were no long-term expectations for the relationship. We were living in Prague, in the moment. And in that moment, it was heartening to have meaningful and personal conversation and tenderness. For me, it was especially enriching, coming as it was on the heels of Amy's rejection.

Amy's break-up announcement had drained me of any personal emotion. Lately, I'd felt attached to the story, yet detached from and even soured to any feelings of closeness or intimacy. It was a dark space I had occupied. While I loved my job, at the end of a long day (or month), you can't tightly hug a story or sensually caress the news. Jennifer's sudden and unexpected arrival in my darkened life had rekindled a lost, internal warmth that could never be found in work—only shared with another.

The story in Prague continued to evolve. Suddenly, as if some East German spigot had been shut off, the flow of asylum seekers stopped. More and more East Germans took to the streets in East Germany, rioting and protesting the Communist oppression under which they lived.

And then the unthinkable occurred.

The embarrassed East German leaders were also embattled, beleaguered, and tired. They summoned the news media to a hastily announced press conference where a spokesman for the East German government addressed the press. When asked about the harsh travel restrictions imposed on their East German citizens, he shocked the room (and subsequently the world) by saying,

"...we have decided today to implement a regulation that allows every citizen of the German Democratic Republic (East Germany) to leave the GDR through any of the border crossings..."

The room filled with confusion. One of the reporters asked, "When does it come into effect?"

The East German, thumbing through his prepared papers as if to search for an answer, responded, "That comes into effect, according to my information, immediately, without delay."

And with that, the dreaded and deadly Berlin Wall—the imposing concrete and steel homage to Communist rule which had stood for over 28 years—was rendered completely useless. Thousands of East Germans flocked to the wall and climbed atop it, which only a day prior would have meant certain death. In symbolic gestures, they hammered away at the hated edifice as if to hammer away at the hated political system which had built it.

That announcement sent shock waves around the world. It resonated most loudly within the Communist countries who had yet to open their borders, who still ruled over their people with an iron fist, as did the Czech Communists. They must have known their flawed political system, like that of East Germany, faced extinction, but they weren't going down without a fight. Meanwhile, we, the Western Press, were still in Prague, waiting and watching.

On a cold and damp November day, the Communist frustration erupted with a vicious beatdown on a group of protesting students... and me.

My soundman John Hall and I were covering a seemingly innocuous protest march. For more than an hour, the students chanted and marched through the narrow cobblestone streets, lit only by old streetlamps whose illuminating glow was diminished by the evening fog. The shops had been shuttered and, eerily, no one was in sight save for the protesters. With a sudden and brazen burst of courage, the student organizers decided to change the route and head to the old city center of Wenceslas Square, a destination that had been forbidden by the state police.

After one fateful left turn, the unsuspecting students marched right into the spider's web where a heavily armed paramilitary force was waiting. Fuming over the developments in Berlin and seething for a fight, they sealed off both ends of the street and proceed to brutally beat the defenseless students with a barrage of clubs, water cannons, shields, and fists.

John and I were the only television crew caught up in the violence. We managed to salvage the videotape just before our equipment was destroyed and we were beaten.

I stumbled through the same foggy, dimly lit streets of Prague I'd stumbled through weeks before after Amy's fateful call. This time, I was in a completely different kind of daze. Semi-conscious, I tried to relive in my head what I had just witnessed. John and I, separated by the melee, reconnected back at our NBC hotel office. The surprising and shocking video became big news and announced the beginning of the end of Communism in Czechoslovakia.

The story also announced and broadcast that John and I had been "brutally beaten." My injuries required that I be flown to Frankfurt, West Germany for tests and observation. Jennifer and I shared a hasty and bittersweet goodbye. We'd grown close over such a short time, and I hoped that we would see one another again. But, in the news business, crossing paths is more by chance than certainty; the where and when are nearly always unknown.

Most of us who cover the news are loathsome to be covered BY the news. We are the light and don't wish to be in the light. But the word was out this time, and I was part of the story. The phones in New York and Rome were ringing with inquiries about my condition, calls coming from everyone from my immediate family to high school friends who were certain I was near death. One of those calls was from Amy. So much had happened since our last call, and I was hurting both physically and emotionally. Doctors confirmed my physical injuries would heal completely. Yet, even after Jennifer's soothing comfort, Amy's wound still stung.

I wrestled with the decision of whether to return her call or not. I couldn't completely dismiss her concern, but I was still outraged by her breaking up with me. I knew I would soon be back in Chicago permanently. I would cross that bridge when I came to it.

* * * * *

Living in the Four Seasons with time on my hands and my furniture still lost in transit, I'd occasionally stop by my empty Lincoln Park condo to meet with workmen and arrange for minor upgrades—things like a fresh coat of paint or refinishing the hardwood floors. As a new American resident and Chicagoan, I also began to receive mostly junk mail, which was interspersed with mail addressed to the former occupant, Amy. She had moved into her apartment shortly after our last call in Prague when she'd phoned to inform me that she was seeing someone else and question whether my return to the U.S.

"made sense."

Her mail posed a quandary; what to do with it? I would've been childish to simply toss it in the trash, but some of it might be important. I did not have a forwarding residential address for her. I knew the grown-up option was to overcome my hurt and phone the law practice where she worked as an associate. I had no intention of revisiting our previous conversation.

Much had transpired in the ensuing three months.

She was caught off-guard and utterly surprised by my call. I was prepared to be received as an unexpected and inconvenient bother to her busy day, but the reception I got was almost... welcoming instead.

"HI. I, um, wasn't expecting... I'm surprised.... How are you? Where are you? I mean, this doesn't sound like a long-distance call... there's not that annoying echo thing."

"You're right, this is not long distance. I'm here... back in Chicago. I followed through on my plans to come home and set up shop as a freelancer."

"Well, how are you? I tried to call you right after I heard about... everyone heard about you getting beat up in Prague. I was worried when I heard. It was a big deal. You made the news."

"Making the news was never my aim, just an unfortunate part of the job. But I'm doing fine, thanks for asking. I'm taking some physical therapy at Northwestern Hospital to work through some of the lingering aches and pains. NBC's been good about paying for whatever it takes, as long as it takes. Anyway... the reason I called is that I stopped by the condo and found some mail addressed to you, and didn't know—"

"OH, well, how is your move going? What's it like being back in the U.S., back home?"

There was a decidedly different and noticeably more caring tone to her voice on this call than on our previous one, and it had nothing to do with the long-distance versus local phone connection.

"Uh, my move is still ongoing. Because it's Italy, I don't have a clue when my things will arrive. In the meantime, I've been camped out at the Four Seasons. So, in that regard, I guess life is good, being back in the U.S." There was no way I was going to allude to my professional uncertainty or inquire into her personal life. The pain was still fresh, the wound still open.

"So, about the mail," I continued. "I'm sure you completed a change of address with the post office, but I do have some stuff addressed to you. Where would you like me to send it?"

"Oh, sure. The mail. Well, just send it to me here at work. Or, I mean, if you're ever downtown sometime, you could just, eh, maybe we could grab a cup of coffee, or, I could meet you and, well, pick it up... if you feel like it."

What the hell was she talking about? A few months earlier, with five thousand miles between us, she'd questioned whether or not we could share the same continent. Now she wanted to meet for coffee. Women can sometimes be a riddle wrapped up in an enigma. If this was about her guilt for breaking it off, I wanted her pity far less than I wanted her mail. But I couldn't articulate that point.

There was a long pause before I responded, "Um, okay. I can meet for coffee downtown. What works for you?"

"Tomorrow morning would be great."

And with that, the long and convoluted history with my wife, ex-wife turned girlfriend, then turned estranged ex-wife girlfriend... would continue for at least one more morning. She suggested we meet near her office at a hip new coffee "shop" called Starbucks. The entire time I'd lived abroad, I had never heard of such a concept, and now it seemed to be taking Chicago—and America—by storm.

Amy was already sitting at a table when I arrived, and she stood to greet me. Our greeting was unpracticed and uncomfortable. On the one hand, I didn't feel like embracing the woman who had shed me like some worn-out and scratchy sweater. On the other hand, there was simply too much history between us to pretend otherwise. I leaned in for a quick, obligatory embrace, leaving plenty of distance between us. It was clumsy, but quickly overshadowed by my clumsiness and total lack of familiarity with the whole ordering and pick-up process at the new Starbucks coffee shop.

Reaching into my coat pocket to retrieve a stack of envelopes, I said, "Before I forget, here's your mail." Gazing up at a confusing menu board listing a mishmash of products with Italian/English names, I then asked, "Where do I go… how do I order a cup of coffee?" I'd just returned from Italy and couldn't make heads or tails of what they were serving.

Amy offered, "Just get in line behind all of those people to order and you pick up your coffee over there, on the other side."

Still trying to interpret the menu board, I asked her, "Okay, what's a tall?"

"Well, that's a small."

"Why don't they just say *small*? And what's an affogato style?"

"I'm not sure, but the person in the green apron can answer that."

I settled on a simple double espresso, fought my way through the crowd to rejoin Amy at the table, and took a sip. It was a watery and bitter version of a beverage with the same name that I had fallen in love with while in Rome. Reflecting on Italian espresso brought up numerous other loving memories. Amy was in many of them, but there was no way I was going to stroll down memory lane with her in a crowded coffee concept. I was there strictly as a mailman and my job was complete. We made small talk, scratching the surface of my relocation to America while avoiding the elephant in the Starbucks—our long-distance break-up. I had no desire to revisit that call nor torment myself with updates about her relationship with some doctor. I stared into the espresso cup I had just emptied. My 15-year relationship with Amy seemed to be just as full as my coffee cup, and I realized it was time to move on with the morning and our lives. I suggested it was time to get back to our respective offices, and we got up from our table and walked outside into the wintery-grey Chicago morning.

We stepped out into a frenzy of pedestrian traffic on the corner of Clark and Madison streets, one of the busiest intersections in the Loop. As I turned to her to say goodbye, the wind kicked up and stung my face. I had to squint against the gale, which was only part of the reason my eyes teared slightly. I wondered if I would ever see her again, and wanted to leave with positive thoughts. "You did it. You're a bigtime Chicago attorney now. I'm sure you'll make partner in no time. Hell, you'll probably be running the place before long. And, as far as you and I are concerned, it's been a wild ride. I've enjoyed it. Well, most of it. Hope you feel the same way. I wish you the best. I mean that."

She stepped forward. Now, there was no space between us. The strong wind that was in my face was at her back. It blew her long blonde hair around her face as she buried her head in my chest and gently grabbed my coat in a half-embrace. She fought back tears, caused not by the wind, to say, "I'm sorry."

"What are you sorry for? I shoulder as much... no, far *more* blame than you do."

Her face was still against my chest as I heard her say, "I'm sorry I hurt you. I'm sorry it ended this way." She lifted her head from my chest and looked into my eyes. I could see tears streaming down both her cheeks. "I learned a horrible lesson that there are some really bad people in this world and... I never meant it to be like this."

"I'm not sure I know what you mean."

"The guy I told you about... the guy I was seeing. It was all just some sick fucking game to him."

"You WERE seeing?"

"He kept telling me I needed to leave you. And if I did, we... he and I would have this wonderful life together. You were in Europe and I didn't know... I wasn't sure you were ever coming back. And, he was here. I wanted to believe him."

The more open she became, the more passionate she became. By now, she was fully sobbing. It was a crazy, busy, rush hour morning, like all rush hour mornings in downtown Chicago. But on this particular morning, while encircled by organized chaos, we were oblivious to the mayhem around us. And vice versa. People hurriedly buzzed past us without even noticing us. We were cocooned in our little emotional world.

With my right thumb, I partially wiped away the tears from her eyes while she continued, "It was all some twisted joke to him. He wanted to see if he could force me to do something. And when I did, he just laughed... and left. It was like this perverse power play. It was a terrible mistake. I couldn't tell you. I wanted to call you, but I couldn't. I called you in Rome after you were hurt, but you never called me back. I knew you wouldn't."

I'd been speechless after our break-up call in Prague. And, now I was rendered silent by her sidewalk confession. I could only hold her as I processed this revelation. Finally, while still hugging her in the middle of a busy corner, I whispered, "I understand. I've seen some shitty people in this world. It's a sad reality. I just never thought they'd come between you and me."

I had been hurt, profoundly, by her breaking up with me. But mine was not a singular pain. Six years earlier, my infidelity while in Beirut (and after) had devastated her emotionally and led to our divorce. We were both responsible for plenty of scar tissue. I had never stopped loving her, and now her outpouring of honesty only made that lasting love more visible.

The reality of the rush hour began to settle in, and we couldn't stay on that street corner forever. I brushed her swirling hair from her still moist eyes and said, "Look, this is all news to me and I'm just a little surprised, which is crazy since I'm in the news business and very little surprises me anymore. I truly appreciate your honesty—so, so much—and I know this wasn't easy for you. I think this all begs for another conversation. Maybe we can continue this sometime at someplace a little more... intimate than Starbucks. What do you think?"

"I think I'd like that, very much."

"Okay, then. Sounds like a..." I wanted to say *date*, but caught myself. That was putting the cart before the horse. I needed to internalize this new info and didn't want to get carried away. I quickly substituted *plan* for *date*. "Sounds like a plan. Let me just figure out where and when. I'll call you."

That surprising conversation stayed with me as I continued to go through the motions of reacquainting myself with my former city while waiting for my lost belongings to materialize. I was still living in the lap of luxury, comfortably inhabiting a room at the Four Seasons. I couldn't complain to anyone that I was growing tired of my enviable address. I would have sounded like the ultimate diva, bitching about an extended stay at the Four Seasons. But living in a hotel, even a grandiose palace, was growing old. I wanted to sprawl out on my furnishing, surrounded by my things. Finally, I received word that my stuff was headed to New York and would soon be headed to Chicago.

Beyond my accommodations, I continued to think about Amy after that Starbucks conversation. A couple of weeks passed, in which we spoke by phone a few times and had a quick downtown lunch that felt more like a meeting than a date. Our climate was slowly warming, but the conversations were more like updates on our careers or my relocation than real and substantial interaction. However, that face-to-face lunch allowed us a chance to gently reminisce about a few of the many happier times. It was not a leisurely and affectionate stroll down memory lane, though. If we were moving closer to one another, it was at a glacial pace, each of us leery of being burned again.

Since I was the party most recently jolted, I would have to get over my pain to move this… whatever this was, along. Amy had already painfully admitted to a regrettable decision. There was little more I could ask of her. Clearly, the ball was in my court, and it was time for me to at least try and turn the corner to see what, if anything, lay ahead for us.

Dinner would determine the next steps, or if there even was one. Not a cramped Starbucks coffee or a business lunch in between meetings, but a romantic and unhurried dinner tucked away in a secluded booth to perhaps relight a recently extinguished and still smoking candle.

"Hi, it's Tim. Hey, do you have a minute to talk?"

"Sure. I'm just going over some endless documents so this is a nice break."

"Did they make you partner yet?"

"You asked me that question a week ago at lunch, and no,

they did not. I'm still a first-year associate. It may be another five or six years before I have to worry about it."

"Well, hang in there. You mentioned lunch. Sooooo, we've had coffee together. We've done lunch. You know, the normal progression for people who are getting to know one another better would be dinner."

"Getting to know one another? I've known you since junior year in high school. We were married for five years and lived together in Europe. I know you better than anyone on the planet."

This was sounding like a stroll down memory lane. I didn't know if I should veer off course or continue down the path. My male instincts told me to veer. Perhaps we could resume the stroll if she agreed to dinner.

"Is that a NO for dinner?"

"No, it's not a no. I mean, yes it's a yes. But when?"

"How about this Friday night?"

She paused to look at her calendar, then said, "This Friday, the day after Valentine's Day?"

"What? I hadn't noticed. (I had.) If your Valentine's week is already filled, we can look at other nights. I just thought—"

"My Valentines week is pretty much like most other weeks, filled with work. This Friday is great. Where would you like to spend *Not* Valentine's Day?"

"I've had plenty of time to discover my Michigan Avenue neighborhood. Evidently, the Magnificent Mile is loaded with magnificent restaurants. There's an Italian place, Spiaggia, I've fallen in love with. It's not quite like being back in Roma, but it's a very elegant restaurant with delicious food and right around the corner from the Four Seasons."

"I've always wanted to try that place. It has an incredible reputation... I mean, for Chicago."

"Did I deserve that? I guess so, but you should know I'm doing my best to conceal my Euro-past and worldly experiences to better blend in back here in the American heartland. Sometimes, those urges are just uncontrollable."

"It's not healthy to control all of your urges. So, you want me to meet you at the restaurant?"

I took Amy's advice and gave into an urge. "Why don't we meet here at the hotel? We've both seen some spectacular hotels and this one's right up near the top of the list. We can have a glass of champagne before dinner. After all, it is Not Valentine's Day and Spiaggia is a two-minute walk. I'll make a reservation for eight. I'm in room 1201. Call me when you arrive."

"Champagne sounds like a good idea and a great start to the weekend. See you Friday."

The anticipation for date night was growing, and so was an arctic cold front from the North. The Friday after Valentine's Day arrived accompanied by howling winds and biting snow flurries. Instead of canceling, Amy braved the weather and managed to find a cab for the gauntlet from her office to my hotel. She arrived in a semi-frozen state; her coat, scarf, and hair were still flecked with snow when she knocked on my door. Just inside my room, she immediately kicked off her high heels and collapsed into an overstuffed chair in the corner of the room. I poured her a well-deserved glass of champagne which, even in its chilled state, managed to warm her.

As she slowly began to thaw, she unwrapped the layers of outerwear. With a champagne flute in hand, she peered out the window and said, "It is particularly brutal out there, even by Chicago standards."

"The easy… and maybe smart thing would have been to cancel. I'm glad you didn't. Thanks for making the trek all the way up here."

"You're exactly halfway between work and my apartment. It's like the perfect rest stop." Resembling a weary and parched nomadic traveler, she gulped down her champagne and, extending her empty glass, said, "I could use a little more, please."

"At your service. It's the least I can do."

As the bottle of champagne was emptied, the storm outside my warm and cozy room intensified. The snow flurries had turned into a full-fledged blizzard—with the snow no longer falling downward, but whipping sideways. The once expansive view from my hotel room was now reduced to a couple of feet. As I stared through the window at the near-zero visibility, Amy joined me, putting her face next to mine. Both of us being veterans of Chicago winters, we knew the conditions would continue to deteriorate throughout the night. The thought of venturing out into Antarctica for an evening stroll was not the least bit appealing to either of us.

Trying to project some thinly veiled false optimism, I encouraged, "The restaurant is literally around the corner. If we bundle up, we can make it with only minimal frostbite."

"I'm still freezing from the first part of my journey. And, I need to use your restroom."

She went to the bathroom while I contemplated our quandary. I was on a first-name basis with the hotel concierge. I could check with them for any last-minute available tables in the hotel's bar and restaurant. That would avoid the need to venture outdoors for dinner. As I picked up the phone, Amy emerged from the bathroom. She had shed her attorney's attire and was now snuggly wrapped in an oversized terrycloth bathrobe embroidered with the Four Seasons logo. She scrunched up the robe's fluffy collar tightly around her chin and neck. "How's room service at this hotel?"

Caught off-guard, I fumbled with the telephone handset as I attempted to find its base... and mine. It appeared my intervention for an alternative location for dinner was unnecessary. She had made that decision, and I was just fine with it.

"Wow, you look really great... I mean, comfortable, and warm. Room service! That's a great idea. Why didn't I think of that? It's a great menu... just like a restaurant. And, the food arrives really quickly and hot... just like at a restaurant. I already said that, didn't I?"

She slowly stepped forward and, as she approached me, her robe was no longer tightly wrapped around her, but loose and opened. She hugged me and I slide my arms inside the robe and around her naked body. I put my hands on her warm lower back and gently puller her close.

So much tumult had occurred in our lives that I just wanted to savor the moment. As we grew close for an eminent kiss, I asked, "Should we order another bottle of champagne with dinner?"

She responded, "I think you should do whatever you like."

I gently pushed her open robe off her shoulders. As it slid to the floor, I quickly undressed and joined her in a mutually naked state. I dimmed the lights and we jumped into the large king bed, enveloping ourselves under the great big fluffy down comforter and cuddling in a cocoon of Egyptian cotton. We were like kids again, back in high school on our sex-filled after-prom night. The Motel 6 had been replaced by Chicago's finest hotel, but the reignited passion was once again feverous.

Our late-night room service dinner was followed by late morning room service brunch. We lingered in bed, avoiding the cold reality outside our window and the uncertainty in front of us. There was no ignoring the long-twisted path we had created and shared. There was also no ignoring the enduring love we both felt even after all of our history. It simply felt good to be back in each other's arms. As a result, we decided to slowly move back into each other's lives.

We were both unattached and maintained separate residences. If either of us thought things were moving too quickly, we could implement the "slow-down option" and reassess. But our separate paths had once again merged and were now headed in the same direction, together.

3

FIRST LIGHT

In some unforeseen twist of fate, my moribund relationship status was suddenly and unexpectedly healthier and more promising than my career status. That was certainly not what I'd had in mind when deciding to leave the security and comfort of NBC News and head out on my own.

Having planted seeds at all of the major networks, I was growing impatient waiting for the phone to ring. The seeds I had planted were not germinating and the waiting was nerve-racking. It was not something I was used to doing. I was used to being assigned to cover network news stories, and that wasn't happening.

It was time for me to cast a wider net, beyond the news networks, and to stop sitting on my hands hoping they would call.

When I'd been a staffer, the word *network* had referred to the company that employed me, covered world news, and informed millions of viewers. As a freelancer, I began to grasp that the same word took on an entirely different meaning. It was no longer just a company or even a noun. It was also a verb. Sure, NBC, CBS, and ABC were networks for whom I hoped to work. But now I realized that *network* could also mean a kind of sup-

port system; a way to better understand the landscape of television, and the many interactive parts and companies that were
working and thriving in Chicago... without me. I needed to tap
into that network and, in the process, network with others like
myself.

The "networks" themselves were one place I could begin to
network. While reminding the various bureau chiefs and assignment editors of my wide-open availability and continued
interest in work, I also began asking for introductions to producers who I might someday work with, as well as the names
of soundmen I might someday hire as part of my crew. A crew,
whether freelance or staff, is comprised of both a cameraman
and a soundman.

When I was a young NBC staffer based in Bonn, Germany,
my soundman/partner was a veteran German by the name of
Fred Richter. In Rome, Italy, my soundman was the worldly
and experienced Massimiliano Matteoli. We were all NBC staff
employees and we worked exclusively with each other. When
the phone rang with an assignment, we would jump into the
car or onto the plane, traveling together and covering the news
together. We were exclusive or "married" to one another and
rarely did crew members "swap" or work with other partners.

When I entered the freelance realm, though, I noticed there
was less relationship exclusivity between cameramen and
soundmen. The business realities demanded more flexibility.
For example, if a cameraman had a slow month, his soundman could look elsewhere for freelance assignments. And if
a cameraman was booked for a ten-day assignment while his
soundman was vacationing with his family in Disneyland, the
cameraman could accept the assignment and hire a different
freelance soundman. As a result, cameramen had a number of

soundmen they would call, and soundmen were called on by many different cameramen.

I wasn't certain when I would get hired, but I was certain that, *when* I got hired, I would need to be ready with a list of soundmen whom I could rely upon. In preparation for that moment, I began meeting prospective sound partners for lunch or over beers. These were enjoyable pre-interview interviews in a non-interview, at-ease setting. The various potential partners answered my questions about their backgrounds and talked freely about the many assignments and shows on which they'd worked.

Many of these guys were Chicago born and raised, and they gladly shed light on both the city's freelance market and the city itself. The freelance world on any side involved making a sizable investment in equipment. Cameramen invested in the pricey camera equipment and soundmen usually invested in their own, less pricey audio equipment, such as portable sound mixers, microphones, and cables—for which they would receive payment. The equipment itself was often a topic of conversation in these so-called interviews, and good soundmen were a valuable resource for "tech talk." These meetings would prove to be a useful window into the latest technology developments, but also into which of Chicago's many retailers were selling and renting professional video equipment and had the best deals and deepest inventory.

I also set my sights on non-network networking opportunities. I discovered some of the many post-production or editing companies that existed in a huge market such as Chicago. Independent producer or cameramen clients would utilize these companies to finish and finesse their video and film projects. The networks had their in-house editing facilities, which was why, as a staffer, I'd previously been unfamiliar with this part of the television industry. But it was helpful to know they existed now, should I ever need a place to edit an independent project. And it was good that they knew I existed, too, should they ever need an experienced freelance cameraman. Most of these companies kept their extensive lists of freelance editors, cameramen, and soundmen just in case a client of theirs needed such services. It could only benefit me to be included on such lists.

In seeing this segment of the television industry for the first time, I began to see a world of television production possibilities beyond world news. Documentarians, advertising agencies, public relations firms, and others were all engaging in television production and post-production projects. This networking allowed me to personally see other avenues of opportunity to pursue while still hoping to break back into network news. It was the kind of world I had imagined existed while living overseas. And now I could almost touch it.

While working FOR a network, I'd never seen the need TO network—to market myself and learn about others. It was almost as if I'd worn blinders as an NBC staffer, performing my one task while working for my one company. As a freelancer, I was beginning to fill in many of the blanks of my new business surroundings. What I needed to do next was fill in my calendar with a freelance booking. A job.

While using my new networking tools, I was "working the phones" with a former network colleague in New York who shared intel on some interesting start-ups that might be a potential road to employment for a hungry freelancer. I was heartened to hear non-network news programs were launching. Like the major networks, they featured anchors who hosted daily programs where reporters in the field would file news and human-interest stories. Unlike the networks, as start-ups, they could ill-afford to employ staff cameramen or purchase expensive camera equipment. These were companies whose business models relied exclusively upon freelance relationships. They were also companies who looked to the major news networks for experienced employees who could make their start-ups a reality. Former network executives, reporters, and producers looking for something new and different were joining forces and signing up for these new endeavors. On that same call, I was told they were also looking for reliable camera crews with network experience to shoot their stories.

I was guardedly optimistic when I was urged to contact an old friend.

Candice Hill had been an editor for NBC News based in the London bureau. We had worked together on numerous stories in the Middle East and Asia while I'd been based overseas. The friend with whom I'd spoken in New York had informed me that she'd left London, and NBC, to return to the States. She was living in Chicago, where she had transitioned from video editing to producing. I was given her number and immediately felt anxious to learn more.

"Hi Candice, it's Tim Ortman."

"Oh my god! I heard you were coming home. Are you officially back?"

"I am. And I heard you got back a few months ago. How is it?"

"It's nice to be home again. I loved living in London, but I'm loving this even more. I can't believe, after all of our crazy globetrotting travels, we both landed back in Chicago at about the same time. Speaking of travels, I heard about Prague. Are you okay?"

"Prague, that feels like light years ago. I'm good, thanks. It does feel a little weird being back. I'm still trying to figure things out. What are you up to?"

"You were abroad a long time... Sometimes it takes a while to adjust. So, what have I been up to? Have you heard of Channel One?"

"No, I have not. But like you said, I was gone for a long time. I feel perpetually out of the loop on so many fronts. I just had my first Starbucks the other day. I predict *that* will come and go like 8-track tapes. It's way too crowded for a simple cup of coffee. So, what's Channel One?"

Candice proceeded to describe Channel One, and its founder, in great detail. Chris Whittle of Whittle Communications had gotten the idea to cover the news and deliver that news into thousands of high school and middle school classrooms throughout the country. Whittle was a successful entrepreneur and media executive who saw millions of American students as an untapped news market. This was a rather large undertaking. It required installing satellite dishes in hundreds of schools and wiring thousands of classrooms with TV monitors to receive and play back daily newscasts. It also required a news-savvy staff of former network personnel to be assembled for the launch. To appear more relevant to their classroom audiences, Channel One hired much younger on-air reporters, in their early twenties, to work with the older and more experienced editorial news veterans.

To offset some of these costs, the Channel One newscasts also contained advertisements, which immediately created controversy. Opponents argued that the kids were a captive audience and shouldn't be forced to watch ads. Additionally, they saw television advertisements as stealing away valuable class time.

I found this to be a valid argument. Kids were (and are) bombarded with ads everywhere they turned. Including ads in the newscasts posed the question, what would the teenage viewers more likely retain—an informative news story or a slick and flashy Madison Avenue TV commercial? Channel One's supporters argued it was an opportunity to deliver news to kids who probably weren't receiving much news, if any. For me, the debate's most convincing point was one of action. If these newscasts, complete with ads, could get kids engaged, then that engagement more than made up for the marketing messages sprinkled within them.

The objectives and approach all sounded legitimate, even admirable. Pragmatically speaking, I also saw it as an opportunity to add a paying client to my anemic list of clients.

After listening intently to the introduction, I responded, "Sounds interesting. It also sounds like there are a lot of moving parts. What's your role with Channel One?"

"It's a national broadcast covering America from coast to coast. They've asked me to oversee news coverage for the middle of the country. To do that, they've hired me as staff to be the Midwestern Bureau Chief, but I'll also be producing stories, as well. The executive producers of the show and the correspondents are staff, too. But the people, the crews and producers who will be shooting and covering the news stories, are all going to be freelancers. The people behind this are serious about it. There's going to be a lot of work to do. There's an opportunity for you here if you're available and interested."

I couldn't believe what I had just heard. Had I just received a concrete offer for freelance employment?

"I've been back for over a month. I've made multiple calls and visits to all the networks... and nothing. Even NBC seems to have lost my number. My gear is complete. My office is complete. I am EXTREMELY available and even more interested. Count me in."

"That's great to hear. As I mentioned, we're broadcasting to high schools and middle schools. I feel compelled to warn you, this may not be the same kind of news coverage... with the same... level of professionalism or the kind of audience that we had at NBC."

"Candice, I know you well enough to know you're not about to sign on to some half-assed endeavor. I appreciate your honesty. It doesn't matter to me whether we're broadcasting to 15 million viewers on *Nightly News* or 1,500 students. It really doesn't. And, frankly, I don't need a steady diet of collapsing Communist governments and revolutions to shoot. This sounds kind of refreshing."

"Excellent. Then look at your calendar. What are you doing next Friday? We have a shoot in Lansing, Michigan covering an Earth Day event."

And, with that, my not so illustrious freelancing career began. I was happy to have a client and be back in the news business. This wasn't network news, but simply news with a twist, and I was fine with justifying the minor twist.

I would work for Channel One on numerous stories in Chicago, Illinois; Lansing and Detroit, Michigan; Madison, Kenosha, and Oconomowoc, Wisconsin; Indianapolis and Bloomington, Indiana; Kent and Columbus, Ohio; Omaha, Nebraska; and Yankton, South Dakota, just to list just a few.

The job of news gathering was much the same at Channel One as at NBC, with a few structural differences. I would receive a call—usually from Candice—asking about my availability. This differed slightly from my NBC days where, as a staffer,

I had only one client and it was assumed that I was always and infinitely available for that one client. In the freelance world, clients could not make that assumption. Another key assumption was that "I" referred to us, as in a crew; cameraman and soundman. Whether staff or freelance, it was always up to the cameraman to secure the soundman's commitment and communicate the shoot specifics to him or her (as soon as I accepted an assignment, I would immediately phone and secure a soundperson). Once my availability was confirmed, I'd go over the length of the assignment with the client, Candace, just as I had done with my bosses at NBC; for instance, departing on Monday and returning on Thursday (with international news, the completion date was sometimes... ambiguous). Travel arrangements would be discussed, as well, concerning whether the journey required a flight or was close enough to be reached by car and where we would be staying. Larger clients like NBC have in-house travel departments to help with these preparations. With Channel One, I made most of my travel plans. Then, after a shoot was completed, I'd submit expense reports to be reimbursed for my out-of-pocket costs, just as I had at NBC.

Once the logistics were determined, the story itself would be discussed. *What are we calling this story? What's the topic and what's it about? Who are the main characters we'll likely interview? What other kinds of video (other than interviews) will we likely shoot? Will we need extra or special equipment for unique circumstances? Additional lighting or microphones for large group interviews?* These sorts of considerations needed to be determined before the crew left for any location. We traveled with every conceivable equipment need, too, as you don't want to be searching for specialized professional video equipment in a small town in Iowa.

The teams that go out into the field to cover news can vary significantly in size depending on the news event being covered and its newsworthiness. An Earth Day celebration will command a smaller group of journalists than, say, a presidential election campaign. But for the kinds of stories covered by Channel One, and many of those by NBC, the team would consist of a standard nucleus. The crew was always at the core of a shoot and almost always joined by an editorial member who had researched the story, made initial contacts for the story, and who would follow the story through the editing phase and to completion. That person was usually a "field" producer. This field role was sometimes entrusted to a more junior, less experienced "associate" producer who would take on similar responsibilities.

Occasionally, a fourth member would join the team in the field. A reporter/correspondent might join the shoot if an "on-camera" appearance from the field was needed in the story, if the scriptwriting demanded their on-site presence, or if they just wanted to delve deeper into and connect more personally with the story. If the reporter was not or could not be on location for the shoot, the reporter and producer would confer in the bureau afterward to write, edit, and assemble the various elements into a cohesive story.

I had learned and retained a few finer points of journalism during my prior life as an NBC staffer. It's a natural occurrence to develop an attachment to a story while shooting and covering that story in the field. While we cannot affect or manipulate the story, some kind of an investment or better understanding of the story is inevitable. Once the story is reported and aired, that bond can (and hopefully does) extend to the audience. It's important to nurture that bond, not exploit it.

Given that the audience for Channel One was made up of

teenagers, no one was certain what that bond would look like. Occasionally, we took our Channel One cameras into the very schools that were watching the Channel One newscasts to assess the connection through feedback from the student viewers. While it's tough to tap into the attention span of a 15-year-old, I watched as our work at Channel One did indeed develop such a connection.

One story in particular which resonated with that younger audience, and which demonstrates the type of connection possible between the news media and an audience in general, was a 1990 story we titled "Kids' Rights." It reported on the United Nations Convention on the Rights of the Child (UNCRC). That convention produced a human rights treaty which set out the civil, political, economic, social, health, and cultural rights of children, and which came into force in September of 1990. The treaty defined a child as any human being under the age of eighteen, which helped generate a keen interest with our audience. The treaty put forth child-specific protection, rights, and needs, and was meant to apply to every child everywhere. It became the most widely ratified treaty in history.[1]

I'd seen that, when stories of relevance and/or significance were reported or "told" (thus the term storytelling) in an interesting manner, all audiences could become more intellectually rigorous—compelling storytelling can make us think. And, from time to time, the Channel One stories like "Kids' Rights" were making kids think. That's a wonderful component of the news.

World Monitor was another interesting news start-up. As with Channel One, I was urged to pursue them as a possible client. It was the broadcast extension of *The Christian Science Monitor*, which was a publication of the Church of Christ, Sci-

---

1   "Convention on the Rights of the Child." Retrieved from https://www. unicef.org/child-rights-convention 5/15/2020

entist. Being a firm believer in the separation of Church and State, I was a little leery of working for an entity that intentionally blended television and religion under the guise of "The News."

To guard against exactly this form of skepticism and dispel any criticism of religious undertones attributed to their reporting, the folks at *The Christian Science Monitor* recruited big-name, well-known network talent to anchor their World Monitor program. They needed someone whose reputation and journalistic integrity would provide a secular foundation, and they found the perfect hire in former NBC correspondent John Hart. Hart was a well-respected and award-winning reporter at NBC News. He realized it was highly unlikely that he would replace Tom Brokaw as the anchor at NBC, so he made the move to World Monitor to become the anchorman there.

With John Hart at the helm, World Monitor became a daily news program that was carried on the Discovery Channel. The show had won a Peabody Award for excellence in journalism and was staffed by a team of former network producers behind the scenes in Boston. The producers would call to book freelance camera crews to shoot stories they were covering. World Monitor's structure closely resembled that of a small-scale network operation. Like Channel One, World Monitor wasn't covering stories with the kind of international implications or global significance that I had covered for NBC News overseas.

They did, however, crisscross the U.S. reporting on interesting stories about interesting people and issues, and I soon become one of their go-to freelance cameramen. I quickly realized my concerns about religious interference were baseless. Everything they did, every story I would work on, held true to many of the same journalistic tenants I'd learned while at NBC. They may have been owned by a church, but they put truth and public interest above any religious interests they may have harbored. This was the kind of news coverage I'd been looking for. It was news for news' sake, not dressed up to deliver some kind of hidden messaging.

After a dormant few months of transitioning from my previous overseas career to my current domestic one, my freelance era had finally and officially begun. It was just barely off the ground, but appeared to be gaining altitude. Channel One and World Monitor were keeping me busy. In between their shoots, I waited for the red "network hotline" to ring. It remained silent.

4

WORK'S SURPRISE

My two clients kept me extremely busy. They would hire me and I would in turn hire a soundman from my growing list of Chicago soundmen and contacts. I also continued to call the major networks and remind them who I was and that I was still very much alive, should they find an opening for a freelance crew. Still, keeping busy shooting news segments for Channel One and World Monitor helped to alleviate the angst I felt and at least partially confirmed that my decision to leave NBC and set out on my own hadn't been entirely fool-hearted.

Having clients who hired my services also reinforced the notion that I was good at my job. Without clients, as doubt had crept in, I'd sometimes lost sight of the fact that I had been hired by NBC News as a staff cameraman at the age of 25. Even having just a couple of paying clients was a good way to reinforce the positive. As I slowly built my new freelance business, I reminded myself that I was having fun doing what I loved to do—where I wanted to do it.

One story in particular turned out to be surprisingly enjoyable.

As a tie-in to the Emmy Awards show on TV, Channel One

decided to produce an informative background story for its student viewers. It was not about the "who," the winners and the losers of the award, but rather the "what," the statue itself. What's it made of? How's it made? Where's it made?

The answer to the last question was Chicago, Illinois. At that time, the industrial north side was home to rail yards, warehouses, and small factories that had been built in the early to mid-1900s. Small to medium one, two, and three-story brick buildings dominated the gritty stretch. Candice booked me and my crew to shoot the segment. She was unavailable to produce the story, so she assigned a young eager associate producer named Jenn to help set things up and assist us with the shoot.

Jenn, my soundman Mike, and I arrived at a modest brown brick building that was home to R.S. Owens & Company. They had carved out an impressive little slice of the trophy business, manufacturing both the Emmy AND Oscar awards. Once inside, we were introduced to one of the owners. He was a jovial man with round glasses, thinning hair, and an expanding waistline. He greeted us with a sincere smile and hearty Midwest welcome. He would be our interview subject later in the day, but he'd proudly escort us on a tour of the facility first. Precision die casting machines and electroplating equipment dovetailed with conveyors to create a fluid and orderly assembly line. At various points, skilled workers assisted the process and inspected the statues.

From Henry Ford's Model T to WWII aircraft to modern-day computer chips and Amazon fulfillment, I have always been fascinated with the efficiency and automated choreography of an assembly line. It might be boring to work on one, but to me, the process is stimulating to photograph. After a brief overview of this particular one, we began to shoot the production process.

My eye was glued to the viewfinder of my camera, intently capturing the stages of the assembly procedure. At the end of the line, finished statues were meticulously arranged on wheeled carts to be sent off to their deserving recipients. Jenn was in awe, ogling the row of carts neatly stacked with a cadre of polished and glistening awards.

To no one, in particular, I heard her say, "Wow. Look at all those Emmy awards."

With one eye still partially glued to my camera, I turned slightly in her direction and lightheartedly commented, "Grab mine and take it to the car, would you please?"

Still in an Emmy trance, she took a step closer to the carts, gazing at the awards, and then said, "It's right here."

Her response brought a smile to my face. I liked that she'd countered my semi smart-assed whit with a whit of her own. If she could stand toe-to-toe with a salty crew, then there might be a future for her in this sometimes rough and tumble news business.

She now had a close-up view of the Emmys. Just inches from the statues, she continued, "T. Ortman, NBC. Didn't you used to work for NBC News?"

Okay, there's a point where the joke goes too far, and she was approaching that point. I paused the recording of my camera. I stood up to look over the top of my tripod and camera to shoot her a look that said, "Enough is enough. Playtime is over. We've got work to do here."

She was still fixated on the Emmys, or one Emmy in particular, and continued, "1988 Sports Emmy Award... Games of the XXIV Olympiad." Turning to meet my serious look with a quizzical one of her own, she asked, "Did you cover the Olympics? I think this is yours."

How did she know that I had covered the Summer Olympics in Seoul, South Korea? Was she some kind of mind reader? Someone had to have put her up to this. I looked suspiciously at Mike, who looked bewilderedly back at me. He set down his audio mixer and boom microphone, and we both cautiously walked closer to Jenn and the first cart loaded with Emmys.

And there it was. A large, NATIONAL Emmy—not the diminutive regional one, but the big boy statue engraved... with my name on it! No one knew what to say, least of all me. Noticing we were no longer shooting and were all gathered around a cart of Emmys, our host approached the crew and asked, "Is there something I can help with?"

"I'm not sure. I think we may have just stumbled upon something that might belong to me." I still had my previous year's NBC News-ID card in my wallet, and I produced it for him to validate my crazy claim.

He looked at my ID, then at the Emmy, and then at me and said, "I'll be darned. That's a first, and let me be the first to congratulate you."

We shook hands, and as it began to settle in that I'd won an Emmy, I asked, "Thanks. What happens now?"

"Well, all of these get packaged up and shipped off to NATAS (National Academy of Television Arts and Sciences) in New York. Then, they'll send yours off to NBC and they'll send it off to you."

I had never won an Emmy before. But I did know, just from being in the business, that only a small percentage of the awards are handed out on TV during the ceremony. We see the recipients in their tuxedos and evening gowns giving eloquent acceptance speeches, but that ceremony applies to only a handful of the vast number of Emmys awarded each year. Most Emmys, especially for technical achievements like camera or the Olympics, are simply given or shipped to the winners, void of tuxedos, speeches, and ceremonies.

What he was saying made sense and it all looked good on paper, but I knew better. The Chicago to New York to New York to Chicago route he was talking about looked full of potholes to me.

I try not to generalize—because I know it's wrong, and because I've seen misguided and mislabeled generalizations hurled at "the news media" over and over again—but I feel as comfortable as my weekend sweatpants in saying that bureaucracies are inherently inefficient. Whether it's the Italian customs department or the U.S. Congress or the National Academy of Television Arts and Sciences that we're speaking of, I fear all are prime examples of how NOT to get things done. Add to that the layers upon layers of bureaucratic management at a cavernous black hole like 30 Rock and NBC, and you've created the perfect blueprint for how to lose track of an Emmy. Just as certain as T. ORTMAN was engraved on the base of that statue, I was equally certain that, once my award—and it was my award—left that cozy little factory, I would likely never see it again.

"That seems like a lot of stops for one statue. I'm right here. Why don't I save everyone some time and effort, and take it off your hands right now?"

He saw my offer as a humorous, even comical suggestion and broke out laughing. "Oh my, that's a good one, but I don't think we can do that. No, we've got to do things by the book... follow the procedures."

"Excuse me. But I know how New York operates. It could get lost in the mailroom or end up as a doorstop for some news executive. I may never see this thing again."

That made him laugh even harder. "Oh, my heavens. Door-stop! Ha, ha, ha! I'm sure NBC will deliver your Emmy to you. Why, they cover news all over the world."

That had been ME covering news all over the world. And, we'd sometimes done it DESPITE the interference from New York, not because of it. At any rate, I could see he wasn't buying it. The pleading of my case was falling on deaf ears, so I would have to bid farewell to my award and keep my fingers crossed.

The freelance assignments continued to come my way after that shoot. Meanwhile, I was unable to shake the nagging thought of an award I'd won, seen, and held... once and nevermore. I couldn't even retell the story. It was so unbelievable that, without the statue physically collecting dust on my mantle, no one would believe me. Only after weeks had passed did I realize that the T. ORTMAN engraved on that Emmy had been a member of the. The last known mailing address for me was Via del Plebiscito—in Rome, Italy. As far as NATAS or NBC shipping and receiving were concerned, I was still living in Italy. My beloved Emmy could be in the hands of Italian customs... the same Italian customs who had lost track of an entire apartment full of furniture. My meager little statue could be collecting dust somewhere with all of the other lost treasures of ancient Rome. I decided to take action. My first call was to the Emmys in New York. I found the number for NATAS and dialed it.

A thick female New York accent picked up. "Hello. National Academy of Television Arts and Sciences."

Attempting to make a long story short, I began, "Hi. I think I may have won an Emmy at NBC. Well, actually I *did* win an Emmy at NBC; you see, I was on this shoot in Chicago and—"

"Hold the line."

New Yorkers. I couldn't even finish my opening statement before being dismissed. I waited on hold until a thick male New York accent came on the line.

"Yeah?"

Once again, I began rambling my convoluted and unbelievable story. However, this time I was allowed to finish.

When I concluded, the voice asked, "What'd ya say your name was?"

"Tim Ortman. O. R. T. M. A. N.," I replied. I could hear fingers typing on a computer keyboard.

"Yep. Got it."

What? I'd found it? I'd finally located my lost Emmy?! "That's great. But wait, why do you have my Emmy? Is that standard procedure... to hold onto it? And for how long? When do you plan on shipping it?"

"No plan."

"What do you mean, no plan? If it is in fact my Emmy, why is *it* in New York when *I'm* in Chicago. I'd much rather it resides with me here in Chicago than in New York."

"Look, pal, I don't give a damn where it *resides*. Until you pay for it, it's gonna stay right here."

"Pay for it? I'm a little unfamiliar with the process—first time and all. I have to purchase my Emmy? Doesn't that sort of diminish the luster of the whole thing? I write a check and I receive an award?"

I could hear him sigh on the phone as though he was talking to a moron. "Luster schmuster. You're not paying for the Emmy. You're paying for the *entry fee* for the Emmy. NBC entered you into the competition, but they didn't pay the $100 entry fee that has to accompany *every* application. Got it?"

"Okay, I think I got it. I write you, eh, or NATAS a check for $100, and you send me an Emmy, my Emmy.

"Yep, that's the way it works."

"I appreciate the education. It's a kind of circuitous, roundabout way to receive an award, but I'll take it. The check is in the mail."

"And once I get it, your Emmy will be in the mail."

I provided him with my office address for the shipping, thanked him, and hung up. And then I waited another couple of weeks, only slightly reassured that I would someday see the Emmy which I'd briefly held months earlier at R.S. Owens & Company.

A couple of weeks later, I was wheeling my equipment in from the loading dock when Michael, the Irish doorman, notified me that a package had arrived. I waited by the elevator doors as he retrieved my package. It wasn't until I read the return address label that I made the connection.... *NATAS, New York, NY.*

"This is it!" I yelled.

"This is what?" Michael screamed back.

"I think it's my long-lost award."

"Well, don't just stand there, lad. Open the bloody package!" Fishing into the pocket of his uniform, he retrieved a Swiss Army knife and handed it to me.

I opened one end and removed an inner Styrofoam sleeve resembling a wine shipper. I opened the Styrofoam container to reveal a bright and shiny Emmy engraved with my name. All of my doubts had been erased. My persistence produced a half-smile externally and a full sense of accomplishment internally.

Michael's eyes widened as he examined the trophy. He asked, "Is that what I think it is?"

I said, "It's an Emmy, and there's quite the backstory that accompanies it."

"I've never seen one before... in person, I mean. Let me get my camera. Stay here. I'll be right back."

Michael our doorman was more impressed with my newfound celebrity than I was. I was just happy to finally have the damn award. If he wanted to capture me and my trophy on film and tell people he knew an Emmy winner, I was glad to assist with those bragging rights.

In a full sprint, he returned to the lobby with a tiny point-and-shoot camera. I was awaiting his direction. Where did he want me standing and in what pose?

Suddenly, without uttering a word, he grabbed the Emmy out of my hand and, in its place, handed me his camera. He pulled the statue close to his face, and with a wide cheesy grin stretching from ear to ear, instructed me, "Okay, I'm ready. Go ahead and take a bunch of shots."

I burst out laughing and happily obliged, shooting an entire roll of film of Michael with *his* Emmy award. Afterward, Michael returned my Emmy to me and I returned his camera to him. I couldn't help but wonder about the letter accompanying those photos back to Ireland.

Dear Family,

No need to worry about me. I'm adjusting to life quite well here in America. It truly is the land of opportunity. I've landed a few odd jobs which I find to be quite... rewarding.

Your loving and successful son,
Michael

5

LIFE'S SURPRISE

Finally, my furniture arrived from Rome. NBC was thrilled to remove me from their relocation budget and I was thrilled to have a place I could call my own. I bid farewell to the Four Seasons staff with whom I'd bonded during my extended stay. My condo was just blocks away from Amy's apartment, and the proximity made it easy for us to see one another on an increasingly regular basis. Any free time we found was spent with each other as our casual relationship slowly progressed into a monogamous, semi-serious one.

Meanwhile, my freelance career was still budding, but the assignments were increasing. World Monitor booked me and my crew to connect with one of their correspondents for an assignment in Colorado. For five days, we would travel through the Western Slope of the Rocky Mountains shooting "slice of life" stories with a distinctly Western flavor. They'd be informative pieces from interesting rural towns rather than the hard-hitting news headlines I'd so often covered with the foreign press corps.

Having never been to that part of the United States, I found both the journey and the stories to be eye-opening and invigorating. Driving on winding roads through vast open spaces, we meandered through the arid high desert of Grand Junction, Colorado and into the canyon country of Moab, Utah. There was majestic beauty in every direction. It was a refreshing departure from Chicago and Rome. Each morning, I'd wake up with deep breathes of crisp, pristine mountain air. On one such morning, I phoned Amy back in Chicago and relayed to her the beauty I was experiencing.

"Morning. You should see this place. I've seen some wonderful spots all over the world, but this trip adds new meaning to "America the Beautiful." Speaking of beautiful, how are you?"

Her response to my question contained a surprising revelation.

"Oh, aren't you sweet? I'm generally good. I do have a slight change in my overall health to report. Well, actually WE have a change."

"What do you mean WE? My health couldn't be better. Maybe it's all this clean air. I feel like—"

"By WE, I meant that I think WE might be pregnant."

My mind was racing as I began gasping for even more of the aforementioned clean air.

"You think? Isn't that kind of an absolute? Either we are or we aren't, right?"

"My home test was positive. I have a follow-up with my OBGYN. But I know my body, and I'm pretty sure I'm pregnant."

Bringing a child into the world is the ultimate responsibility, but abortion and adoption were never options for either of us and were never discussed. I'd always wanted children and was relatively certain Amy felt the same, although we hadn't had a lengthy heart-to-heart discussion on the subject. Having such a conversation *after* conception seemed a little moot. Needless to say, this was not how either of us had envisioned family planning. One thing was certain; slowing down was no longer an option.

Our semi-serious relationship would have to get kicked into high gear and launch into fast-forward mode.

Even though I was stunned by her surprise "Breaking News," my knee-jerk reaction was to stay positive, and I reassured her with, "Well, that's... great."

My glass-half-full support was met with her glass-half-empty worry. "You really think this is... great?"

Given our on-again, off-again history, the concern in her voice was warranted. I, too, was painfully aware of that history. Still reeling from the startling news, I quickly began to see this as an opportunity instead of an obstacle.

"Yes, I do. This is all new head-spinning news. Let's wait to hear from your doctor. But, if you are... if *we* are in fact pregnant, that's a good thing. It's a wonderful thing. This could force us to grow up and really commit to each other. We've always loved each other, but we maybe took that love for granted and treated it too casually. We have something special. And, bringing another life into the world is pretty damn special, too. It's something fantastic, and I think we'd both make fantastic parents. I'm probably sounding like a cheerleader here and I don't mean to. I'm just being honest."

"I agree, this could be a fantastic thing, but I'm also a little scared. Actually, I'm scared as hell, and I'm just being honest."

"I hear you. I'll be home in a couple of days, and by then, we'll know for certain. This is potentially a game-changer, but not a negative or unwelcome one... just a surprising one. I know we haven't talked about it much, but I'd love to have a child with you. And if you'll entertain one more sports metaphor, we'd make MVP parents. I know it. This all begs for a lengthier conversation than a morning chat from Grand Junction, Colorado. Give some thought to what I said. I'll call you tomorrow and then be back home day after tomorrow. I love you. Don't be scared."

Amy's home pregnancy test and intuition were spot-on. We were pregnant.

Amy's initial fears were replaced with genuine excitement about being a mom. As for so many first-time parents, seeing our daughter's beating heart on the first ultra-sound elevated that excitement. Brought to our senses by the pending birth of our daughter, we did the unthinkable and remarried.

Being older, wiser, and more mature the second time around, we chose the grown-up, middle-aged option for our wedding ceremony... and eloped to Las Vegas. Amy chose an ivory, not so formal dress. With her already showing a small bump in her abdomen, she and I walked down the aisle at the Silver Bells Wedding Chapel. Joined only by my older brother Jeff and his wife, the Reverend James Cotton presided over our nuptials. With his blessing and a hearty "Halleluiah! Can I get an amen?", we walked down the aisle and into another heartening chapter of life.

* * * * *

On January 14, 1991, Alexa Marilyn Ortman entered our lives and made the world a much better place. Amy had moved in with me, returning to the familiar and cozy one-bedroom condo she'd occupied while attending law school. It was so cozy that our newborn daughter's crib was sandwiched into our not-so-master master bedroom. As a more lasting solution, we would eventually purchase an old three-story home in a historically

German neighborhood on Chicago's nearby North Side, which was undergoing gentrification. Over the next five years, the three of us would reside in an ongoing construction site.

While still in our tiny condo, we gleefully shared our new parenting duties. Amy took full advantage of her law firm's maternity leave policy to dote over our baby daughter. I was also guilty of over-adoring her. I thoroughly enjoyed pushing her stroller through the park, the weary midnight and early morning feeding shifts, and, after Amy's tutorials, changing Alexa's diapers. We both found parenting a newborn to be an exhaustive delight.

Exactly two days after Alexa's birth, a major international news event occurred. The six-month preparation for war, known as Operation Desert Shield, would become a very real war known as Operation Desert Storm. President George Herbert Walker Bush—or, Bush 41—had warned Iraq's leader, Saddam Hussein, that his invasion and annexation of neighboring Kuwait would not be tolerated. But the Iraqi army stayed put in Kuwait, refusing to heed the warnings of an imminent war with an American-led coalition consisting of 35 nations.

Desert Storm was a much larger military action than that of the international peacekeeping forces I'd covered during the war in Lebanon. My intellectual curiosity had me wondering what it was like to be on the ground in Baghdad; what were the similarities and what were the differences compared to conflicts like what I'd seen in Lebanon? I knew many of the journalists on assignment there and part of me longed for the wartime comradery I'd once known. I had only been back a year, but the infant daughter in my arm and the bottle of formula in my hand were my primary focus. I wasn't about to pack up my TV gear and head back overseas to cover the war in Iraq.

When it was my turn for Alexa's bottle feeding, I was able to watch LIVE coverage of a U.S.-waged war from the comfort of my couch as my baby daughter nursed in my arms. As a first-time father and veteran cameraman, I found this to be both enthralling and mind-boggling. This was the first war in which the U.S. military played a dual role as a conquering army and, simultaneously, a front-line news agency. They had equipped their high-tech weaponry with video capability, making it possible for viewers to watch images from precision-guided missiles as they closed in and destroyed enemy targets. POV video from the pilot's perspective was shown as fighter jets took off from aircraft carriers flying sorties over Iraq and firing their weapons. Recent advancements in night-vision equipment provided viewers with the ability to watch fighting day and night. The grainy, green, night-vision images gave an entertaining *Blade Runner* feeling to watching war. And the Army distributed this material to the news networks, who in turn broadcast it to the world. It was patriotic, must-see TV news.

Desert Storm was big news for all of the American news networks. But in 1991, CNN was the only player in the 24-hour-news space, and it was a space they'd occupied alone for ten years. When Iraqi authorities expelled Western reporters from Bagdad, CNN was allowed to remain in place (thanks to producer Robert Wiener's contacts). Once communications were cut, CNN was able to stay on the air thanks to a separate or back-up audio system (known as a four-wire). And in the early moments of the war, that foresight allowed for anchorman Bernard Shaw to report live via radio from a suite in the Rashid Hotel. *"The skies over Bagdad have been illuminated..."*

Desert Storm was a made-for-TV war. It not only changed how war would be covered, but CNN's coverage of Desert Storm foreshadowed how news would be covered—wall to wall, bumper to bumper. News was no longer delivered sunrise to sunset. It was now "round the clock"... uninterrupted.

This was where I and many in the news business grasped the mesmerizing power of 24-hour news.

Desert Storm would not and could not last forever. But the mechanisms for 24-hour coverage had been put in place, and other networks were anxious to mimic CNN's round the clock success. War or no war. Five years later, Fox News Channel and MSNBC would follow suit with their brand of 24-hour news.

To an entrepreneurial freelancer with lengthy network credentials, all this added airtime to fill would translate into more assignments, more coverage, and more live shots, which would translate into more income. However, in the days following Desert Storm, I was not focused on the distant future and eventual expansion of 24-hour news. I was focused on the immediate future of being a dad and building a business. The non-network client base I'd created with Channel One, World Monitor, and others were paying the bills and even slowly expanding. I was grateful for their ever-increasing assignments. But, for the previous seven years, I had been a staff network cameraman. That was what had defined me and how I viewed myself.

To truly justify my freelance endeavor, I would have to break into the big news networks back home. I viewed those networks as my window on and into the world of real news. Any client base I created that lacked such network clients was a hollow base. Any success I may have achieved without the inclusion of the news networks was a failure. For me, covering the kind of network news that had become so ingrained in me would be the only real measure of success.

6

REVITALIZATION AND REALIZATION

Finally, my networking paid network dividends. My former employer was the first to open the door and invite me inside—or, *back inside* network news. The NBC Chicago bureau had both cameramen and soundmen on staff, as well as established freelance crews who capably handled the workload. I'd long been assured I would eventually receive a call to work me into the rotation. Without such a call, I'd become frustrated in the ensuing months and had begun to skeptically view those assurances as a courteous dismissal. I'd never been so happy to be so wrong.

A nostalgic look back at the halcyon days of automobile travel was my first network assignment after returning to the U.S. Before we GPSed our way from coast to coast on super-highways that stretch everywhere, Americans traveled at a more leisurely pace. The famed Route 66 was the first intercontinental road linking Chicago to Los Angeles. It wandered through urban and rural communities and, in doing so, connected both. My soundman and I joined an NBC producer and correspondent to shoot a wistful video essay that retraced those romantic journeys through the heart of America.

The opportunity to shoot video on the picturesque backroads

of America is photographic gold to a cameraman. Seizing upon such an opportunity can let one's creative side shine through. There's a saying in television news: "You're only as good as your last story." Making the most of the Route 66 shoot was more than simply getting my foot in the door. It provided a new client (and former employer) with eye-catching video evidence that I did belong and that I merited future assignments.

There are numerous criteria used to evaluate a freelance news crew. Professionalism, reliability, integrity, punctuality, personality, and congeniality are all components of that client-vendor relationship. But *talent* tops the list, and for a cameraman, it's difficult if not impossible to fake talent. Different stories pose different challenges, visually. In a basic sense, talent is the ability to see things others might miss and then to "frame" those images and capture them with a camera lens to realistically and honestly show the viewers a sight and visually tell a story. The written word, sound, lighting, and editing all work together to create the final product. But it becomes much easier with quality moving images.

With that first NBC shoot, my talent was confirmed and I was no longer on the outside looking in.

NBC quickly became an important client. I was soon in their mix of trusted freelance cameramen. Being on the "inside," my presence was a reminder to the executives and decision-makers in both Chicago and New York. "Oh yeah, this guy used to work for us overseas. He's one of us." That reminder allowed me to climb the ladder of freelance hierarchy and quickly advance past my competitors, who didn't possess my experience as a former NBC staffer (and some might even say my talent as one).

About this time, the news magazine phenomenon was rapidly gaining traction. CBS had *60 Minutes*. ABC had *20/20*.

These two programs were the award-winning and prestigious crown jewels at CBS and ABC. As hour-long news magazine programs, they allowed for longer-form news reporting. A news story on the *Evening News* might run 2:30 (and far less today), whereas a story on *60 Minutes* could run 15 minutes. To capitalize on the success, all four networks were experimenting with *60 Minute* and *20/20* knockoffs.

Real Life with Jane Pauley was one such experiment at NBC. It wasn't intended to be an exact copy of *60 Minutes*. Instead, it launched as "news magazine lite," with a positive side. Regardless of its news approach, it was an added demand on the resources of the news division and would require, to some degree, employing trusted and professional freelance crews to help shoulder the added burden... and the cameras. I became one of those trusted freelancers who were hired and relied upon to shoot segments for *Real Life*. The longer format allowed us the luxury of spending numerous days in the field producing and shooting stories. We profiled a hugely talented and successful black choir comprised solely of inner-city kids, and reported on the impact Indian gaming was having on Native American tribes, as well as the shocking rise of teen athletes using steroids. And there were many, many other such stories. The proliferation of the news magazine format allowed broadcast journalists to cover more news in a more in-depth manner. Not every news event is going to be Desert Storm. But these magazine stories were all news-worthy topics, and I felt fortunate to be part of their coverage. By adding *Real Life* to *Nightly News* and *TODAY*, I also felt fortunate to have three means of income being generated from a single network client.

A similar experiment occurred at ABC. Eager to build on the success of its network mainstay *20/20*, ABC created *Primetime*

Live. Hosted by Diane Sawyer and Sam Donaldson, *Primetime* focused more on breaking news with the interaction of a live studio audience. Back in New York at the network headquarters, additional producers were being hired to staff all of these additional programs, and some were jumping ship from network to network. The reputations (and good fortunes) of some of us freelance cameramen were spread by word of mouth from producer to producer, and subsequently from network to network. If you had climbed to the top of the call list at one network, you were soon at the top of the call list at many of them. Fortuitously, I was soon in the mix at both NBC and ABC, where I was increasingly receiving assignments for *Primetime Live*, whose producers focused on hard news topics.

One such story required our team to spend weeks shooting in Chicago's bleak ghettos. The cold and grey winter skies made those gloomy neighborhoods appear even more so. The video was very real and gritty, as it peered behind the curtain of American affluence. Groups of lost men void of direction gathered around trashcan fires on neglected streets in front of neglected and crumbling, barely inhabitable buildings. Crime and violence were pervasive in these neighborhoods (and, sadly, still are today). Yet, that was not the focus of this in-depth story. This particular story uncovered the horrendous practices of abusive slumlords who preyed on the poor. In the process of covering the story, we interviewed people who had never been interviewed before and gathered stories that had rarely been told. We profiled the dedicated work done by unsung heroes at food banks to nourish the indigent and hungry. It was a side of American life not often seen, and it was difficult to see. These were dark stories about hopelessness—the kind that are depressing to cover and watch. But, in doing so, we utilized one of journalism's most hopeful tools. We provided a voice for these voiceless and desperate citizens.

It had been 14 months since my return. With ABC, I added another network client to my growing resume, which was an affirmation that, just perhaps, my freelance experiment was worthwhile. More than that, I was reminded that the industry in which I worked, the news media, was an extremely worthwhile endeavor both in this country and beyond.

As 1991 was winding down, the networks had turned their focus from the last major story, the recent battle in Iraq, to the next major story, the 1992 elections and the battle for the White House. CNN had started something called *Special Assignment*. It wasn't a news magazine show, but rather a select unit of producers and correspondents dedicated to magazine-like, longer-form reporting. Profiling presidential candidates and their records was a perfect fit for and a preferred topic of *Special Assignment*.

On this note, I was pleasantly surprised to receive a call from Atlanta. CNN was looking for me. Apparently, another word-of-mouth recommendation had resulted in another network contact. I never inquired as to how I had surfaced on their radar; I was just happy to be a blip on their screen. *Special Assignment* wanted to hire me and my soundman to shoot a profile on a rising political star in nearby Nebraska. I was available for the dates in question, so we packed our gear and flew to Omaha, where we met up with the CNN producer and correspondent for our "special assignment."

Senator Bob Kerrey was first elected to the U.S. Senate in 1988. Before that, he had served as Governor of Nebraska from 1983-1987. Before that, he'd been a U.S. Navy SEAL who'd won a Purple Heart and the Medal of Honor for heroism while fighting in the Vietnam War. He was an unpretentious and straight-talking civil servant and humble war hero. With the 1992 presidential election in his sights, he announced his candidacy for president in late 1991 and became one of the Democratic front-runners. As journalists, we must remain independent from any candidate, but I did find Senator Kerrey to be a genial gentleman whose middle-of-the-road politics would appeal to many. However, with mediocre performances in both the Iowa caucuses and the New Hampshire primary, his chances soon faded.

The CNN *Special Assignment* story added even more momentum to my network discovery. Additionally, it provided me with a taste of what it was like to cover American politics. Some find politics distasteful, but I found them fascinating—and I knew a mere taste would never suffice to satisfy my growing appetite. While these added news magazine shows and longer-form news reports were an immediate boon to my freelance business, they most benefitted the American news consumer. There was only a limited amount of content you could cover with one morning news program and one evening news program. These added programs provided coverage and made for the airing of more and more varied news topics. We were in the business of news and information, and, at that time, business was expanding in a favorable direction.

Today, there are still excellent examples of the once prolific news magazine show. *60 Minutes* just celebrated its 52nd anniversary. Yet, so many others have been canceled due to declining ratings or repackaged into something entirely different—such as the true crime and courtroom drama. With a loyal audience following and an unending supply of grizzly murder stories, shows like *Dateline* continue to chug along as a reliable profit center for their networks. The gruesome murders they retell are a far cry from the news reporting they once performed, however, and represent a divide from what they were and what they are now.

In 1990 and '91, I'd steadily built up a healthy mix of clients comprised of network news and non-network programs. These were supported by additional clients from corporate, educational, and medical television. I was very busy and, as a result, happy. My active schedule was matched or even exceeded by that of my wife, whose demands at the law firm were outpacing my assignments. Both of our schedules were "enhanced" by our hectic home front.

We had purchased and moved into a 100-year-old, three-story home in a German neighborhood on Chicago's North Side. The house had endured a century of neglect and was in desperate need of repair. This was major reconstruction versus cosmetic makeover. In TV terms, the undertaking was like transitioning from *My 600-lb. Life* to *Project Runway*. But through all of the cracked plaster, drafty windows, creaking floors, and leaky roofs, the structure offered a glimmer of potential charm... and plenty of much-needed space for Alexa and our expanded family of three. Importantly, it fit our budget; that of a second-year law associate and a freelancer who had sunk most of his savings into a dream—and expensive camera gear.

Our only option was to reside within the house of horrors during its transformation.

Alexa was one when we moved in. She celebrated her first birthday with fellow toddlers in a construction zone that doubled as a dining room. She took her first steps wobbling between toolboxes and two-by-fours. Amy and I lovingly and vigilantly wiped the constant drywall dust from her highchair. We weren't alone, though. Chicago is a rich patchwork of ethnic neighborhoods. Our German neighborhood bordered a Polish neighborhood to the West, which is where we found Alexa's nanny Danuta, who was a Polish-speaking version of Mrs. Doubtfire. During the workday, she would shelter Alexa from the steady stream of craftsmen and workers. Danuta was equal parts caregiver, security blanket, and traffic cop. The construction was a constant inconvenience for Amy and me, but for an inquisitive toddler, the large floorplan offered a playground of discovery as long as we were mindful of the circular saws, nail guns, power drills, and belt sanders. (With the inevitable starts and stops, the renovation ended up being a four-year project which would tax any marriage, including ours. But any frustrations we felt during the construction were replaced by a sense of accomplishment upon completion... or maybe it was just relief.)

With my work, I was no longer focused on cold-calling prospective clients, as I'd had to do upon my return from Europe. Most of those prospective clients had become actual clients, in fact, but with one notable exception.

Within the news business, CBS was quietly revered and sometimes referred to as the "Tiffany Network." Visionary and driven founder William S. Paley had built a massive and hugely successful empire. Over the years, the network news division there had included some of the most respected names in broadcast journalism—Edward R. Murrow, Walter Cronkite, Eric Sevareid, Howard K. Smith, William L. Shirer, and many others contributed to making *CBS News* the leader. During the mid to late 1980s, the ratings gap between the three broadcast networks had tightened, with Tom Brokaw and *NBC News* taking the #1 spot. But CBS was still an illustrious and historic place for television news. It was also the one network where I remained on the outside looking in. I was determined to respectfully but regularly knock on their door and remind them of my existence. They, in turn, politely responded that they'd survived over 60 years without my services and saw no reason to change "at this time."

After I'd spent two years trying to court CBS, a friend of a friend introduced me to a young up-and-coming producer at CBS Chicago. Glen Dacey was impressed with my foreign experience and the fact that I was working for all of the major networks *except* CBS. Unlike NBC and ABC, which gave greater autonomy to the individual bureaus for staffing needs, CBS required that all of their freelancers be hired out of New York. Glen graciously offered to put my name in the New York hat from which freelancers were pulled. I expressed my whole-hearted appreciation while concealing my genuine skepticism.

About that time, a rape trial occurred in my backyard.

Boxer Mike Tyson had been one of the most dominant and feared combatants the sport had ever seen. At 20 years old, he became the youngest undisputed world heavyweight champion. He won his first 19 fights by knockout, most of them in the first round. In 1990, a 42-1 underdog and unknown challenger named Buster Douglas beat Tyson to claim the title. It was one of the biggest upsets in the history of sports. Any sport. Before Douglas, Tyson had vanquished all challengers with amazing ease. After Douglas, however, he would suffer a much more damning defeat outside of the ring.

In the summer of 1991, Tyson visited Indianapolis, Indiana for the Miss Black America beauty pageant. During that visit, he invited an 18-year-old contestant to his hotel room, where they had sex. She accused him of rape, and he was arraigned on charges of rape and criminal deviant conduct; a trial date was set for February of '92. I saw this as a most serious fight for

Tyson, but did not connect any dots to myself.

Someone on the CBS news desk in New York looked at a map and determined that Chicago, a three-hour drive from Indianapolis, was the most logical place from which to staff the coverage of the Tyson rape trial. That same someone must also have noticed a post-it note containing the name of some new Chicago freelancer. Regardless of how the magic happened, my phone rang and, just like that, I was part of the CBS News family, albeit on a temporary trial basis (pun intended). It's not what you know but who you know, and my timely introduction to Glen had just paid a dividend.

Because I was booked a few days in advance of the trial, this would not be the kind of shot-out-of-a-cannon departure which is so common to breaking news and natural disasters. There would be time to pack leisurely and kiss Amy and Alexa goodbye.

I was receiving more and more news assignments from the networks. The very nature of news is unpredictable, so trying to create a predictable schedule a month or two in advance was difficult at best. A trial, for example, was on the courthouse calendar months in advance. The networks knew it was coming and they usually knew its expected duration. Other magazine assignments offered the same luxury of advanced notice, but the fluidity of news dictates that those who work in the business of news need to be flexible and respond to the breaking nature of their business. It is an inherent part of the news process. As a freelancer whose income was only earned when I was on assignment, it was a delicate balancing act. You wanted to be available for the network breaking news. But, if you were available, you weren't working.

As I was prepping for the Tyson trial, my phone rang again.

NBC was calling. "Hey, Tim, we want to send you to Indianapolis next week for this Tyson trial. Not sure how long it will take; probably three weeks, max."

Sheepishly, I responded, "I would love to, but I just received a call earlier today from CBS for the same assignment. I'm sorry I'm not available."

Matter-of-factly, and now somewhat rushed, they responded, "Damn them! Just kidding. Not to worry, we'll get you on the next one. Gotta run."

And, later that same day, ABC called wanting to send me to Indianapolis. Had I missed something? Had little green aliens landed at the Indianapolis courthouse? Had it been struck by lightning and then leveled by a twister? I'd thought I had developed a fairly well-honed news sense, but I'd initially seen Mike Tyson's troubles as something that would headline on the budding sports network ESPN or maybe CNN with all of their airtime to fill (in '92, they were still the only 24-hour news operation). I concluded that all three broadcast networks had called not because of my nascent popularity, but rather out of interest in a salacious celebrity rape trial. Pragmatically speaking, the really big news for me was that I'd been hired by CBS.

We checked into the Indianapolis Hilton and met up with the CBS News team. I immediately recognized correspondent Bob Faw from his years of on-air reporting and astute writing. Producer Ingrid Arnesen was smart and serious while simultaneously foreshadowing a wicked sense of humor. For years, I'd competed against CBS on news coverage. Regardless of the story or the journalists assigned, they were always prepared and professional. Now, as a team member, I could see that Bob and Ingrid were all that and much more. We were all prepared to stay in Indianapolis for the duration of the trial and nobody could predict that time frame; the best guess was about two weeks.

Superior Court Judge Patricia Gifford presided over the trial. Tyson had assembled a high-profile $5,000 a day legal team for his defense. The prosecution was led by Greg Garrison, a fiery, red-headed trial lawyer who hadn't lost a case in almost 20 years. At that time, Indiana did not allow cameras inside the courtroom. The principal video each day would consist of the courthouse arrivals and departures of Tyson and his legal team, as well as the Garrison team. On day one, we arrived at the courthouse steps at 6 a.m. to get a prime position for the arrivals. We were not alone, and were soon joined by other camera crews... many other camera crews.

The trial would last 13 days. Judge Gifford ran her courtroom in a strict but fair and even-handed manner. The defense team claimed that the sex had been consensual and that the accuser was after Tyson's money. The prosecution pounded away at Tyson's history of lewd and offensive behavior. Tyson's testimony was a disaster and contributed to his downfall. Each morning, we would prepare a story or "spot" for *CBS This Morning* and each afternoon we would prepare a spot for the *CBS Evening News*. ABC, NBC, and CNN all did the same. During the trial, 400 news media members from the U.S. and 13 foreign countries would cover the events. The world was watching.

The former champ was eventually convicted and sentenced to ten years, a sentence that was reduced to six. With time off for good behavior, he would spend a total of three years in prison.

From the opening gavel to the final sentencing, the trial was very much a news story deserving of coverage. Yet, at times, that coverage seemed to deviate from the standard journalistic path of who, what, where, when, and why. In '92, the term "date rape" had recently entered the mainstream of the American lexicon, which fueled the interest in and debate surrounding the Tyson case. Some of the reporting attempted to villainize Tyson and dramatize the whole trial (even without cameras in the courtroom), and in doing so went well beyond reporting on guilt or innocence.

I was ecstatic at the opportunity to work for CBS. Adding them to NBC, ABC, and CNN completed the sweep for me. In horseracing terms, it was like winning the Superfecta (the most difficult wager to win), or, in baseball, it was akin to hitting for the cycle. I would work on many, many more assignments for each of those four networks and even others. The Tyson trial was rewarding in that it was such a lengthy assignment, and in freelance parlance, the longer the assignment, the bigger the paycheck. Yet, in terms of news relevance, I quietly questioned the amount of airtime and resources thrown at this one story. The coverage simply didn't fit the crime. In my previous ten years, I'd worked on stories where network journalists and tabloid journalists had stood side by side and reported on the same story—with the former dealing in facts and the latter in lurid ambiguity. One story with two markedly different versions. However, in this story, the line between those two began to blur.

It's human nature that causes passersby to gawk at a car wreck engulfed in flames. To some degree, the media circus that engulfed the Tyson trial fanned the flames of sensationalism, increasing the tabloid rubbernecking—but at the expense of real journalism.

Mike Tyson's rape trial would leave the door ajar for other spectacles to become spectacular news.

In January of 1994, Detroit hosted the U.S. National Figure Skating Championships at Cobo Arena. Even in an Olympic year like '94, the U.S. National competition is rarely noticed outside of the major sports media, and it's certainly not covered by the major network news media. But because television is a visual medium, certain visuals can enhance a story and even change the narrative. Such was the case in Detroit in 1994.

Nancy Kerrigan was one of the favorites to win the national competition and make the U.S. Olympic team. In the moments following a practice round, she was found sitting on a hallway floor just off the ice rink, holding her right knee and tearfully screaming, "Why? Why? Why?" Those images were recorded by a camera crew for Intersport, a Chicago-based sports and entertainment company, and they would become a visual and audible clip that would be seen by countless millions. Kerrigan had been the victim of an unidentified assailant who'd beaten her twice on the knee with a metal baton before fleeing. That was just the tip of the iceberg.

As a Chicago-based company, Intersport hired me to travel to Detroit and shoot some additional follow-up elements of this growing story.

As the plot unfolded, Kerrigan's archrival Tonya Harding was implicated in the attack. Her ex-husband Jeff Gillooly and bodyguard Shawn Eckhardt had hired the assailant, Shane Stant, to shatter Kerrigan's knee, thereby removing her from competition. It turned out, Stant was a terrible hit man—as in, he was incompetent. He failed miserably at his objective and only succeeded in bruising Kerrigan's leg. The mere fact that these morons attempted such a boneheaded move turned a little skating saga into national news. While the traditional news media reported on the who, what, where, and when, the tabloid news media speculated on the seedier why. That speculative question of motivation moved the story's focus from Detroit to

Harding's hometown of Portland, Oregon(beyond my Midwest jurisdiction), where the media staked out her home and the skating rink where she practiced.

To capitalize on the growing appetite for such stories (which our media had created), stories began to take on a certain hue. Harding was the unpolished, trash-talking, chain-smoking girl from a broken home on the wrong side town while Kerrigan was the polished and elegant product of a loving family. Harding was a "bull in the china shop" powering through her performances while Kerrigan was a lithe ballerina on skates. In the wake of the attack, creating these subplots created a villain vs. victim, good vs. evil storyline that dramatized and scandalized the story well beyond any news boundaries.

This opened the door for rampant media speculation. What did Tanya Harding know? When did she know it? Was she in on the attack? Did she order the attack? The news media rushed to answer these burning questions without having the hard facts to support an answer. The conclusion? HARDING HAD TO BE IN ON IT!

It was scandalous infotainment. The mainstream news media at first resisted, but was eventually sucked into all the salaciousness. Respected publications like *Time, Newsweek*, and *The Washington Post* and all of the news networks followed suit. The lines between trusted and tabloid media at times became so blurred that it was difficult to distinguish fact from fantasy.

The media maelstrom continued to build and even added international intrigue to the story's appeal. Six weeks after the attack on Kerrigan, both she and Harding skated for the U.S. team at the XVII Winter Olympic Games in Lillehammer, Norway. When Harding and Kerrigan took to the ice for their first practice, 300 photographers were shooting an event that would normally have attracted 30. When they skated in the final competition, 48.5 million viewers were watching, making it the highest-rated Olympic event, EVER. In the end, Kerrigan finished second—barely edged out not by Harding, but 16-year-old Ukrainian Oksana Baiul. A tearful Harding finished a disappointing eighth.

It was made for TV drama, distorted by an exaggerated lens and an embellished storyline. It was even made into a biopic movie, *I, Tonya*. But it wasn't deserving of such round the clock news coverage from the mainstream news media.

I was in my late thirties—too old and experienced to be disillusioned by headline-grabbing news. As a foot soldier on the frontlines, I never assumed myself to possess the big picture perspective of the network generals back in New York. But my news compass had been shaped, in part, by my many years of working overseas. Covering an assaulted figure skater and disgraced boxer with the same news fervor as the fall of Communism or a regime change seemed a little incongruent to me.

"Is this really news?" I wondered. I allowed myself brief moments of contemplation, but mostly I would simply smile all the way to the bank. I was riding a crest that included all four major networks. The news business was a labor of love and business was good. Yet, for the very first time, I began to question the object of my affection.

If Mike Tyson and Tonya Harding tarnished the adulation I felt for my industry, there was another story on the horizon that would leave many of us questioning the direction of news. Four months after the Lillehammer Olympics, a double-murder occurred in Brentwood, California.

The O.J. Simpson trial was unlike anything before it. The murder investigation and ensuing ten-month trial would seize hold of America's attention for a year and a half. I was based in Chicago at the time. With a plethora of staff and freelance personnel available in the Los Angeles market (many of whom I'd consider close friends), I did not participate directly in the O.J. coverage. I don't want to elaborate on stories on which I did not work directly, and yet, the O.J. trial was such a seminal moment in news coverage that it begs at least a brief mention.

To contextualize the coverage, start with the fact that there were only two 24-hour news channels in 1994—CNN and Court TV (which would later become TruTV). CNN had seen their post-Gulf War ratings dip dramatically. The O.J. story was a story about celebrity, murder, money, sex, and race. It was human drama that had the potential to reclaim at least some of those lost ratings. It immediately became story #1 at CNN and Court TV, and just as immediately, the viewers tuned in to watch.

The cameras in the courtroom played directly into TV's visual appeal. Witnesses became characters while the hordes of viewers became instant jurors. The hungry viewers couldn't get enough. *The Guinness Book of Records* lists the Simpson case as the "most viewed trial" of all time. Each day, on average, 5.5 million Americans watched the live courtroom coverage. And once they tuned in, there was no turning back. The story became so engrained in our culture that people were less likely to watch or read other news. It made it difficult, if not impossible, for the networks to focus their coverage on other deserving stories, for fear of losing "O.J. viewers." If they dared, the negative change would be reflected in the overnight ratings the next morning.

If the Tyson trial and the Harding/Kerrigan story had at times blurred the line between tabloid and mainstream reporting, then the O.J. trial fused the two together. Sometimes, the mainstream media even seemed to follow the tabloid lead. One of Simpson's defense attorneys, Gerald Uelmen, observed, "What I realized is, this is entertainment. This is not news."

The Simpson trial also exploited a fairly new tool of the 24-hour news toolbox, one that's been invaluable and irreplaceable ever since. The expert panel discussion proved to be an inexpensive way to speculate and keep the discussion going... which is a great way to keep viewers tuned in.

In local news, there's a popular adage used to describe coverage that maximizes local ratings. "If it bleeds, it leads." Networks had always striven to deliver broader, deeper, and more thought-provoking coverage than that. But O.J. was one story that bled, and it led. It led all news as well as our nation's consciousness for a year and a half, and even longer. It was over-the-top, hyper-news coverage. The news media gave the viewer what they craved and, in doing so, the networks were rewarded with higher ratings and a healthier and more profitable bottom line. At the same time, they abandoned their higher calling of actually serving the public interest instead of simply pandering to it.

The O.J. trial was a news event that launched a number of news careers and enhanced many more. Once it was all over and there was time to reflect, however, I know there was an abundance of journalistic embarrassment and even remorse for the level of coverage that had been dedicated to one horrific story. For better or worse, O.J. helped create our world today where 24-hour news is the norm, where "reality" shows are everywhere, and where entire networks are dedicated to true-life crime dramas.

7

A Palate for Politics

There were stories I was assigned to that made me question the intense level of coverage; stories I found unimportant that became imperative; stories I thought minor which, in the eyes of the network, were major. My job was to cover those stories, *not* to assign coverage to those stories. As a disciplined photojournalist, I kept my opinions about coverage to myself. As a small businessman, any media "frenzy" in which I participated was to my benefit and at the expense of the subject of that frenzy. Fortunately, stories labeled as frenzied, hyped, and spectacle were still few and far between.

Between Tyson and O.J. and well beyond, the vast majority of network stories on which I worked reminded me of the many reasons I found the news media to be an immensely fulfilling industry. So many of those stories confirmed to me that: 1). It was a useful and at times even honorable way to deliver information; 2). It was reliable, accountable information reported without "fear or favor"; 3). It was information that people needed and could use to make informed decisions; and, 4). It was information whose collection methods were not compromised or intimidated by power. As a member of the press, I discovered that following American politics was an exemplary exhibition of the latter two points.

While working abroad as a staff NBC cameraman in the foreign press corps, I enjoyed every political story I covered. Living and working in foreign countries, I found that these were always stories about foreign elections whose outcome had a direct impact on America. During the Cold War, German elections for chancellor would determine how staunch an ally the U.S. would have in West Germany. The German Bundestag (Parliament) elections determined the deployment of American nuclear cruise missiles on German soil. In a far different corner of the world, the Philippines, widowed housewife Corey Aquino ran a true grass-roots, island-hopping campaign through impoverished villages to win country-wide support and upset the longtime dictator Ferdinand Marcos. With enormous American Navy and Air Force bases there, the Philippines represented another important U.S. ally and the election results would determine our military capabilities in Asia. In each of those election stories, and others, I was always fascinated with the interaction between candidate and voters, as well as the discovery of which issues the voters found critical and which ones were seen as inconsequential.

Early on, I realized the importance of covering democratic elections around the world. However, the elections we have right here at home are by far the most important, with a rippling effect felt in every corner of the world. During the presidential election of 1992, I encountered firsthand the traveling roadshow that is our brand of campaign politics. It's a journey that takes a fortunate few through small towns and major cities to press the flesh and get candidates' word out to the American electorate. In '92, that journey had incumbent Republican

President George H.W. Bush and his V.P. Dan Quayle as the odds-on favorites. A crowded Democratic field comprised of two governors and three senators vied for the Democratic nomination. And, a third option was offered to the American voter. Wild card and Independent candidate Ross Perot was on the ballot. My U.S. political baptism would have me witness the fight from not just one or two sides, but from all three sides and angles.

Iowa is considered the backyard for a Chicago-based freelancer. In election years, the Iowa caucuses are always the first test for presidential wannabes, and it's where I joined the campaign. CNN was the prism through which I would get my first glimpse at a run for the American presidency.

Jerry Brown had served two terms as California's governor from 1975-1983 (and subsequently from 2011-2017). He had unsuccessfully run for president twice before. 1992 would be his third and final attempt. He was a longshot when our CNN political team met him in Dubuque, Iowa. Undeterred, he was full of energy and new ideas, and embraced the opportunity to address not just Iowans, but all of America through CNN... and my camera. On a cold January morning, our team of correspondent Brooks Jackson, associate producer Matt Saal, and my camera crew met up with Brown and his small campaign staff at their hotel. During a lengthy interview, he talked about the need for campaign finance reform and his (then) radical flat tax. Afterward, we followed him outside and into the Iowa winter, "on the stump" as he walked the pick-up truck-heavy Main Street of downtown Dubuque.

Dubuque is a quaint Midwest town that looks like it was frozen in time 100 years ago. Brown ducked into shops and diners and into the lives of ordinary Iowans to talk politics. During election years, it's not uncommon to see politicians strolling the streets of Iowa towns looking to meet and greet voters. On this occasion, the townsfolk, dressed in brown Carhart jackets and worn Levi bib-overalls, warmly greeted the smooth-talking California governor. He was passionate about his plans for the country and they listened intently, albeit with a slight hint of skepticism for the city slicker from Sacramento.

The back-and-forth was honest and respectful. But regardless of the message from the candidate ("This will make your life better.") or response from the voter ("How will it hit home in Iowa?"), the engagement was representative of American democracy and it was on full display in Dubuque. For most American voters, their only acquaintance with political figures is through their television or computer screens, their perspective limited to a debate stage or paid political ad. Yet, in places like Iowa, that introduction can be a personal one. It can be real and raw, and allow for an unvarnished look at the person asking for your vote.

Sadly, for Governor Brown, his campaigning and our CNN coverage had little to no impact on his candidacy in Iowa. He finished a disappointing fifth place in a five-horse race. After that poor start, he would run a resurgent national campaign and gain momentum, but only manage to finish in a distant second place for the Democratic nomination.

As the Democratic primaries came to a close in June of '92, a little-known governor from Arkansas had outlasted a crowded field and was the presumptive Democratic nominee for president. During the primary campaign, he dodged claims about draft-dodging Vietnam and sexual promiscuity. He was a charismatic campaigner with a southern drawl who ran as a centrist "New Democrat"—a term coined by Southern Democrats to win back white voters who had defected to the Republican party to elect Reagan and Bush. But it was an ambiguous term to most everyone not from the South. And, even though Bill Clinton was a five-term governor of Arkansas, outside of Arkansas, not much was known about his accomplishments and failures there. Much of the campaign rhetoric had been focused on the man while little was known about his record.

CNN Special Assignment called to book me for a lengthy shoot in Arkansas. The documentary was entitled *Bill Clinton of Arkansas* and would be produced by Richard Cohen. I wondered... *could* this be *the* Richard Cohen?

The Richard Cohen I had heard of (but not worked with) was a major deal at CBS News. In 1981 when Dan Rather replaced Walter Cronkite as anchor, Cohen was Rather's producer. It's worth noting that Cohen is married to the classy and smart correspondent and anchor Meredith Vieira. For years, they were a true network news power couple. However, his ability to marry a beautiful, brilliant, and successful wife was not the reason for my reverence towards him.

Due to a love of politics, Cohen moved on from Rather to run all presidential campaign coverage for CBS News. The job was a dream job for Cohen, who was a well-known figure around the news networks for good reason. He possessed a brilliant journalistic mind as well as an in-depth understanding of the power of television. He also spoke his journalistic mind, which led to disagreements between him and senior news management at CBS (including the anchorman). Even within the same network, differing opinions are nothing new, and a diversity of thought can lead to more thought-provoking news coverage. But that's not always the case. Somehow, Richard's star at CBS began to diminish and eventually get extinguished altogether. After more than a decade of political stewardship and keenly insightful production, he was out at CBS.

CNN immediately wooed him to join their network. He was a proven and accomplished producer talent. They needed a "hook"; a meaty assignment or story into which Richard could sink his political teeth. George H. W. Bush had been vice president for eight years under Ronald Reagan, and president for four. He and his record were well-known. To many Americans, the Democratic candidate was more of an enigma—or at least a mystery. Clinton had lived a newsworthy career... to Arkansans. But he was now on the mainstage of politics and Americans needed to know more. With his run for the White House looming large, a comprehensive examination of and accurate reporting on his record as a governor was the project that brought Cohen to CNN, and vice versa. And, I was the guy hired to shoot this documentary. I felt mildly honored to have been selected, knowing that recording and detailing the experience of a presidential nominee while working with a living TV legend could be a weighty assignment. But from the moment I first met Richard in Little Rock, I knew it would be an infinitely rewarding ten-day shoot. He was confident without being cocky, and frankly, most people with his resume and accomplishments (there are few) own egos the size of New Jersey. He did not.

For all of us involved in the story, it would be a discovery. But Cohen was focused and disciplined in his examination, and resistant to chasing loose leads, exaggerations, and hyperbole. He wanted just the facts on Clinton's gubernatorial time, both pros and cons. Richard had a sharp sense of humor that was frequently on display with our crew. In tenuous interviews, he'd use the same humor to put a jittery interviewee more at ease. After that, his piercing questions would get right to the heart of the matter. On the few occasions an interviewee appeared tense, it had nothing to do with the glare of my lights or the scrutiny of my camera lens. It was Richard, whose reputation as a revered news pro preceded him. He'd done his homework and was always prepared and engaging.

Richard had brought along associate producer Matt Saal to help with some of the logistical coordination. For Matt, working with Richard was like getting an accelerated Ph.D. in journalism. I'd worked with Matt in Iowa on the Jerry Brown story, where we had immediately gotten along, so our extended four-man crew quickly gelled. We caravanned in two cars, crisscrossing the state to collect information and report on Clinton's accomplishments and failures. We also wanted to hear what the people of Arkansas had to say about their leader. Beginning in the capital of Little Rock, we spoke with both friends and foes about his overhaul of the education and welfare system in Arkansas. We traveled to Hope and Hot Springs to get a sense of what his childhood had been like. We visited Fayetteville, home to Tyson Foods, Inc. to find out the state of chicken in Clinton's home state. Paper was big business there, too, so we traveled to El Dorado to shoot massive paper mills and speak with the management of International Paper and Georgia Pacific. This all helped create a picture of Clinton's relationship with the business community. And then we spoke with environmentalists for their take on Clinton's environmental record. We drove to and through places like Pine Bluff, Eureka Springs, and Mossy Lake, speaking with locals for their input at every stop along the way. We even drove through the dusty streets and saw the dilapidated shacks of tiny Helena—once dubbed "The Blues Capital of the Delta," but which had deteriorated into an impoverished, rural part of the state.

At the conclusion of our ten-day, fact-finding mission, our

snug-fitting jeans made it clear we had all enjoyed too many home-cooked Southern meals consisting of barbeque, beer, catfish, grits, and chicken-fried everything. Additionally, each of us had a much clearer picture of Governor Bill Clinton. Richard took a wealth of material back to the CNN offices in Atlanta, where he helped craft the hugely informative documentary, *Bill Clinton of Arkansas*, the aim of which was to present a clearer picture to the American voter. It was not a glossy campaign ad or an endorsement of one candidate or another. It was a meaningful and useful news program whose journalistic aim was to inform the voter (without fear or favor) so that they could make a more educated decision. That's all. And I left Arkansas with something else... the respect and sincere admiration for one more dedicated network news friend.

On my next campaign stop, I would get on the bus. Literally. Four weeks before the election, NBC hired me and my soundman to be their crew covering Vice President Dan Quayle on a three-day Bush/Quayle bus tour through the tightly contested state of North Carolina. I would learn that traveling with the White House is altogether different from covering the Iowa caucuses or shooting an independent documentary in Arkansas. Everything is bigger and more intense. The V.P. was accompanied by a sizeable and always busy staff. And wherever the Veep goes, there is always a cadre of Ray-Ban-wearing, Glock-carrying Secret Service agents.

The press had their dedicated tour bus where every network, national paper, and major magazine was represented. Some members had been following the V.P.'s campaign for months. My crew was new to the Bush/Quayle press corps, but we were welcomed aboard and treated like we belonged. When all of the members of the government, security, and press were assembled, it made for a massive, multi-vehicle caravan. Unencumbered, we rumbled down North Carolina highways and backroads like a highly secured parade that stopped for no one.

This trip would visit Greensboro, Fayetteville, and the tiny hamlet of Rocky Mount. I had covered world summits while living overseas. The security and protection of world leaders at those events had been enormous and impenetrable. But aside from brief and well-choreographed photo-ops, the press had never gotten close to those leaders. It had been coverage from afar. The campaign stump back home was different. While campaigning, the supporters were close to the candidate, the press was close to the candidate, and as a result, the dutiful Secret Service was simultaneously everywhere and invisible. It's quite the task to let a candidate like the V.P. move relatively freely through a crowd while surrounding him with a heavily-armed bubble. And for every agent you saw, there were numerous others surreptitiously moving in the crowd and on the perimeter of the event. The campaign days and nights were long ones, with 14-hour to 18-hour workdays being the norm.

At the campaign stops and rallies, the Vice President would often walk the "rope line" shaking hands and kissing babies with hundreds of ecstatic supporters and well-wishers before ascending a stage to address the cheering, flag-waving crowd. "Is this crowd pumped up?" the Veep asked his followers. His inquiry was met with a thunderous *YES*. "Is this crowd fired up? Is North Carolina going for George Bush? Is the South going for George Bush? Is America going for George Bush?" With each question, the frenzied crowd bellowed affirmatively and in unison. The race had tightened, so his attacks on his Democratic opponents were frequent, centering on Clinton's character and lack of trustworthiness.

I heard that same speech multiple times over those three days. It could have become monotonous and boring, but for me at least, it never did. It wasn't that I supported what Mr. Quayle was selling. On that bus tour, I was ambivalent. Neutral. It wasn't about one side or the other. It was about the interface between candidate and voter. It was about the kind of genuine interaction that makes our political system the envy of the world, and it was enlightening, never boring, for me to witness it firsthand.

Election night is always a special night for me. Whether on assignment or in a recliner at home, I'm constantly mesmerized by watching the elections play out with the results trickling in from across the nation. You have to love the process if not always love the outcome. As in 1980 and '84, 1992 would find me working on a campaign story on election night. NBC had hired me as part of their coverage of the Ross Perot headquarters in Dallas, Texas. Perot was a Texas billionaire who ran as an Independent. Many voters viewed his third-party candidacy as an exciting alternative to the staid two-party traditional options. A mere five months before the election, he was leading in the national polls with 39% of the vote (Bush had 31% and Clinton had 25%). Then, in July, Perot abruptly dropped out of the race. He claimed the Republicans were planning to smear his daughter's reputation and ruin her upcoming wedding. It was a strange and unproven accusation. It was even more strange when he abruptly re-entered the race a month later. By then, his candidacy had suffered irreparable damage due to his diminishing credibility. His once commanding lead in the polls had dipped to a distant third place.

Three days prior to election night, we checked in to the Versailles-Esque Grand Kempinski Hotel in North Dallas. The lighting survey and set-up, as well as the preparations and testing of the live satellite equipment, involved a lengthy, multiday process. There was also an election-eve rally where Perot and his supports predicted a surprise victory.

The actual election night would be spent with Perot supporters in the cavernous yet opulent grand ballroom. Well, not exactly *with* his supporters. They would be milling on the floor of the ballroom with cocktails and canapes in hand. As has become "Standard Operating Procedure" on election night, the broadcast news media—meaning every news network as well as all of the local stations from near and far—occupied cramped positions on a series of crowded risers in the back of the ballroom, the cameras pointing towards a stage and podium where the candidate would hopefully speak—eventually. The walls of the ballroom were adorned with gigantic television screens. On those many screens were displayed the ongoing election results and projections from the four networks (ABC, CBS, CNN, and NBC). Lisa Myers was our NBC correspondent. Throughout election night, she gave live "hits" or updates on the mood and/or expectations from the Perot headquarters, and these were inserted into the main coverage hosted by Tom Brokaw back in Washington.

Desirous to "get it right," the networks are extremely cautious and calculated, employing a scientific methodology before predicting a winner in any given state. Within minutes or even seconds of each other, all four networks are generally able to project the same winning candidate for each state. While this system is not always 100% guaranteed accurate (we'll get to 2000 Austin, Texas in a later chapter), on that evening in Dallas, all four networks reported identical results showing Clinton out to an early lead. Bush was close behind him, but Perot was lagging behind both in a distant third place, gathering a smattering of votes without winning states and their electoral votes, which determine elections.

Needless to say, the mood in the Perot HQ was not a festive one. I cut a path through the tangle of cables, tripods, light stands, and people on the risers to facilitate a much-needed bathroom break. I navigated my way from the ballroom to a large and extravagantly decorated hallway, beautifully illuminated by crystal chandeliers and sconces. The hallway was like a separate palatial wing that housed the restrooms. To successfully reach the men's room, I had to circumvent a group of ten or so bejeweled Dallas matrons huddled in the center of the hallway near the powder room. As I approached, I noticed their sequined gowns were uniformly snug and perfectly hemmed to reveal their sparkling $1,000-a-pair Jimmy Choo fashion footwear. (Thanks to Amy, I'd been previously enlightened and educated on this celebrity shoe designer.) Their big brown hair-dos were sprayed perfectly in place. Their long red nails were a perfect match for their over-applied lipstick and their glitzy and gaudy, pave necklaces pointed directly to the plunging necklines of their eveningwear.

I did not recognize any of them as members of the press.

Nope, these were tried and true Perot supporters, and it was obvious they were pissed. As I maneuvered past them, their conversation became clear.

"Did you see those results up there on those big TV screens? Why, I mean, I don't believe a word of it!"

"I know. They have Ross in third place!"

"Why, I declare, I bet he's winning this whole damn thing and we wouldn't even know it by watching the lying reporting."

"It's the media, I tell ya. You just can't believe a thing they say."

Fortunately for me, no one in the group noticed the media credential swinging from the lanyard around my neck; otherwise, I could've been torn apart limb by limb. My pace picked up considerably as I ducked into the men's room. I stood over a marble urinal in a conflicted state of laughter and disbelief. *Really? The entire broadcast news media colluded to "throw" an election?* The mere thought was ludicrous. But these women had moved beyond thought to articulate the absurdity of a media coup. And they believed it! I'd been astonished when nut-job conspiracy theorists had announced that the Apollo 11 lunar landing had been staged. But this Perot conspiracy was ever more "out of this world" than a faked moon mission.

I concealed my press credential in my shirt pocket and braved the hallway, hoping to once again evade the ire of the haute couture, media-hating mob.

When I returned to my NBC position on the press platform, veteran producer Art Lord was there. Art was a respected fixture in the LA bureau. His reputation as a dedicated producer had been cemented during the Vietnam war, after which he'd returned home for less hazardous news assignments. I'd worked with him before and always enjoyed his experienced perspective. He was informing us of our upcoming live "hits" from Dallas, which Washington had scheduled.

"Okay, guys, they'll be coming to us at 8:35 for another live update. We'll have about four minutes of cross-talk back and forth."

I replied, "Sounds good. Audio, video feed, and comms (headset communication back to the New York studio mothership) have all been checked out and confirmed. We are good to go." Looking for his take on what I had just heard, I added, "Hey, you're not gonna believe what I just overheard."

With thousands of supporters on the floor and hundreds of media personnel on the risers all chatting simultaneously, the room's din was loud. Art leaned in for clarification. "What did you overhear?"

I shared with him the conversation I'd just heard. Pointing to the many giant TV screens around the room that were airing the network broadcasts, I said, "They think we're just making up all of this shit."

Art burst into laughter. "And that's news to you? I hate to break it to ya, but we're not universally loved."

"That part, I get. I've been shot at, shelled by warring militias, and beaten by commie thugs. I was under the impression it was because they feared the truth we were reporting. I've never had anyone take aim at me for making it up."

"We're an easy target. They see or read something they don't like and it's much easier to blame us than confront the cold, hard truth. Their guy is getting his ass kicked tonight. Instead of that being his fault, like maybe he shouldn't have dropped out of the race for two months, it's our fault. The hope is that your lady friends you encountered in the hallway represent the lunatic fringe. Look around. Most of these people aren't thrilled with these election results. But they realize we're just reporting the news. We just call it like we see it. At least, that's the hope."

"I was caught by surprise with the whole, 'Ross could be wining and we'd never know it' comment. I never heard that one before. I guess while living overseas covering wars and revolutions and famine and the like, I've been living a pretty sheltered life. It took the Grand Ballroom of the Grand Kempinski to open my eyes."

The following morning, Ross Perot gave a moving concession speech. Its tone was unifying and hopeful. He congratulated

Governor Clinton (to the boos of some in the crowd) and addressed the many challenges that lay ahead. He urged his supporters not to be discouraged, but to work together with the new administration and move the country forward for the benefit of all. His message was positive and void of the kind of media bashing I'd heard the night before. He chose to take the high road instead of assessing blame.

The 1992 presidential campaign was my first deep-dive into U.S. politics, and it was an eye-opener on many fronts. I'd experienced the very real adulation felt by so many voters for their candidate. There'd been long, grueling days chasing after candidates and chasing down the facts behind them. I'd listened to the same canned speeches from the same candidates in a seemingly endless loop. I'd discovered that a small but virulent strain of distrust exists for the press. In the end, I walked away with a greater admiration and deeper passion for the way we elect our leaders.

Even after the votes had been tallied and the winners announced, there would be one more ride on this campaign trail... a post-election assignment. I traveled to Washington, D.C. as part of the team covering the Clinton - Gore Inauguration. Dignitaries, supporters, partygoers, and journalists descended on D.C. Presidential inaugurations are always a significant news event and an even more significant party, and I was invited to the party this year... I mean the coverage.

It is a massive, live television undertaking requiring coordination with and approval from an even more massive security operation. From the capitol building to the White House and everywhere in between, camera placements are omnipresent for the historic swearing-in ceremony. I would occupy one of those camera positions. But it wasn't at the Capitol. It wasn't at the White House. It wasn't even along the parade route. It was *in* the parade route. My assignment, my camera position was INSIDE the motorcade and broadcasting live from directly in front of the presidential limo as the presidential parade crept its way along Pennsylvania Avenue from the Capitol to the White House.

That kind of mobile satellite technology was fairly new at the time. Our moving camera position was a specially outfitted flatbed truck. We would be driving past high-rise buildings and through a metropolitan downtown while maintaining a constant, rock-solid, undisturbed video signal... of POTUS. There were many technical hurdles and line-of-sight transmission issues to overcome. After a long week of set-up and rehearsals in sub-zero temperatures, we were ready.

It was a frigid but brilliantly sunny morning on Jan 20, 1993, when we boarded our flatbed truck. Our satellite tech, my soundman, and I took our places on board and tested our equipment for the thousandth time. There were only so many camera trucks allowed amidst the bullet-proof limos in the motorcade. As a result, we shared our platform with ABC News. Space was at a premium. Just before the motorcade left the Capitol, we took on one more very important passenger. We were joined by *TODAY* anchor Katie Couric, who had been reporting on the swearing-in ceremony. She added an invaluable editorial voice to my up-close video. Reporting live for that duration at that event can be pressure-packed, but she performed flawlessly. At one point, the new President and First Lady emerged from their presidential limo and walked among the cheering crowd and throng of Secret Service agents. Our proximity, being in the midst of everything, seemed to exaggerate everything, including the excitement.

I was on assignment. This was my job. But I felt fortunate to be taking part in a once in a lifetime, riveting ride. The artic environment had little to do with the goosebumps I felt. They would eventually dissipate, but the memories would not.

Afterward, we were assigned to cover one of the countless balls that take place throughout Washington on inauguration night, which made for a seemingly endless day. As I watched and recorded the attendees dancing into the early morning hours, I saw that their feet may have been tired, but their mood was jubilant. The Democrats had won the White House, the Senate, and the House of Representatives. These were the winners. They were now in power. I could not help but think of the other side, the Republicans. I'm sure their mood was much more somber. This was my first working trip to Washington, but I began to view it as the ultimate company town. The company is politics, and you are either on the inside or you are out. This was simply my observation, seen through the eyes of a political neophyte. But it seemed better to be a cameraman heading back to Chicago than a politician on the outside in Washington.

The 1992 presidential campaign and election offered my first in-depth taste of political coverage. They proved to be a mouthful, though, and I was salivating for more. There would be plenty of news to cover in between presidential elections, but I had already set my sights on 1996.

8

NEW AND REWARDING

Network by network, assignment by assignment, I was building a domestic resume that included all of the big-four broadcast news organizations. The adrenaline rush I'd fed off while covering international stories years earlier had been replaced by a more fulfilling and lasting high with the creation of a sound business. It was a very small business with only one employee—me (two if you counted the many soundmen I regularly employed). The gratification grew as more and more companies called to hire my services.

What began with Channel One and World Monitor had been enlarged to include all of the news networks. And to that mix, I was adding corporations, the medical community, and public relations firms. These "non-network" clients were anxious to bring a network look and approach to their video projects. By employing the right freelance camera crews and tapping into their production and lighting knowledge, big-business CEOs and MDs could resemble network anchormen and women on camera. The workload was as much as I could comfortably handle with a healthy and diverse client mix that would keep me in demand for the foreseeable future, always remembering that "you're only as good as your last shoot." This worry and neurosis is always languishing in the brain of a freelancer.

I wasn't the only one climbing the ladder of success. I was part of a select group of cameramen who had discovered the freelancing model and were enjoying growing success. Beyond my niche and within my own family, my accomplishments were eclipsed by those of my wife. Amy was experiencing a meteoric ascension as a corporate attorney at a major Chicago law firm. In the male-dominated world of a law firm, a respected, smart, beautiful blonde female is a... hot commodity. Her brains and beauty had turned heads, and she was promoted to partner in record time.

But, oftentimes, such success comes with a price. Partnerships like hers were often referred to as having "golden handcuffs," where a significant salary and bonus were linked hand-in-hand to 80 or 100-hour workweeks. As a result, it's not uncommon for some young partners to contemplate a less demanding legal career; one where they leave the law firm to practice law "in-house" at a corporation. My work featured lengthy assignments, with long hours and demanding travel, but I also enjoyed down days in between assignments. Amy's long days were back-to-back-to-back. It made sense that she would someday desire a less stressful work environment, yet one where her legal talents were still valued. Chicago was a big place and home to many corporations. I was certain she would find the right opportunity when the time was right.

Alexa was growing up quickly. She had gone from the terrible twos to the fantastic fours, graduating from infant playdates to preschool. Her electric personality was evident early and constantly on. Her energy was boundless, and she frequently transferred it into dancing... all the time and everywhere. Our endless home renovation was nearing an end. A truly WOW feature we had added was a beautiful, custom-milled, solid oak spiral staircase that ascended through a vaulted ceiling and into our upstairs bedrooms. The architectural marvel was lost on Alexa, who viewed the hand-carved and meticulously finished banister and spindles as her private dance barre, fearlessly swinging from it like a four-year-old ballerina. The house was a zoo in constant motion with two busy parents, an energetic preschooler, a nanny, and ever-present tradesmen.

Our home renovation wasn't the only building we'd undertaken. We were building new friendships with other new parents and neighbors. We were building relationships with Amy's coworkers and clients within the Chicago legal scene and I was constantly forging new alliances with a growing list of clients and coworkers in my network news and video production space.

Creating and running my own small business was vastly different from my staff employment on many fronts. Obviously, as a staffer, I'd known nothing about client development and maintenance. I'd had only one client. NBC. As long as I'd showed up for work and done my best, the client had been "maintained" and happy, and my job had been safe. With a variety of clients calling, I had a variety of clients to please. This was something else I could not have foreseen until I was knee-deep in clients. Just doing my best during a shoot wasn't always enough. Follow-up calls were needed to ensure the client who'd seemed happy during the shoot hadn't somehow changed their mind afterward.

There was no fool-proof textbook recipe for landing a new client. Word-of-mouth recommendations were proving to be a bankable means for generating new clients, but it was impossible to know from where such an endorsement might come. Was it the executive producer, producer, associate producer, or talent? Perhaps even the caterer or make-up artist might mention or recommend (or condemn) me next? Everyone involved had to be impressed in the hopes of a favorable review.

Crew compatibility was another key element of providing an outstanding work environment on a shoot. Think of the cameraman-soundman dynamic as the dynamic between characters in a western or crime genre "buddy movie." Doesn't matter whether it's Butch and Sundance or Crockett and Tubbs, cowboys or cops; it's a similar dynamic. Two different individuals blend their personalities and assets to form a single unified and enjoyable team.

Every shoot involved me AND a soundman or partner working together to record pictures and sound. *Together* meant professional seamless interaction. There could be no friction or mistakes. And, there were times when the crew could even set the mood. News coverage can involve long hours and somber stories. An insightful and cohesive crew can interject a modicum of comic relief or levity, reminding everyone that they're just covering news and not curing cancer.

With every soundman I hired, every crew I assembled, I tried to account for some degree of that buddy system. Within a few years, I had expanded my list of soundmen to include Gary Wahlgren, Bill Laing, Mike Bidese, Dennis McGuire, Bob Downing, Danny Gianneschi, Rich Pooler, and others. They were all highly qualified, dependable, and conscientious sound recording specialists with their independent strengths who worked with me to form a likable team. And, they all had relationships with numerous other cameramen, which only increased their earning potential. There was no one partner I had, but many available team members. It was a win-win situation that worked for everyone.

Given the amount of time we spent together on assignment, those relationships felt like family at times—a very extended family with multiple personalities and idiosyncrasies, but family nonetheless.

One evening, I was at home preparing dinner in my construction-site/kitchen. Amy was on her way home. I was holding Alexa in my arms, a glass of wine in one hand while I juggled a couple of pans on top of the stove with the other, when the phone rang.

I answered the plaster dust-covered phone, pinching the receiver between my shoulder and neck while continuing dinner prep. "Hello."

"Hi, is this Tim?"

"It is. Who is this?"

"My name is Steve. I hope I'm not getting you at a bad time." The caller's voice was shaky and uncertain. If this was some cold-calling telephone solicitor, he was really bad and unrehearsed at his job.

"Well, it's not the best time. I'm in the middle of a few things right now."

Undeterred, the caller continued, "Okay. I just wanted to say that I got your name and number from Susan Franks, who suggested I reach out and give you a call."

The name he'd just dropped revealed the caller was no run-of-the-mill solicitor. Susan Franks was the Numero Uno contact at NBC News in New York for all freelance hires. She worked on a small but specialized team responsible for hiring all freelance crews domestically. For instance, when a *TODAY* producer needed a crew for a three-day shoot in, say, Cleveland, that producer would complete a "Crew Request" listing all of the specifics of the shoot. That request would then be submitted to

Susan's team, who would begin calling vetted and proven crews in that region to be hired for the Cleveland gig. This occurred multiple times a day, all across the nation. Susan had become an expert in evaluating and categorizing who the most talented and trusted crews were across the U.S. Steve the caller had my attention, at least fleetingly. But what exactly was his connection to Susan, I needed to investigate further.

"Well, Susan is one of the best in the business. How well do you know her?"

"I don't. I called her out of the blue. But she took my call and said you were one of the best cameramen in Chicago and a genuinely good guy, and that I should turn to you for answers."

"One of the best, eh? Not sure that's the case, but I'm flattered. Right now, what I am is an overwhelmed cook and distracted dad. What do you mean? Answers to what?"

"Well, I mean like how to break into the freelance market as a soundman here in Chicago."

Aha! So, this was some kind of solicitation. The picture was becoming clearer. The guy had cold-called Susan, who'd probably cut short their call by giving him my name. And now he was calling me. Alexa was squirming out of my arms. My neck was throbbing from holding the phone against my ear and the sauté pans were burning. I needed to cut to the chase and cut short this call.

Hurriedly, I continued, "Steve, right? Look, I wish I could help you, but I really don't have any answers for you and I'm not in a position to train and hire new soundmen. I have a dozen or so guys I'm currently working with."

"Yes, it's Steve. Steve Azzato. I'm not asking for training. I recently graduated from Columbia College with a degree in audio arts. I was just hoping you might show me where or how to start."

Just then, Amy walked in the door, dropped her briefcase, and began venting about work. I feared my call with Steve would last forever if I didn't pull the plug. "Columbia College, not familiar with it. Steve, I'll call Susan in the morning and thank her for the recommendation. You should follow up with her, as well. Wish I could do more. Gotta run. Good luck."

I should've been grateful someone had sought my advice, but that was lost in the hectic, post-workday dinner preparation stress. Besides, this was my business we were talking about and I wasn't in the business of charity.

The following week, Steve called back. Slightly miffed, I asked, "Look, did we not have this exact conversation last week? I thought I made it clear. I'm not in a hiring mode. I have plenty of established soundmen I use, many of whom I've known for years. Bringing you on would be at their expense and I'm just not going to do that. Besides, you said you're right out of college. So, do us both a favor and lose my number."

"Well, yes, I did recently graduate from Columbia College. But before that, I worked as an engineer. This recent pursuit is just something I've always wanted to do... and I want you to know that I really appreciate your time on last week's call. Should you ever find the need to bring on another soundman, I'd love the opportunity to work with you. As I mentioned, New York certainly had high praise for you."

The angrier and more irrational I became, the more courteous and complimentary he became. He was infuriatingly considerate.

Steve continued to "check in" and "circle back" with polite, patient, and unsolicited follow-up calls. Early on, I feared he might be stalking me. Had I covered his rape trial? Had I dated his sister? Eventually, though, I grew to realize he was genuinely and keenly interested in a career in the television news business and he saw me as a possible gateway to that elusive path. That was a privileged position in which to be. In four short years, I had built up my modest reputation as a dependable freelancer and crew for hire. I vividly recalled the earlier days when my cold calls had fallen on deaf ears. I was fortunate to have an abundance of professional soundmen I could rely upon, but what was the harm in adding one more? Was Steve's polite perseverance beginning to soften me up?

When he called next to circle back with me, I was ready to throw him for a loop.

"Hi Tim, Steve here. I realize you said you're not in a hiring mode at the time, but I wanted to circle back and see if anything has changed."

"Steve, glad you called. What are you doing on Tuesday, October 11th?"

"Uh, Tues... October 11th? Let me check... I am... available. Why?"

A couple of weeks earlier, I had been contacted by the Lands' End clothing company and booked for a corporate shoot at their headquarters in Dodgeville, Wisconsin. I knew it would be a low pressure and relatively stress-free shoot, void of any demanding network deadline. I hadn't yet booked a soundman for this one-day job and its one-day wage wouldn't be missed by my regular sound guys. Additionally, I knew the commute to rural Dodgeville would be a leisurely, three-hour drive through Wisconsin's bucolic dairy country; another stress-free time where I might get to know Steve from Columbia College.

"Why? Well, I have a corporate shoot on the 11th and I was hoping we might work together."

"Work together? You and me? On an assignment? I think that

132

would be... great. I look forward to it and I promise I won't let you down. I'll be prepared. I mean... I'm already prepared, but I'll be ready when the day comes, uh, when the shoot, eh, on the day of the shoot—"

"Steve, it's a corporate shoot in Wisconsin. We're not going into battle in Lebanon."

"Of course. Yes. Well, should I meet you there? Would you like me to drive into Chicago and meet you there? How should we do this?"

"You mentioned you live in a northern suburb, right? Why don't I swing by and pick you up on the way to Wisconsin?"

"Perfect. This is great. And, thanks for the opportunity."

I picked him up at his newish, multi-level home in Libertyville, one of Chicago's many comfortable northern villages. All the homes on his cul-de-sac had a similar suburban curb appeal and immaculately maintained landscaping. When I first met Steve, he was not what I was expecting. I'd incorrectly assumed an inexperienced guy trying to break into the networks would be youthful. The guy I met was about my age, 37. He had thick black hair and a solid build, the result of good genes; not a strict gym regiment. Similar to in our phone calls, he was courteous and polite while he endeavored to bridle an irrepressible enthusiasm. After the personal introductions and pleasantries, we jumped into my Chevy Suburban for the three-hour drive to our shoot location.

I've found there to be a common character flaw that runs through many who are employed in the television news biz. My college Psych 101 course does not qualify me to psychoanalyze my coworkers, however, insecurity sometimes drives people to volunteer their unsolicited resume and accomplishments. If I'm burning to learn that you broke into TV in a 500-watt university radio station, I'll ask. Otherwise, it's probably not relevant or of interest to anyone... but you. Steve did not suffer from this malady. He was, at once, easy to talk to and mostly avoiding himself as a subject. Instead, he inquired (politely) about me and my background. When I did turn the focus on him, I was surprised to learn he had worked at the in-house video production department of Abbott Labs, a hugely successful pharmaceutical company. The coursework at Columbia College had been the equivalent of post-grad study to build on his resume at Abbott. His experience had been acquired in a studio environment, but he yearned for more location experience; the kind so prevalent in news coverage. We had a lot in common. We both came from tight-knit Midwestern families with multiple siblings. We were both parents to small children, although he had three to my one. We even had similar tastes in music. The entire three-hour trip breezed by.

We arrived at the location eager to work together. On smaller news stories and corporate shoots, the cameraman often takes a lead production role by playing both cameraman and director. Steve was familiar with the professional level of equipment and took my direction well. He was quickly up to speed and performing like a veteran soundman. The client, the Land's End people, were happy with the outcome of the shoot, which made me happy. I had added another client and found another reliable resource in Steve. After our initial shoot, I knew he would easily dovetail with the many other soundmen I'd worked with over the years. Exactly how and where he would fit into the overall hierarchy was uncertain.

The timing would benefit us both, though, as I was about to undertake a project that would require all the help I could muster.

The Land's End shoot was a corporate departure from what had become a steady diet of network news shoots. NBC, ABC, CBS, and CNN were all calling with regularity. The dream had always been to have too much work; too many clients calling with too many conflicting assignments, to keep me busy always and indefinitely. I was now living that dream.

Be careful of what you wish for.

I was a network cameraman at heart and that was the beating heart of my business. Still, I enjoyed the diversity that came with developing and working with non-network news clients. My heavy network workload was diminishing that ability.

One of my first corporate clients was the historic and iconic department store chain, Marshall Field and Company. In the late 19th and early 20th centuries, Marshall Field had built a massive retail empire in Chicago and had become one of the richest men in America (think Amazon long before the internet). His flagship store was completed in 1906. It's an ornate, 13-story granite structure featuring an enormous grand hall with a vaulted ceiling and multiple soaring atriums. It provided the ideal retail location for shooting their corporate video projects. The parent company was Minneapolis-based Target Corporation and I was their go-to cameraman when the Minnesota folks came to Chicago for productions.

The Marshall Field store had been contacted about participating in an educational project that they initially found worthwhile. They kicked the idea upstairs, or up north to Target, who found the project even more worthwhile and committed to paying for the production costs to shoot and edit a pilot. As their camera crew in Chicago, I was hired to shoot the pilot. To learn more about the shoot and the much larger project, a production meeting was set where all the principals could meet. The cordial meeting took place in the famed Cape Cod Room in Chicago's historic Drake Hotel.

The venerable Cape Cod Room was a seafood restaurant and oyster bar on the arcade level of the Drake. It opened in 1933 and was a steadfast throwback to a vintage era. With its nautical theme and long wooden bar, it was a favorite of celebrities over the years and one of the places to see and be seen among the city's upper echelon.

I joined a small group for dinner to discuss strategy and requirements for the project, which was called *Enter Here*, and it was an ingenious and ambitious venture. Like the Channel One undertaking a few years prior, high school students were the target audience, but that's where the similarities ended.

One of the people at the meeting was the creator and driving force behind *Enter Here*, Jim Crumley. He was an intellectual free spirit with shoulder-length hair, a soft-spoken voice, and a super-keen mind. He was a former freelance writer who'd harnessed his free-thinking and freelance writing skills to carve out a highly profitable niche in the publishing world. He wrote textbooks that were published by huge firms like Houghton-Mifflin and others. These were complex works for college readers and distributed nationally. He was so good at it, and the demand so great, that he built an entire team of free-spirited intellectuals to supply that demand. He then purchased a spacious, four-story Victorian structure in the heart of Evanston, Illinois just off the Northwestern University campus to house his team of writers. From top to bottom, it was an impressive operation.

His active and inquisitive mind was always on the look-out. Having mastered the college and high school level, he looked elsewhere for his next teaching opportunity. He realized there was no real comprehensive course taught or textbook written on how to get a job, and he saw a video series like *Enter Here* as both an opportunity and a natural extension of his textbook business. He knew there were millions of American high school students who had neither the means nor the interest in attending a four-year university. What they did have were questions about what careers were out there and what was right for them. Jim sought answers to those questions.

Enter Here aimed to profile 100 different jobs and careers which did NOT require a college degree. There were ten different disciplines or categories in play, and within each category, ten different jobs (and individuals performing those jobs) would be profiled. A retail salesperson at Marshall Field was the first video shot. It would act as a blueprint or pilot for the other 99 videos which would follow.

Tom Betting was also at that meeting. He was an easy-going freelance producer/director and creative type who was void of the ego and idiosyncrasies often associated with such titles. He was based out of Minneapolis and enjoyed a close relationship with the Target Corp. I'd enjoyed working with him on Marshall Field and Company videos in the past. Since Target was underwriting the first video, they brought Tom and I together for the *Enter Here* pilot.

The requirements for that first shoot were straightforward and not too challenging. But as the overall project began to take shape, the challenges became more evident. This had never been intended to be a "Chicago Only" project. Chicago's a thriving commercial center and was a popular location for the shoots, of course. But, to accurately depict the diversity of the many career options available to high school students, the project would have to be national in scope and thus require travel across the country.

Additionally, Jim voiced his preference for an aggressive shooting schedule, hopeful to have everything shot and "in the can" within a year or so. This was the sort of guaranteed income that's so rare in the freelance world. But I was confident my phone would continue to ring from network bookers, as well, and taking on such a project would certainly require me to abandon those same network clients I had painstakingly nurtured over four years. Yet, the more I learned about Jim, the more I admired and liked him... and the more I wanted to be a part of his team and dream. Could I maintain my current client list of heavy-hitters and take on another major one? Could I have my cake and eat it, too? It was a dilemma.

Albert Einstein once said, "In the middle of difficulty lies opportunity."

Enter Here was an opportunity disguised as a dilemma. Jim was looking for more than a cameraman to shoot his videos. Yes, he needed that, but so much more. He was looking to me for a management role—someone who understood the ins and outs of production and could take control to coordinate and manage the many demanding shoots across the country. If, in addition to that, I could shoot some of the videos myself, that would be icing on the cake.

Two camera crews shooting simultaneously would be able to meet the rigorous requirements of the demanding shooting schedule. To truly take control of and oversee the project, I would have to expand and reinvest in my company. I remembered hearing, "You must spend money to make money." I purchased a second camera package. Not all cameramen had the desire or means to purchase expensive professional video equipment, and it would be from this pool of talented but camera-less cameramen that I would hire a few select cameraman to shoot with one of my cameras while I shot with the other. This enabled me to contribute as a cameraman, manage the process, and maintain responsibility for the overall quality of the shoots while receiving the equipment rental income for all hundred video shoots.

Jim, Tom, and a close colleague of Jim's, Kathleen Ermitage, comprised the editorial team who worked tirelessly to identify the specific jobs included in the series. They then contacted numerous companies regarding the subjects, locations, dates, and times for the hundred shoots. As that information was confirmed, it was communicated to me. I then assigned crews (either me or someone else) to each shoot.

The series eventually took us to Charleston, South Carolina; Nashville and Memphis, Tennessee; Madison and Milwaukee, Wisconsin; Austin and Dallas, Texas; Las Cruces, New Mexico; Hartford and New London, Connecticut; Los Angeles, California; Portland, Oregon; and Washington, D.C. Many of the shoots occurred simultaneously in different cities. As a well-traveled former network cameraman, my knowledge of the challenges and demands posed by life on the road gave me added value. As a staffer at NBC, I'd watched and learned how to cancel, amend, rebook, reroute, and create from scratch my travel itineraries, which came in handy while working on *Enter Here*.

Acting as both a production manager and cameraman allowed me to work on various *Enter Here* shoots while also continuing to accept news assignments from the networks. I could have my cake and eat it, too. Most of my network news assignments necessitated a fair amount of responsibility. Managing the production teams for every *Enter Here* shoot was, at times, nerve-racking, and required a different kind of responsibility. It's one thing to be responsible for my behavior and that of my soundman/partner. Making and meeting travel schedules, crew calls, and acting professionally and respectfully while on set has always been second nature to me. But to have that same responsibility for other camera crews on other shoots brought with it an added dimension of personal accountability. However, that managerial challenge forced me to grow beyond being a skilled cameraman. It was interaction and oversight that would serve me well in many future endeavors. And, it was the first real opportunity for me to expand beyond a cameraman and crew leader role, into that of running a production company with its many different facets. In doing so, it allowed me to dream big and wonder about eventually tackling things like post-production and writing roles. But, for the moment, my plate was full with all I could handle.

Simultaneously booking and moving two separate crews around the country was like moving pieces around an ever-expanding chessboard. To simplify things, I began working predominately with one soundman, Steve. The more I worked with him, the more I found to like. He was professional in his approach and eager to learn the nuanced differences between on-location shooting and the studio shoots from his previous years of experience. That eagerness manifested itself in an enthusiasm I had rarely seen at the networks.

The news profession can be an exhilarating industry where fascinating assignments open the doors to exciting locations. Shooting *TODAY* live from Paris, Munich, Zurich, Vienna, and Venice while traveling on the famed Orient Express is just one of many examples from my background. To be certain, not every assignment is like going aboard the Orient Express, and some may even border on... well, boredom. Yet, many of us lose sight of the interesting world in which we work, growing complacent or even jaded.

Steve was the refreshing flipside of that jaded coin. To him, every assignment was a newfound adventure, every location a new frontier. Even after a 15-hour day when everyone was tired and frowning, he managed a smile. If I needed a spare light, new camera battery, or videocassette, he'd gleefully grab it from the production vehicle and quickly return with a "What else can I get or do?" look. He was the lovable Labrador Retriever of soundmen and a joy with whom to work.

Shooting the *Enter Here* project was an exhausting 16-month long process. After each shoot was completed, I would deliver all of the videocassettes to Jim's office. Once everything was shot, my role was completed. After that, the story for each video would be written and edited, a process that would be repeated 100 times. Then, the 100-episode series would be sold and distributed to numerous high schools and school districts around the country. It was a critical and financial success for its creators. Jim, Tom, and Kathleen and I would stay in touch and continue to work together from time to time.

And, there would be many more new frontiers for Steve and me to visit.

9

TERROR AND ERROR

As expected, Amy was courted by one of the law firms' corporate clients. No company, large or small, likes having their best and brightest talent "poached" by their clients, and her law firm was no exception. But as long as the clients remained clients and continued to spend millions of dollars on legal fees, the firm could only acquiesce to the brain drain and smile approvingly. The specific clients interested in Amy's legal skills were a couple of businessmen who had become uber-wealthy from Blockbuster Video during the heyday of video cassette rentals, long before Netflix and video streaming. Moving on from Blockbuster, Scott Beck and his Blockbuster partner Saad Nadhir purchased a small, Boston-based casual restaurant chain that held a significant upside. Amy was part of the legal team that completed the transaction. The new owners planned to turn the chain into a national and international juggernaut of a brand, which would require an in-house legal dream team to navigate a franchising law minefield and a Wall Street IPO. Amy was selected and invited to be part of their dream team.

Their lucrative offer to lure Amy away from the intense competition and endless hours of the firm was more than tempting. It included a highly attractive salary, a less grueling pace of work, and normal hours... as well as stock options potentially worth millions. (That "potential" proved to be a mighty big "IF.") This would have been a no-brainer, had the company been Chicago-based. It was not. Boston Chicken had changed its name to Boston Market and moved its growing operations to Golden, Colorado. The contemplated move would require our young family to uproot itself and move west. We would have to exchange the Chicago skyline for Rocky Mountain vistas, rush hour traffic for wide-open spaces.

There were changes other than the local landscapes with which I was wrestling. I had established myself as a "Chicago-based" freelancer. All of the networks had a bureau presence in Chicago at that time. My network assignments were products of the many ties I'd formed and the bonds I'd made with network folks in both Chicago and New York. They'd grown familiar with me being based in Chicago and my ability to cover network news in the busy Midwest. The proposed move would cause me to move from the 3rd largest TV market to the 20th; from a bustling city to a western "cowtown." The many trusted soundmen with whom I'd worked and whom I viewed as extended family were part of a Chicago family. The many non-network contacts I'd made and cultivated were Chicago contacts. Those diverse contacts had grown into clients—corporate, educational, and medical clients—because of my presence... in Chicago. Without that presence, my relationship with those clients would wither and die. Just as I had ascended to the top of the Chicago ladder, I would have to start over at the bottom of the Denver totem pole.

Thirteen years earlier, when I had been offered a network promotion and incredible opportunity, Amy had dropped everything to travel to Europe for me. We were much younger then. Because I was too immature to fully appreciate her incredible sacrifice and too distracted by my early success, our relationship and marriage didn't survive. In the spring of 1996, it was Amy's turn for recognition, promotion, and success. I could only attempt to reciprocate the level of support she had provided me. It seemed selfish and short-sighted to wallow in a "But, what about me and my career?" sentiment. I was thrilled for her and excited for us. Any fears I may have harbored needed to be silenced. As Horace Greeley once said, "Go West, young man."

Amy negotiated her employment agreement and we made the preliminary travels to assess housing and school districts in the Denver area. I had committed to a couple of assignments with NBC News that I needed and wanted to complete before saying farewell to the Windy City once and for all. Our move west occurred in two different stages. Amy and our five-year-old daughter Alexa made the first relocation wave while I tied up some loose ends in Chicago. Those loose ends were a Summer Olympiad and a Democratic National Convention.

In July, I traveled to Atlanta with my new close friend and loyal soundman Steve to work on the XXVI Summer Olympic games for NBC. In 1988, I had worked on the XXIV Summer games in Seoul, South Korea, (which had earned me that Emmy I told you about). In both games, NBC held the American broadcast rights or was the "host network." Working for the host network comes with certain privileges not afforded to other media outlets. You're given special access to venues and events. I was looking forward to sharing those perks with Steve, as it was his first Olympics. The first stop was accreditation where, as NBC employees, we were provided with special credentials—a reminder we were working the Olympics and not attending the Olympics.

Olympic coverage is divided into two departments. NBC Sports is the behemoth division responsible for the daunting task of showing live coverage of every competition from every venue and conveying "the thrill of victory and the agony of defeat." We were part of the much smaller team employed by NBC News. Our news coverage would be seen on *Nightly News*, *TODAY*, and the newly launched MSNBC.

Sports covers everything from high jumping to equestrian show jumping, from boxing to fencing and everything in between. Olympic news coverage can include anything from drug testing suspensions to snarled traffic jams (always an Olympic headline). In Atlanta, there was one story more newsworthy than all the others combined.

We were averaging 15-hour workdays and we'd been doing that for 12 straight days. Working the Olympics was both exhilarating and exhausting, and it was about to become even more so. I was sound asleep in my hotel room in the early morning hours of Saturday, July 27th when my phone rang at 1:30 a.m.

It was the overnight news editor. "There's been a bombing at Centennial Park. Get down there immediately. Shoot what you can. We'll send a producer to meet up with you and keep you posted when we have more details."

I woke Steve and we grabbed our gear, jumped in the crew car, and raced down to the park. The explosion had just occurred and the scene was pandemonium. We were like salmon swimming upstream, slicing against the current of concertgoers who were running away from the stage as we were running towards it. The police had just established a perimeter around the park, which was now a crime scene. Understandably, they closed access to the entire park. The downtown Atlanta streets were echoing with the sounds of sirens as ambulances sped to the bomb scene and then, just as quickly, sped away carrying the injured to nearby hospitals.

In the hours immediately following the bombing, the facts surrounding the incident were unknown or sketchy at best. Steve and I stopped some of the fleeing spectators for quick soundbites. Most were visibly shaken and disoriented. Everyone was on edge. Would there be more explosions? The early morning hours ticked by nervously. We were joined by producers and correspondents who gathered info and tried to clarify the murky details. It was soon made clear that this had been an act of domestic terrorism. We followed the story for 21 straight hours that first day before returning to our hotel, where we collapsed.

The next day, the games resumed, but far from normal. Flags were flown at half-staff. Athletes were temporarily evacuated from their Olympic Village accommodation to safeguard against additional bombings. A cloud of concern hung over the entirety of the games.

The day after the bombing, media outlets were reporting that the bomb, hidden inside a backpack under a park bench, had first been discovered by an unnamed AT&T security guard. That guard would soon have a name and a different title: Richard Jewell, Hero.

Everybody was instantly clamoring for an interview with the humble hero. *TODAY* was one of the first to get Jewell on the set. During a live interview, Katie Couric commended him, saying, "You were in the right place at the right time and you did the right thing, Richard."

At that time, *Nightly News* sometimes used a story type called "In Their Own Words." It removed the correspondent from the story and let the interview subject talk and tell their story, using just... their own words. It was the kind of storytelling vehicle that would work ideally with, say, an "aw shucks," regular-Joe security guard who'd found a terrorist bomb and, in the process, saved a bunch of lives.

Eric Wishnie was a young, Chicago-based producer and a close friend. We had both traveled from Chicago to work the Olympics for NBC News. He was given the assignment to interview Richard Jewell for an "In Their Own Words" segment on *Nightly News*. He called me and assigned Steve and I to shoot the interview with Richard Jewell. Three days after the bombing, on July 30th, Centennial Park reopened. Eric, Steve, and I met Jewell at the park in the morning to begin setting up. It provided the perfect location for our videotaped interview with the Olympics hero.

The recent Clint Eastwood film about Richard Jewell was a long time in the making. It received mixed reviews and suffered at the box office. Yet, it was a passionate work about a story that was near and dear to the director's heart. The actor cast in the lead role, Paul Walter Hauser, possesses a striking resemblance to the man I encountered during that 1996 interview. Houser is a mirror image of Richard Jewell and brought back vivid memories of that time.

The real Richard Jewell who I met was an unassuming thirty-something who carried more than a few extra pounds. No one would have mistaken him for one of the Olympic athletes. Dressed in his white AT&T shirt with SECURITY written across his broad shoulders, he had the matter-of-fact walk and talk of law enforcement. He was humble and respectful, proud but not boastful. He was called "odd" by some, but that was never evident to me. He seemed to enjoy his new-found fame while simultaneously keeping it in check.

During Eric's interview, Jewell carefully walked us through the events that had led up to the explosion. He was methodical in describing the details and modest when referring to himself. Eric was a talented interviewer; one who listened throughout, took notice of key soundbites, and knew when it was "in the can" without droning on and on, repeating the same questions.

He announced, "I think we've got it. Our work is done here. Richard, that was fascinating stuff. Thank you."

Jewell responded politely in his Georgian accent, "Well, I appreciate that, sir. Glad I could be of help."

I interrupted the farewell pleasantries with a cameraman concern. "Hang on. I think we should shoot a little B-Roll of Richard before we pack up and head out of here."

"B-Roll" is a standard production term dating way back to the old days of film cameras. It refers to extra footage shot to supplement interview footage. It allows for greater flexibility in the editing process; to "cut away" from the talking head to some other action/shot.

Eric disagreed. "B-Roll—what for? We have all the footage from the morning of the bombing. Not to mention endless footage from the Olympics."

"True. It's just a habit of mine. We always shoot tape of the interview subject doing his or her thing. You don't have to use it, but at least we'll have it."

"And I won't use it. Like I said, we already have plenty of footage. But I don't want to come between you and your many years of cameraman training."

"Many years? Is that a reference to my senior, 'old man' status on this crew?"

"Think of it as an homage. Look, knock yourselves out. Shoot as much B-Roll as you want or as much as Richard can tolerate. But since this is for tonight's broadcast, I need to get back to the broadcast center and start editing. Pop out the tape of the interview and I'll take it with me. That way, you guys can linger shooting your valuable B-Roll and I can get back to work editing."

"*Our* valuable B-Roll," I reminded him.

"Whatever. See ya back at the newsroom. Richard, thanks again." Eric ran off and headed back to the International Broadcast Center where NBC and many other news organizations were based. We were by far the largest news presence in the center.

It was just Richard, Steve, me, and the thousands of people who had returned to Centennial Park. No bands were playing that morning, so we had conducted the interview off to the side of the main stage. For our B-Roll purposes, I directed Richard to walk along the stanchions that separated the stage from the crowds. He happily complied. He surveyed the mass of people with a protective, crowd-control-like presence. We shot this action from several different camera angles; from in front of him, from the side, from behind him. We did so knowing that it was unlikely the footage would ever be used, but that we'd have done our job properly.

After thirty or forty minutes of shooting, I was comfortable we had shot enough never-to-be-viewed B-Roll. We thanked Richard for his additional time. It was early afternoon and we had time for a quick late lunch before heading back to the NBC newsroom at the broadcast center to drop off our remaining videotape and await any other assignments. Steve and I were just finishing up a deliciously greasy meal of Southern fried chicken when my phone rang. It was Eric calling from the newsroom.

"Did you get B-Roll of Jewell?"

"Of, course. We're just—"

"Bring it back ASAP. I'm in editing room three. Come see me as soon as you get here."

And with that, he abruptly hung up. His entire demeanor had changed, which was incredibly unlike the Eric I knew. Something was up.

We parked our crew car and walked through security and into the NBC newsroom just like we'd done every day for the previous two weeks. The newsroom of an Olympic network is always a beehive of activity, but at that moment, it was a swarm of commotion. Everyone was working the phones trying to get confirmation of something. People were screaming across the newsroom at each other. I noticed a fellow cameraman with his camera mounted on a tripod, shooting a newspaper. I leaned over his shoulder to take a closer look at the paper. It was a special afternoon edition of the July 30th *Atlanta Journal Constitution* (AJC). In big, bold print, the headline read:

"F.B.I. Suspects 'Hero' Guard May Have Planted Bomb."

Peering up from the viewfinder of his camera, he looked at me and said, "All hell is breaking loose."

I blurted out, "Holy shit!" I was still clutching the videotape of our hero… turned suspect. Steve and I headed for edit room three.

Eric and an editor were in a small, dark, windowless room hunched over a couple of TV monitors. They were frantically cutting (editing), or more accurately, *re-cutting* the Richard Jewell interview. Given the new details, the story had taken on a different angle. They were on edge and the mood in that tiny room was a tense one. I tried to slightly ease everyone's temperament by announcing our arrival with, "Can anyone use some worthless B-Roll of a security guard?"

Eric swung around in his desk chair and barked, "Not fucking funny! Not fucking now. We're an hour from air and this entire story, this entire *lead* story, has been turned upside down. May I *please* have that goddamn tape?!"

"Sure, here ya go." I wasn't done yet, and while handing him the tape, I had to add a smart-ass reminder, "Be careful with this. It's the only one I... *we* have. Jewell is the one in the white shirt with SECURITY emblazoned across his back. You can't miss him."

Normally, my dear friend Eric was one of the most humorous, fun-loving colleagues with whom to work. But, in that moment, pinned up against a deadline, he was laser-focused on the changing Jewell story, and rightly so. It looked as though there was a huge break in a hugely important investigation. He turned to look over his shoulder and shot me a piercing look that strongly suggested we leave his editing domain immediately.

Shortly after the AJC published that paper, both CNN and NBC went on the air with their reports naming Jewell as a suspect. Most everyone else soon followed with similar news stories. At that point, Richard Jewell virtually disappeared. His previous TV interviews were all live. We were the only network to have taped an interview with him, and we were the only network with B-Roll of the one-time Olympic security guard guarding his post. For months to come, the Richard Jewell story would dominate the airwaves with developments and debate. There was plenty to talk about... but nothing to show, save for a few minutes of B-Roll shot one morning at Centennial Park. Those images would be aired over and over and over again. If only freelance cameramen received royalties for their B-Roll.

When that story shifted and Jewell became a "focus," I remember thinking at the time, "What could cause such a drastic change in the story? What could cause such a dramatic transformation of a person from hero to villain?" I knew Tom Brokaw as one the most experienced, disciplined, and respected journalists in the entire business. If he said it, it had to be true. But, to whom or what was this dramatic development attributed?

Good journalism is only ever as good as the sources of information. Whenever possible, those sources should be double or even triple-checked. Concerning the Richard Jewell case, that source was extremely vetted. And, it turned out, there were three sources for that information.

EFF, BEE, and EYE—or, the **F**ederal **B**ureau of **I**nvestigation.

NBC News, CNN, the AJC… everyone reporting that Jewell had become a suspect in the investigation had received their information from the federal government; from senior officials within the freaking FBI!

Long before J. Edgar Hoover, law enforcement liked to "get their man" and crack the case. Hoover created Public Enemy #1 to motivate the FBI to get their man. Obviously, the FBI was eager to solve the case of an Olympic bombing on American soil. In doing so, there was a rush to judgment, and a rush to "profile" who could've done this. A rush to identify suspects.

The news media is in the business of reporting news. That sometimes means breaking news, too. It is a competitive business with some news media even feeling possessive of certain stories. *The Washington Post* must've felt like they "owned" the Nixon-Watergate story.

That same sense of ownership may have motivated *The Atlanta Journal Constitution* to break the story first on Richard Jewell's journey from hero to suspect. They were the hometown newspaper. *The Atlanta Journal Constitution* was committed to covering the Atlanta Olympics and aggressively covering the Olympic bombing. CNN was the Atlanta-based cable news network, and they, too, had a special interest in news from the games. NBC was the host network and our news division had more people than anyone covering news of the games. We were the real home team.

NBC News is a key player in the much larger news media. NBC and others rushed to own the story and get it first, and in doing so, we as the news media got it wrong.

That error is an indelible stain on all of journalism, particularly for those of us who so vociferously exclaimed "SUSPECT!" in the name of news. It was a terrible chapter for the news business and far worse for the life of Richard Jewell. For eighty-eight days, he and his mother endured torturous and relentless scrutiny by two of the most powerful institutions in American—the government and the news media. For the remainder of the games and long after, a horde of local, national, and international press camped outside the apartment where he and his mother resided. They became prisoners in their own homes.

I'd worked on some investigative reports for magazine shows where staking out a criminal or conspirator had been needed to get surreptitious video of the story's antagonist. In tragic news stories with multiple deaths, I'd had to stake out hospital ERs for ambulance video of first responders and victims. I've never enjoyed the stakeout-side of network news. It is, however, a necessary evil.

Fortunately for Steve and me, we avoided the stakeout scene outside the Jewell apartment. In the absence of concrete information from the FBI regarding their investigation, there was little else to shoot on the Richard Jewell story. But the Olympics continued, and there were plenty of other Olympic stories to shoot that last week of the Atlanta games.

Prior to and during the Atlanta Summer Olympics, I had shared with some of my New York and Chicago contacts that, in the fall, I would be relocating to Denver due to my wife's incredible career opportunity. Everyone's response was universal. *"While you're in Atlanta, you absolutely must meet Jack and Roger."* Jack Chesnutt was the bureau chief and Roger O'Neill the correspondent of the NBC News bureau in Denver, Colorado. While the networks were dismantling and closing their overseas bureaus, they still maintained active offices in many American cities. New York, LA, Chicago, Atlanta, Miami, Dallas, and Denver were all home to NBC News domestic bureaus. Jack and Roger from Denver happened to be in Atlanta covering the Olympics. Fortuitously for me, Steve and I spent most of that last week in Atlanta working on stories with Jack and Roger. They were knowledgeable and road-tested pros whose different personalities and styles complemented one another— Roger more focused and serious, Jack attentive and more relaxed. Our work together finished off the Olympics on a high note. I was concerned about my prospects in Denver and, while not guaranteeing my future success, they painted a more hopeful picture for the future. Before Atlanta, I'd known no one in Denver, but in one week I had doubled my network contacts to two. Still, I contained my exuberance.

After the closing ceremonies, everyone assigned to cover The Games moved on. I returned to Chicago to shoot many more news stories (and one big one) before having the finality of packing up and moving to Denver. But when the Olympic torch was extinguished, Richard Jewell's life remained mired in hell, and it was a hell that would last for another three months. On October 26, 1996, the U.S. Justice Department finally announced that Richard Jewell was no longer a suspect in the Olympic Park bombing. After being cleared, Jewell sued several media companies for defamation. He and his attorneys negotiated settlements with many of those companies (including NBC) for undisclosed amounts. He eventually returned to law enforcement, working as a sheriff's deputy in West Georgia and a police officer in Pendergrass, Georgia. He died of a heart attack in 2007.

The damage he and his mother suffered could never be undone. Many of us who worked on that story felt remorseful. As he often does, Tom Brokaw said it best when he tweeted, "Richard and his mother went through a painful time which I deeply regret. I hope we all learned a lesson, including the FBI which was my principal source."[2]

There certainly is a valuable lesson to be studied. But to do so requires we look back and learn from the past in a world that has little time for retrospective reflection.

---

2   @tombrokaw (2019, December 25)

10

Relocation on the Campaign Trail

I had barely one day to unpack before launching into a dizzying sequence of assignments that would conclude with the 1996 Democratic National Convention at Chicago's United Center. My last month in Chicago would prove to be my busiest. I viewed it as the storm before the calm; a deluge of work in Chicago before an anticipated dearth of work in Denver. And I would only have to deal with one crazy busy schedule—mine. While I was in Atlanta, Amy and Alexa had met the movers, packed up our house, and headed west to set up our new home. I would join them after the convention.

The house was empty, save for my television equipment, which I was still using, and our wine collection, which would be the last thing shipped via refrigerated truck. Cameras and Cabernet would be the last to go. I was constantly working, so I had little time to miss all of the material possession that had been comfortably placed in our Colorado home. In between the constant assignments, there were numerous farewell drinks and dinners. I was moving just three states away and would be working in the same business, but there was a feeling of finality that signaled an end of something.

For two short years, I had worked extensively with Steve Azzato. We'd become closer than most crews who work a lifetime together. There was an unspoken awareness that that bond would soon be severed by a regional divide, as Denver cameramen don't work with Chicago soundmen. Our busy work schedule kept us preoccupied, postponing the inevitable Chicago blues. At the end of long days, I would come home to a rented bed and glass of wine and just collapse.

The convention was quite the culmination. It was the re-election run for the Clinton-Gore team, and everybody who was somebody was in attendance. The same could be said for the networks. NBC had a huge, although not exactly Olympic-sized, staff to cover the events. The President declared, "Hope is back in America."[3] He promised to build a bridge to the 21st century while creating 20 million more jobs. My busy schedule earlier in the year had conflicted with many of the Republican primary battles. Working the convention provided me with a much-needed shot of politics. I had not been booked to cover either the Clinton or the Dole campaign leading up to election day. I knew that could change, but saw this as my only real glimpse of politics for the 1996 season.

I walked through our completely remodeled but now barren 100-year-old house wearing a melancholy expression—equal parts smile and frown. I recounted the many fond memories created under that roof while a long-postponed sadness finally engulfed me. As I loaded up my camera gear and clothes, I felt like a character in Jackson Browne's song "The Load Out."

Let the roadies take the stage
Pack it up and tear it down

---

3   "Hope is Back in America." *The Washington Post.* (1996, August 30) Retrieved from https://www.washingtonpost.com/archive/politics/1996/08/30/hope-is-back-in-america/b446537c-ea85-4642-880c-87d14c3c054c/

They're the first to come and last to leave [...]
They'll set up in another town

Sure enough, there was "another town" that lay ahead. Denver was the future, Chicago the past. Looking over my shoulder or into the rear-view mirror was inevitable, but to dwell on it made little sense. At six in the morning and with the Rocky Mountains in my sights, I saddled up in my Suburban and drove the 1,100-mile, 18-hour trip in one day, arriving in our new home of Evergreen, Colorado by midnight.

As "The Mile-High City," Denver rests at the base of the Rocky Mountains. Twenty minutes west and 2,000 feet higher in elevation, Evergreen is nestled in the foothills of those same mountains. Pine tree forests sprouted everywhere and herds of elk roamed freely through the wooded neighborhoods as if they owned the place, which they pretty much did aside from the homes.

Many of those homes were large stone and beam, custom structures sitting on an acre or more of land. That kind of scenery didn't exist in Chicago. Those kinds of homes certainly did exist in Chicago, but mostly in the toney "North Shore" suburbs where the city's wealthy elite resided... which had been mostly out of our reach. With Denver's cheaper cost of living and Amy's new Associate General Counsel salary and relocation allowance, that lifestyle was suddenly accessible, at least initially. It was our hope and belief that eventually I would resurrect my career in Denver and my temporarily moribund business would take root, bear fruit, and we'd return to the dual-income means of the past. And it was only a hope. Any loose ends with any Chicago clients had been neatly tied in a bow. There were no clients, network or otherwise, and no assignments or shoots on my calendar.

It didn't take long for Amy, Alexa, and me to adapt to our new city/country living. Alexa was quick to make new friends in her kindergarten class at an idyllic public school. Bergen Meadows Elementary was aptly named, as it sat in the middle of an actual meadow frequented by the resident elk herd. Even better, the Evergreen Public School District had SAT scores and graduation rates on par with some of Chicago's best private schools.

Almost immediately, Amy was up to speed in her new job. She'd become acquainted with the owners and senior management during the acquisition of the company. And, since her former law firm was a feeder for the legal department, she already knew many of the attorneys with whom she'd be working closely. Better yet, she loved the new challenges and environment.

So, what about the formerly in-demand, Emmy award-winning, out-of-work cameraman?

I knew that I needed to tap into the Denver market just as I had done in the Chicago market six years earlier. But I hated receiving cold calls as much as I hated making them, for fear of being as welcome as a 1-800 phone solicitor. The best point of entry into Denver was through the one team that already knew my name, Jack and Roger. They responded to my call by inviting me to the bureau to see their operation and meet the team.

Compared to Chicago and most other bureaus, Denver was a small but productive operation comprised of five dedicated staffers. Patti Burke was the young but eager bureau coordinator who seamlessly performed a multitude of tasks that made life less complicated for Jack and Roger. Ray Farmer was the down-to-earth cameraman with a keen eye and genuine smile, for whom the glass was always half full. The multi-tasking David Jackson was both Ray's soundman and the bureau editor/tech wizard. There were few problems he couldn't solve. Having been a staff cameraman in my previous life, I knew there could come a time when the workload would be too much for Ray and David to shoulder alone. And I hoped that, when that time came, I'd be called upon. Of course, I wasn't the only freelance cameraman in town… just the newest. I would learn later that the existing pool of freelance talent was highly suspicious of the new interloper from Chicago with network credentials. I was hoping to get my foot in the door and they were hoping I'd break my leg in the process.

Shortly after that visit, NBC did call. However, it was the political desk in Washington, D.C. inquiring about my availability. I was still unpacking boxes and adjusting to my new environs. Needless to say, I was surprised to hear from Washington, but there was a little over a week left in the '96 presidential campaign.

I knew the assignment editor, although not well. She cut right to the point. "Tim, what's your availability for the next week or so?"

"I'm available. But I must tell you, I'm no longer in Chicago. I recently moved to Denver."

"Yes, we're aware of that." The Washington bureau and political desk, like the government, knew everything about everybody. "We've recently encountered a situation with our crew assigned to the Vice President."

The media that covers and travels with presidents and vice presidents require a higher level of security clearance than most. It's usually a long-term assignment—particularly on the campaign trail, where a revolving door of personnel is frowned upon.

"Okay. Situation?"

"Yes. Bruce and Chuck are with the Gore campaign. Chuck's

father has fallen gravely ill. We need to get him off the campaign and back to Miami to be with his father. Bruce isn't comfortable working with another soundman under these circumstances, and we need to get another crew credentialed and onboard Air Force Two, like immediately."

Bruce Bernstein and Chuck Stewart were the colorful, long-time crew based out of Miami. They were beloved industry-wide and so well-known as to be identified by just their first names. They'd been NBC staffers who'd taken a cash buyout or "early retirement." It was a way for NBC to reduce headcount and salaries without simply firing valued employees like Bruce and Chuck. They'd had no intention of actually retiring. So, with the windfall cash from their early retirement settlement, they'd purchased camera equipment and immediately gone back to work for NBC, making more money as freelancers. They were veterans of numerous presidential campaigns and consummate entrepreneurs. They also had a thriving T-shirt side business whose catchy slogans were worn by both the news media *and* campaign staffers. They were loyal and exclusive to one another, too, which explained why Bruce would leave the campaign due to an illness in Chuck's family.

"We need you on the campaign in two days. Who are you working with?"

I didn't have a Denver soundman, yet. But I feared telling her that might send the wrong message, given the urgency and importance of the assignment. My last soundman had been Steve. "Steve Azzato. Although, he's in Chicago—"

"I'll let you two work out the logistics of your rendezvous. You both just need to be at Scott Air Force Base in Belleview, Illinois to meet Air Force Two first thing this Saturday. Have Steve call the political desk ASAP with his personal information so we can get it to the Secret Service. The producer traveling with Gore is Lydia Ramos. She'll be contacting you shortly. Bye."

I immediately dialed Steve's number. *Please answer and please be available.* At the same time, I yelled upstairs for my wife. "Amy? Honey, I have good news... I'm no longer unemployed!"

Steve dropped everything to team up with me on the assignment. We'd known that someday our paths would once again cross—just not so quickly. We met in St. Louis and took cabs for the short drive across the Mississippi River to Belleview, Illinois. At Scott Air Force Base, we met up with our producer Lydia Ramos and the Clinton/Gore campaign staff, who issued us our credentials as members of the White House Traveling Press. We were officially the NBC News crew covering the Gore campaign and were immediately swept up into the whirling maelstrom of endless campaigning. This was a far more intense experience than my previous bus tour with then V.P. Quayle in 1992. Over the next six days, we would hit *seventeen* different cities, making at least one campaign stop in each.

Saturday. Day One: We began at a rally in Collinsville, Illinois, then drove to Rock Island, Illinois, and then got back on board Air Force Two for a four-hour flight to Sacramento, California. Food and drink were always in ample supply (sleep was the lacking ingredient), and Steve and I shared a few beers on that evening flight with my news colleagues who made us feel welcome and part of the "team." After Sacramento, we were back on board Air Force Two for another transcontinental flight to Detroit, Michigan. We slept on board the plane.

Sunday. Day Two: We arrived in Detroit at dawn. We were all escorted to a 20-plus vehicle vice presidential motorcade that transported us to a downtown hotel. Each member of the press was shown to their hotel room. My initial reaction was, "How thoughtful of the campaign to allow us a brief nap." Turned out, the room was *not* for sleep or even rest. It was for us to shower. After a thorough but brief cleansing, we were all back in the motorcade for four more campaign stops at inner-city churches around Detroit. Each of the predominantly black congregations enthusiastically received the Veep for Sunday worship. After the church services, we were back on Air Force Two for a flight to Boulder, Colorado. After Boulder, we headed for an evening rally in Milwaukee, Wisconsin. At this point, I began to wonder if the Clinton/Gore campaign needed to hire a travel agent who had a better command of American geography. The travel schedule made no sense; traveling east to fly west, then back east again and then west and back east again. It was all incomprehensible, but who was I to question the route?

On the flight to Milwaukee, it was my turn to learn the skilled art of "tray surfing." This is a competition banned on all commercial flights, but sometimes permitted on campaign aircraft. As the plane is lumbering down the runway and gaining speed for takeoff, the surfer stands on a food serving tray and "surfs" down the carpeted aisle. The speed of the aircraft acts as the inertia or power of a wave propelling the surfer downhill. It is a sport best performed after the lubrication of a few Heinekens.

Here, it's worth noting the then configuration of the Air Force Two aircraft. The communications area was at the front of the plane, just behind the pilots. The middle of the plane was for staff and the personal quarters for the V.P. and his family. The rear third was for the press... and Secret Service. Any lunacy performed by the press was always contained to the rear third of the plane and happening under the watchful eye of the Secret Service.

Someone (probably Bruce and Chuck) had temporarily installed a ghetto blaster and portable JBL speakers in the overhead carry-on bins. This system provided the musical entertainment on longer flights. DJ honors were handed out on a rotating basis, and from Boulder to Milwaukee, it was NBC's turn to spin the records. My successful initiation into tray-surfing created a feeling of confidence in me. Steve and I decided on the classics. I inserted a Rolling Stones CD and hit play.

With "Honky Tonk Woman" blaring from the overhead bins, Al and Tipper Gore appeared in the press cabin. I was told that this was not a rare occurrence, as they often mingled with the press "after work." Because we were the new kids on the block, replacing Bruce and Chuck, they welcomed us on board the campaign and asked about the health of Chuck's father, which struck me as particularly caring.

The press had labeled Al Gore as being stiff and rehearsed. That may have been one side of him. But onboard Air Force Two, I watched as he went "off-script," spontaneously interacting and joking with the press corps. It was a different Al Gore than the one I had read about. Then Tipper approached me and asked, "Whose music is this?"

I instantly and vividly recalled that she and other Washington wives had created a committee that had successfully lobbied the music industry to apply PARENTAL ADVISORY labels on music with violent, drug-related, or sexual themes. And now, I was playing rebellious music about loose women. Yikes! Before answering, I looked around to see if any of the Secret Service agents were reaching for their Glocks. They were not. I was safe for the moment.

"Um, well… it's mine. I'm the one who chose the Rolling Stones. Um, I'm sorry…"

"Hang on just a minute." And with that, she spun around and headed to the middle of the plane with the promise of returning.

Steve and I looked at each other confusedly, not knowing what had just transpired. Were we in deep trouble with the Second Lady? Would we be banished from the campaign in Milwaukee? Damned Rolling Stones! If only I'd played it safe with the Backstreet Boys.

She quickly returned with a drink in one hand and a CD in the other. She took a sip, handed me the CD, and said, "Well if that's all you got, play this instead." She handed me a copy of Jackson Browne's *Running on Empty*, an album about life on the road. She'd spent so much time on the campaign trail, it spoke to her, and with my years of travel, it always spoke to me, as well. I hit "play" and the whole traveling press corps began to dance and sing in unison, "Looking out at the road rushing under my wheels..."

We were not in trouble. We were inside the ropes covering the Veep and enjoying the perks of our job.

Monday. Day Three: After a few hours of sleep in a Milwaukee hotel, we raced off early in the morning for a rally in Racine, Wisconsin. That was followed by a flight to Cleveland, Ohio, and then we were off to Gore's home state of Tennessee for a frenzied series of campaign stops. Knoxville was the first stop, followed by Nashville and then Chattanooga. The Clinton-Gore team was way up in the polls over the Dole-Kemp team. Everywhere Gore appeared, he was met by enormous, raucous crowds of cheering supporters. The decibel level was turned up in his home state.

The Chattanooga event was held at a converted airplane hangar at the airport. As part of the throng of press, Steve and I descended the stairs at the rear of the aircraft on our way to the camera/press platform. My camera hung from my right shoulder at the end of a sturdy and padded camera strap as I balanced the tripod over my left shoulder. A song pumping from the gigantic loudspeakers in the hangar froze me in my tracks. It was familiar to me. I'd heard it over and over, but couldn't put my finger on what it was.

I turned to Steve and asked, "What is this song? Who's singing?"

"I don't know. I'm not familiar with it."

We continued to make our way to the hangar, still hearing the familiar song that had taken control of my brain. Grasping at straws, I turned to a Secret Service agent whom I'd befriended on the plane and asked, "Doug, help me out here, do you know who sings this song?"

"Help you out? What do I look like, a DJ? I'm with the Secret Service. You're on your own, Tim."

And then the music stopped as the stage was cleared for the keynote speaker... the Veep. The roar of the crowd grew in anticipation. We made our way closer to the press platform, where a reserved space awaited each network and press organization.

Our path took us by the stage, where suddenly I accidentally walked straight into and was confronted face-to-face with the answer to my question.

Back when we were in high school, Kim Ritchie could often be found strumming a guitar. She moved to Nashville to write songs and play in honky-tonk bars. At one such performance, she was discovered by an executive from Mercury Records who signed her to a record deal. Her first CD produced three hits on the U.S. Country Top 100 chart. We'd played it endlessly at home and in the car. But I'd had a brain freeze upon hearing it in Chattanooga. And now, I was standing face to face with the writer/performer.

"Hey! That was you! What are you doing here?"

"Oh My God! Well, I'm warming up the crowd for ... the guy. I can't believe you're here in Tennessee. What are *you* doing here?!"

I tugged on my lanyard and said, "Well, I'm traveling with the guy, covering him for NBC. I love your music. And it looks like I'm not alone. Things are going well?"

"Yeah, things are going really well. And, it looks like for you, too, traveling with the Vice President. Wow. Like, this is your job? Where are you these days? Didn't you marry someone from high school?"

While the rowdy crowd clapped and chanted "FOUR MORE YEARS," Kim and I strained to hear one another and get caught up on the last twenty years. All of a sudden, I felt a very strong tug on my right elbow. It was a female staffer on Gore's press team.

She scolded me with, "What are you doing? You're kind of holding up the show. And, you're going to miss the Vice President's speech if you don't move your ass and get into place right now!"

"Gotta run, Kim! Keep cranking out the hits!"

The staffer cut a path for me through the thick crowd and escorted me onto the press platform, where Steve and the other twenty members of the press were tightly gathered. I placed my tripod on the place where NBC RESERVED had been written on a thick strip of silver tape. I snapped my camera into place on the tripod and pressed the "record" button just as the Vice President walked on stage.

Steve whispered in my ear, "What was that all about?"

I responded with, "That song I was asking about... I'll explain later."

Once we wrapped in Chattanooga and were back on the plane, I found the press staffer and apologized for being late to the platform. She was understanding and minimized any issue. There was a genuine respect for the press corps and what they did. We were the mouthpiece, the loudspeaker for the candidate's message. This staffer had a job to do and understood that so did we. She kept a watchful eye out for both. There was a sense that we, the press and the campaign—while staunchly independent—were working together, not against one another.

The next to last stop on our long day in Tennessee was Memphis, once home to the King, Elvis Presley. Late in the evening, our motorcade pulled up to a Grand Ole Opry-like country concert hall. The rally there mirrored the other twenty or so rallies of the last few days. While the remarks were old news to us, it was new and inspiring to the supporters in attendance. It was our job to cover every move the candidate made, every speech he gave, no matter how redundant. After the event, we all returned outside to the motorcade and awaited the V.P. and his staff. It was standard procedure that every news organization had their own vehicle and driver—usually a minivan to accommodate both passengers and equipment. When we returned to our crew vehicles, all of us were surprised to find a bottle of champagne sitting in our respective cars. It didn't matter that there were no cups or glasses. We tipped the champagne to our lips and drank straight from the bottle, passing the bottles around among the press corps like college kids at a tailgate.

After meeting with local politicians, Al and Tipper Gore emerged from the concert hall and into their shiny black, bulletproof limo. We jumped into our vehicles and the motorcade sped off, back to the airport. Our final stop was Carthage, Tennessee—Al Gore's hometown. The next day was Election Day and the Vice President wished to vote in the town where he'd grown up.

But a funny thing happened on the way to the airport.

When traveling in a presidential motorcade, you never encounter another vehicle. For obvious security reasons, all intersecting roads are closed; all highway on and off ramps blocked. It is truly a traffic-free commute. As we whisked down the highway unencumbered, heading back to the Memphis airport, the motorcade took an unexpected and unannounced "detour." We darted off the highway and into what appeared to be a residential neighborhood. Steve, Lydia, and I were all perplexed. The motorcade stopped on a tree-lined boulevard. Thinking this was yet another campaign stop, we grabbed our gear; I shouldered my camera and ran to the front of the motorcade. The rest of the like-minded press did the same, still photographers and cameramen frantically squeezing off frames of nothing in the evening darkness. We were met by Tipper, who was emphatically waving her arms above her head.

"Everyone, put down your cameras! Stop shooting. This is not an official event. Al just wanted to get his picture taken with you guys."

After I took the camera from my shoulder and looked around, I could see we were standing on Elvis Presley Boulevard, smack-dab in front of the gates of Graceland. With Tipper acting as official photographer, we all stood shoulder to shoulder around the Vice President, squeezed into the frame, and said, "CHEESE!"

The V.P. had wanted *his* picture taken with *us*. It was a pleasantly surprising photo-op, and the grins each of us wore in that photo were a product of our genuine surprise... and at least partly from imbibing numerous bottles of champagne.

We awoke early on Election Day of 1996 to cover Al and Tipper casting their ballots. We then boarded Air Force Two for a flight to Little Rock, Arkansas, where we would spend election night. It was no surprise that Clinton-Gore won reelection, and the Arkansas capital was awash in celebration. The next day, we took our final journey on Air Force Two, accompanying the White House Traveling Press Corps back to Washington, D.C. Steve and I would once again say goodbye and head to Chicago and Denver, respectively, with a few more war stories added to our resumes.

The campaign relationship with the mainstream media of 1996 looks like a bygone era today. The champagne and photo-ops I've described weren't attempts to win over or manipulate the news media. By then, Clinton-Gore was 20 points ahead in all of the polls. Victory was a forgone conclusion. During their first term, the Clinton administration had received plenty of honest but negative reporting, and it would worsen in the second term (i.e. impeachment). The Gore team wasn't trying to buy "good ink." They were simply recognizing who we were and appreciating the job we performed.

As the mainstream media, at every rally, we were treated as a respected part of the process. That ride along with Al Gore was certainly my most in-depth and up-close campaign experience, but far from being my only such experience. In addition to the other campaign stories I've recounted in this book, there are additional political stories I'd worked on that are not contained within these pages. I'd covered Democrats, Republicans, Independents, incumbents, and first-timers alike. Never was I made to feel unwelcome by the candidate or campaign.

I'd heard stories from colleagues who'd covered the 1984 presidential campaign of Reverend Jesse Jackson. With growing support but no money, that was a bare-bones and underfunded effort that lacked everything except rhetoric. The days were long, the travel cramped and grueling. When there was a break, the "refreshments" normally provided to refuel the traveling press were rarely offered (and one can't simply jump off the campaign for a quick bite). The tired and hungry media openly complained. But the "harsh" treatment of the press was a result of the campaign's economic hardship and not a symptom of any intention to punish the press.

I have never covered a Trump rally. But from my many colleagues who have, I'm told the same mainstream media is now viewed with contempt and hatred—repeatedly singled out for attack by an angry and rabid crowd, and called the cause of our problems by the man at the microphone.

As the news landscape has increased and the reporting voices multiplied, the trust and respect between candidates and media have eroded. This downward spiral is compounded by the anonymous, online voices and international hackers who are hellbent on muddying the waters and ruining a once trusted process. Covering politics should always be a search for the truth. Without trusted and illuminating reporting, that search is done in the dark.

11

THE EPICENTER OF NEWS

After the Clinton-Gore reelection, I returned to Denver and resumed networking with prospective television clients in my new market. There weren't many. I was hoping to establish myself as a qualified cameraman, much as I had in Chicago six years earlier. The good news was, this time I had both an international and domestic news resume to boast about. The bad news was that Denver, being a fraction of the size of Chicago, would only generate a fraction of the news and work to which I had grown accustomed. But perhaps, over time, I would become the backup for Ray Farmer, the bureau's staff cameraman, receiving the assignments for which he was unavailable.

My new friends at NBC News Denver informed me that development wouldn't be "over time," but rather immediate—and that I would likely be so busy as to incur plenty of so-called overtime. I was cautiously optimistic. Their news forecast sounded bright, but even experienced news veterans like Jack and Roger couldn't have forecast the series of news tsunamis that were building in the not so distant future and headed our way.

A year and a half before Amy's career moved us to Denver, a despicable and deadly act of terrorism occurred. On April 19,

1995, a truck bomb ripped through the Alfred P. Murrah Federal Building in Oklahoma City, Oklahoma, killing 168 people and injuring more than 680. Fifteen of the victims were children enrolled in a daycare on the building's second floor. This bombing stands as the deadliest act of domestic terrorism in our nation's history. Timothy McVeigh and Terry Nichols were apprehended, charged with murder and conspiracy, and would be tried separately. In April of 1995, I was still wearing two hats for the ambitious *Enter Here* project, acting as both production manager and cameraman. I loved the added responsibility and professional growth that the project demanded, but my schedule was so busy that I was unable to break away and cover the bombing story out of Oklahoma City. However, I would be heavily involved in the next phase of the ongoing story.

To provide the defendants a fair trial, the trial venue was moved to Denver. This was the kind of story that would play prominently every day in the morning headlines and nightly news. To cover it properly, Jack and Roger knew their small market bureau would require assistance. Additional correspondents, producers, editors, and engineers would all be needed. With only one camera crew on staff, they would also need to add several more crews to cover the consecutive trials of two despised terrorists, with no end in sight. The viewers, and thus the networks, would insist on gavel-to-gavel coverage.

Jack asked if I would commit to NBC for the indeterminate length of the trial. He needed a crew upon which he could rely, and my NBC qualifications and recommendations made me a perfect fit. Ray would be involved, but also needed to be available for other news coverage and assignments that were sure to surface in the Rocky Mountain West area during the trial. Plus, I also think that Ray—as a staffer who could pick and choose his assignments (to some degree)—expressed a desire not to be shackled to the mind-numbing duty of trial coverage. His creative eye and gentle demeanor occasionally desired the wide-open spaces and mountain locations commonly found in Denver's backyard. For my part, I was flattered Jack had approached me for the open-ended commitment. With this assignment, he had opened the door for me in Denver. It would be up to me to make the most of it. As the trial ebbed and flowed, other crews would be added on a temporary basis. As long as I excelled at my job and proved reliable and dependable, I would be there throughout the lengthy proceedings. For a Denver-based freelance cameraman with network credentials, the sound of the judge's gavel was opportunity knocking. I replied to Jack's inquiry with a hearty "HELL, YES."

I would need a reliable professional sound partner for this long-term commitment. I had met and briefly worked with a handful of local Denver soundmen, all of whom were more than qualified. But my favorite and most tried-and-true soundman resided 1,000 miles away in Chicago. Steve Azzato.

Amy and I had plenty of room and an unused guest suite in our new Evergreen home. I floated the idea of having a live-in guest for the foreseeable future. Most wives would understandably balk at such a prospect. Because of Steve's universal likeability and Amy's understanding and support for my opportunity, though, she offered zero opposition to the idea. Her only question was, "Just how long is this assignment?"

My journalistic training allowed for only one fact-based and honest response. "I don't have a fucking clue."

I made the call to Steve and proposed the unconventional work relationship. There would be breaks in the trial coverage and time for home visits back to Chicago. But, being gone for months at a time would cause unusual difficulty for his wife Kathy and their three kids. Still, the opportunity for such guaranteed network income and, to a lesser degree, the chance to "get the band back together" made it an easy sell. With Kathy's approval, he drove from Chicago to Denver and set up semi-permanent residence in our home.

There were a number of pre-trial motions to cover that kept us all busy in anticipation of the actual McVeigh trial, which was set to begin in March of 1997. But before the jury was even selected, the McVeigh trial was eclipsed by another horrific, headline-grabbing death in nearby Boulder, Colorado.

The day after Christmas in 1996, Patsy Ramsey phoned 911 to report a missing child and what was initially thought to be a kidnapping. Seven hours later on that same day, in the basement of their home, Patsy's husband John discovered the murdered body of their six-year-old daughter, JonBenét. The child's hands had been bound behind her back with duct tape. She had been strangled by a garrote around her neck—made from a piece of chord and a wooden handle—and her skull had been cracked. It was a horrendous crime. My daughter Alexa was almost the same age as JonBenét; they were both six years old and in kindergarten. With each bizarre, gruesome, and sickening detail that emerged, the knot in my stomach grew and tightened. As a result, it was difficult for me not to empathize with the grieving family.

The Ramseys were an affluent, upper-class white family. It was Christmas. The warm glow of the Christmas lights adorning the exterior of their gingerbread house-like Tudor mansion belied the horror that had occurred inside. The home sat in a picturesque neighborhood in picturesque Boulder. The adorable, blonde-haired and blue-eyed JonBenét had been a child beauty queen, winning many crowns at an early age. Those details and the horrible nature of the crime created a frenzy of coverage. It became tabloid fodder and stayed on those same front pages for years to come.

The local NBC station KUSA had footage on that first day and night from outside the home of the initial police arrivals and investigation. NBC had access to that tape, but to supplement it, in the days and weeks following the murder, Steve and I peeled off from covering the McVeigh pre-trial motions to covering the JonBenét story. We shot video of the Ramsey home, neighborhood, and the downtown Boulder office building where John Ramsey ran Access Graphics, a computer services company. Almost immediately, the Boulder District Attorney's Office was besieged with questions from the media about developments in the case, and regular press conferences were held, which we regularly attended.

Interest in the story wasn't limited just to the tabloids. Home video from JonBenét's many beauty competitions showed a heavily made-up little girl dressed in cowgirl outfits and princess costumes as she bounced across stages. Television is an image-driven medium, and those videotape images drove demand for more and more coverage of the murder investigation. The *TODAY* show displayed an almost unrelenting interest in the story. The show's senior producers in New York were asking and at times insisting on daily updates to the story. They needed new details to accompany and justify the replaying of the beauty pageant footage.

Almost immediately, the family members became key suspects in the crime. At early press conferences, the Boulder Police Commander said they were "under an umbrella of suspicion." The District Attorney said, "Obviously, the focus is on these people... call them what you want to."

There was a short, almost incoherent ransom note found in the house. It fueled the "Who Dunnit" speculation. Handwriting analysis cleared John, but could not eliminate Patsy as the note's author. The suspicion increased... and the appetite for the story grew.

It was revealed that shoddy police work had botched the crime scene, ruining valuable forensic evidence. Meanwhile, the police were pointing fingers at the District Attorney for a botched prosecution. Infighting broke out between the DA's office and the police department. At times, they seemed to be conducting parallel but separate investigations of the same crime. The problem was complicated by the fact there were sources from the DA, the police, *and* the Ramsey family, as well... all with different theories and agendas. This was a goldmine of gossip for the tabloids who were in the business of speculation. But, for a news division dedicated to reporting verifiable facts, it was a minefield. For their part, the NBC journalists in Boulder did an admirable job of attempting to separate fact from conjecture. Still, the nation's appetite grew and *TODAY*'s demands for frequent updates continued.

After the early flurry of revelations in the initial probe, the investigation, like many investigations, went "underground" and quietly progressed at a snail's pace. There was little to report on, and even the frequent press conferences ceased. But the editorial tug-of-war continued with New York clamoring for more and Denver insisting on reporting news only when there was news to report.

All this came on the eve of the McVeigh trial. The Denver news scene was suddenly presented with two separate but major news stories taking place in two separate but nearby towns, Boulder and Denver, which were a short 45-minute drive apart.

Both stories were of huge national interest. Any concerns I'd harbored regarding the inactivity of my Denver-based career immediately and forever disappeared.

JonBenét's murder was grotesque and tragic. However, the main news event was taking place at the Byron C. Rogers Courthouse back in Denver, where Chief U.S. District Judge Richard Matsch presided over the McVeigh trial. The judge had banned the presence of cameras in the courtroom. This was not uncommon in federal trials, and when you blow up a federal building—killing 168 federal employees, citizens, and children—it is most certainly a federal crime. The judge allowed a closed-circuit TV feed to be viewed in a courtroom back in Oklahoma City, but ordered the media to be banned from that courtroom and TV feed. The news media would have to rely on sketches from inside the courtroom. There would be very little video to help tell the story of the United States v. Timothy McVeigh and subsequently the United States v. Terry Nichols; two historic trials.

The one regular source of video would be the "comings and goings" at the courthouse as the teams of attorneys for both sides arrived and departed each day. This footage would be predominantly comprised up of video, with very little audio. Judge Matsch had issued a gag order, prohibiting the attorneys from discussing the case. Knowing the arrival and departure shots were such valuable images, both the government and the news media made preparations.

The camera crew "scrum" is a common scene on newscasts. On numerous occasions, I've been involved in the tornado of camera crews jostling for position while simultaneously backpedaling directly in front of a walking subject or subjects. To avoid this sort of daily scrum, the government, together with the news media, created a press "pen." A fence of metal stanchions was erected. On one side, the arriving and departing attorneys walked unencumbered in and out of the courthouse. On the opposite side, our network news crews lined up and recorded the parade of attorneys in a relatively orderly manner.

There was nothing surreptitious or sneaky about this network "stakeout." It was out in the open, pre-arranged, and choreographed. Everyone had a job to do, and this was a compromise that satisfied both trial participants and media participants. Because it took place each day during the trials, the camera crews settled into a workday routine. Lining up at the fence was like arriving at the office and greeting one's coworkers. Even if we all worked for different networks, the press pen was like a shared office where we collectively spent a great deal of time.

As the McVeigh story moved from pretrial to the actual trial, the news coming out of Boulder slowed. The JonBenét story remained a horrible, tragic, and bizarre murder of national interest, but it had become an *unsolved*, horrible, tragic, and bizarre murder of national interest. After the initial few months, there was little to report regularly. The DA and Police Chief grew tired of standing before a horde of news media to report that there was nothing new to report. Yet, the story and case remained anything but solved. Meanwhile, the initial, frenetic back and forth motion of the two stories we were covering never felt schizophrenic to Steve and me. They were two vastly different assignments, and although both of them were tragic, they were stories where we were able to separate ourselves from the sadness... mostly.

For the most part, the national focus shifted back to Denver and the trial. NBC was the only network to employ a staff camera crew in Denver (Ray & David). The other networks employed freelance crews (or incurred travel expenses to fly in staffers) when the need arose... like for a terrorist trial. As a result, the Denver freelance community was well-established, tightly knit, and mildly competitive. The crews had all rotated among the different networks and everyone knew each other. Most of the freelance crews in the pen had, from time to time, worked for NBC. Enter Tim and Steve. In crew terms, I was the new kid on the block and Steve was a Chicago interloper. Yet, we were NBC's lead crew and eating the proverbial lunches of those other crews. The trials would be a lengthy and lucrative assignment, and some of those crews saw a past source of income suddenly disappear. The initial grumblings, cold shoulders, and knives in our backs were inevitable.

Luckily, the daily routine in close proximity with those peers helped melt the early ice and build mutual respect. There are vast differences between covering a courtroom drama in Denver and a battle in Beirut. However, it's been my experience that, if you cover the same story with the same people day-in and day-out, unless you're a complete asshole, you can't help but build relationships and form a bond with your news colleagues. That kind of camaraderie helped fast-track our assimilation into the mix. Soon, we were just another crew.

There was one colleague for whom that bond was felt almost immediately. Scott Gordon "Gordy" McLean was a long-standing CBS freelancer. He and his soundman Paul were the first call for CBS when it came to stories anywhere west of the Mississippi River. He was confident in his abilities and comfortable in his own skin. From our first meeting, he never viewed me as a threat, unlike the many other freelancers who first viewed me with skepticism at best and contempt at worst. Gordy and I were the same age, having jumped into news coverage in our early twenties. As a result, we shared a lot of common ground. We both possessed a big picture view of the news business. While able to keenly focus on the job or assignment at hand, we also understood the much larger role of news; from where it had come and the direction in which it was heading. Like me, he had ventured out and taken on demanding roles in non-network series, much as I had done in acting as production manager/producer/ cameraman on the *Enter Here* project. He was married to a smart career woman who'd started her talent agency specializing in camera crews and production personnel. They were worldly and well-traveled, just as Amy and I were. His two daughters were slightly older than Alexa, and we lived a mile from each other in the same Evergreen neighborhood. All of this could have been a passing coincidence. But when we discovered that we shared a similar global appreciation for wines, drinking from and collecting out of the same regions, varieties, and producers, our friendship was forever forged.

While all four networks were fully represented at the trials, their coverage was run differently. CBS and CNN had no bureaus in Denver. Everything was run out of New York and Atlanta, respectively. ABC operated a bare-bones skeleton bureau out of Denver. The joint venture between NBC and Microsoft, MSNBC, had been launched just eight months before the trial (about the time of the Atlanta Summer Olympics). As a result, NBC was the only media outlet with both a broadcast news division in NBC News *and* a 24-hour cable news operation in MSNBC, which made NBC News the dominant player in Denver.

The one-two punch of having both broadcast and cable news required additional resources, particularly of the humankind.

As profitability became more and more of a focus within the news division, so also did financial accountability. Contrary to practice in decades past, each program, like *Nightly News* and *TODAY,* had to create detailed budgets... and stick to those budgets as best they could. As a start-up, MSNBC also had its own very elaborate budget. From management's perspective, accountability is good, as it reveals where the money is being spent. What's missing from this equation is an awareness of the uncontrollable variables inherent in news coverage.

Big news, whether planned or breaking, requires resources. A detailed spreadsheet listing the many news-related expenses can look buttoned-up and definite in a board meeting. But it can be an entirely different exercise when those resources are allocated in the field. When three related but different entities, like *Nightly News*, *TODAY*, and MSNBC were all clamoring for the same resources, things were bound to be spread thin. Jack had done an incredible job of preparing for the McVeigh trial coverage, bringing in and hiring additional people. Adding an entirely new client like MSNBC and an entirely separate story like the Ramsey murder compounded his job immensely. There was no dress rehearsal. This was "fly by the seat of your pants" network news coverage. I recall many long days that were bookended by early morning and late-night live shots. Eventually, some years later, there would become a more predictable rhythm to the demands of broadcast and cable news. But, in that first year, Jack was asked to master a juggling act never before seen—and he did so admirably.

Aside from the human resources, there were facility concerns that required an agile approach. The Denver bureau was physically located miles from the courthouse, making the commute problematic in the event of late-breaking news A suitable studio located close to the courthouse was needed—one where we could control the many variables like changing weather and lighting, and where reliable and high-quality audio, video, and transmission could be managed and guaranteed daily. Such a location would be critical for our many correspondents who were reporting live and conducting interviews. And, such a location didn't exist in downtown Denver.

During the pretrial phase of the McVeigh story, Jack and Roger had scrambled to look for office space adjacent to the courthouse that could house an array of reporters, producers, and associate producers while also doubling as a soundstage... one that didn't require a five-year lease. Somehow, they not only found an ideal location, but negotiated temporary lease terms that New York could live with since these were additional and unforeseen costs not included in the previous year's budget projections. In other words, projecting network news forecasts can be as scientific as palm reading.

The office space was perfect. It was on an upper floor in a modern office tower that was a block from the courthouse. The windows faced west, looking out onto the Denver skyline and the foothills of the Rocky Mountains. Eventually, that view would provide the perfect backdrop for the countless live shots and interviews resulting from the trial. But the space was designed for business tenants, not TV tenants. As the trial began, Steve and I were charged with converting a portion of the office space into a network television studio. We hurriedly split our time between coverage at the "pen" and building out the new studio space. Additional lighting needed to be hung from the suspended ceiling. Soundproofing was needed to separate the ambient noise of the "newsroom" portion from the "studio" portion. Because the afternoon setting sun blazed through the windows like a laser, we needed to apply a series of transparent but darkening films known as "gels" to control the sun's blinding effect. Working with the satellite engineers, we needed to conspicuously route our audio, video, and communication cables through the workspace to their rooftop transmission space. It was a challenge we enjoyed, and within a couple of days, our office space was a broadcast center.

Suddenly, there was a great amount of airtime to fill with Denver stories and very little video to show. The McVeigh trial could offer sketches, courthouse arrivals and departures, and the standard reporter's on-camera wrap-up. And with the news updates having slowed on the Ramsey story, there was even less to show on that story, save for the endlessly played beauty princess footage.

Still, we needed to feed the beast.

To help fill the void created by the increasing demand for Denver news, NBC did the only thing they could and borrowed from the cable news playbook authored by CNN; they called upon "expert" analysts. At the time, cable news was a brave new world for most of us outside of CNN. My sense was, initially, that the producers just needed a warm body in the chair to fill up the airwaves. The "talking head" experts were retired FBI agents or "profilers," attorneys, or authors—usually the same Denver fixtures over and over again. After getting the hang of cable news, the shows started to branch out and book a more diverse range of experts who offered sometimes different but still well-informed perspectives on the developments in the McVeigh trial and Ramsey case. The journalistic intent was always to advance the story. More accurately, it was sometimes simply a matter of filling up the airwaves and the cable spectrum.

As the guy behind the camera who was shooting the growing ranks of experts, it was all new to me... and not to be confused with the news. For 15 years, when I'd focused my camera on an "expert," it had been at the correspondent who'd covered the event, written the script, and reported the facts of the story, not his or her opinion. Now, I was pointing a camera at an expert, expressly for his or her opinion.

This was a natural extension of cable news. The formula would grow from an interview with a single expert analyst to an entire panel of expert analysts. Just like network correspondents, these experts would go on the payroll of the network. However, they weren't being paid for their journalistic experience and independence. They were being paid for their insight and their opinions. This was a key development in the evolution of the news business. Within the same news network, and sometimes within the same news program, you could find both a correspondent reporting on the facts and an expert giving their opinion. The two were not individually labeled as "NEWS" and "OPINION" or "ANALYSIS." It was and is understandable for the average viewer to become confused and regard both as news—when, in fact, they are not.

We package the food we consume with very detailed labels and nutritional information. Perhaps our news needs the same information listing its most basic yet vastly different ingredients. The late great CBS Anchorman Walter Cronkite said it best when he said, "Objective journalism and an opinion column are about as similar as the Bible and Playboy magazine."

No one has ever been charged with the 1996 murder of Jon-Benét Ramsey. The following year, the family moved from Boulder to Atlanta and in 2006, Patsy Ramsey died of ovarian cancer without ever knowing who killed her daughter. That same year, new DNA evidence exonerated the family of JonBenét's death. The Timothy McVeigh trial ran from March to June in 1997. He was found guilty on all eleven counts and sentenced to death by lethal injection. Terry Nichols' trial began in September and concluded in January of the following year. He, too, was found guilty, but was spared the death penalty and instead sentenced to life imprisonment without the possibility of parole. Because of the unspeakable crimes they had committed and the many lives they had ruined, their freedom had come to a very deserving end.

The irony was that the coverage of these different tragedies and the insufferable loss of life had afforded me a new life as a Denver-based freelancer. I was already somewhat grizzled from all that I'd seen in the name of international news coverage, and these stories would add to that hardened exterior, but for me, that glass was more than half-full; it was overflowing. Those early assignments had helped establish me in the Denver media market. Steve and I were enriched by both the significant compensation we were paid and the many lasting friendships we formed during coverage. Additionally, I witnessed the arrival and implementation of cable news at NBC. It was a very fortuitous time, and while I would always have a fondness for Chicago, Denver soon felt like home.

There was barely a hiccup on my career path. Amy and I resumed our dual-income earnings. I decided to invest in both myself and my career, as there was a new and exciting digital editing technology that was transforming the industry. Avid Technology was revolutionizing the post-production world with something called non-linear editing. The old-school analog editing made it difficult and cumbersome to make changes while editing videotape. If you finished "cutting" a 3:00 story and needed to make a change to the first minute, the entire story from that point on had to be rebuilt. Non-linear technology made it simple and easy to apply such a change. You simply inserted your change and the rest of the story was digitally rebuilt for you. This advancement vastly increased the storytelling power and creativity available to editors and producers. The more I learned about this new technology, the more I coveted it.

The networks, being behemoths, were slow to experiment. It would take years for them to fully switch over to non-linear editing. I had spent years building and cementing my reputation as a top network cameraman. As much as I secretly wanted to try my hand at producing, it would've been foolheartedly to suddenly abandon my camera in the hopes of instantly transforming into a network producer. I hoped to marry the storytelling skills I'd learned in the news business with a comprehensive knowledge of this new tool. That combination would enable me to cross the threshold from cameraman to producer for smaller, non-network clients and projects. All I needed was to purchase the $250,000 editing tool and find a non-network client or two.

I needed to look no further than my own family. Boston Market's meteoric growth had been exponential. Their stock price was soaring, which allowed for additional expansion of their restaurant chain. And, they had so much leverage power that they were also in "acquisition mode," looking for other restaurant concepts that they could gobble up and acquire. As a means of getting into the breakfast market, they bought four regional bagel chains and converted them into their own Einstein Brothers Bagels concept. Boston Market was growing and running two different restaurant concepts. Both chains were looking for a video production company to hire and assist them with the creation, production, and delivery of training and communications projects that would be distributed to their respective restaurant teams, franchisees, and investors. There are expensive Madison Avenue ad agencies and Hollywood production companies engaged in the business of flashy television ad campaigns. The training and communications business can be lucrative, but flies below their radar—it didn't fly below mine.

Amy had introduced me to a new coworker of hers and a neighbor of ours. Rob Schlacter was tall, athletic, and affable with a proclivity for laughter. He'd been an area developer for Boston Market. His operational expertise had helped grow the northeast region into one of the most profitable in the country, and in the process created a financial success story for himself. With the formation of the new Einstein Brothers Bagel brand, the company wanted his talent on the inside. He was hired as a V.P. for operations and relocated to Colorado with his family. The entire family was easy to like and we socialized frequently.

In the restaurant business, no matter how delicious the food, the guest experience is always affected, positively or negatively, by the service and performance of the staff. To help educate staff and improve that component, restaurant companies produce and distribute "Best Practices" and "Guidelines" videos. It's an entertaining and engaging way to teach their staff—far more so than having them read a training manual. Rob wanted to create a series of training and communication videos for the staff at the many Einstein Brothers Bagels restaurants.

Sometimes, success is based on who you know, not what you know. And sometimes it's both.

My skillset, past client list, and expanded start-to-finish facilities made me the perfect fit for the job. I worked closely with the Einstein Brothers team to write, shoot, edit, and produce videos that clearly conveyed corporate messaging to individual restaurateurs and staff. Those initial videos were extremely well-received, and created an appetite for more at both Einstein's and Boston Market.

I had moved from my small garage space to an expansive, high-tech office park in Golden, Colorado. My new, enlarged space offered room for the addition of both editing suites and production meeting rooms. The added square footage could handle the demands of my new client list and projects while allowing for future expansion, if needed. I formed a production company, High Road Pictures, Inc., to officially embark on this new direction. By adding post-production (editing) services to the production (camera) services I'd already offered, my small production company became twice as marketable. Building my nucleus of freelance producers, cameramen, soundmen, editors, and graphic artists also allowed me the luxury of offering clients and prospective clients an all-inclusive, start-to-finish video production solution. This allowed me to stretch my legs creatively, so to speak, with writing scripts and producing and managing entire projects in an executive producer role. Beginning with Einstein Brothers and Boston Market, the clients who contracted me to provide these expanded services were smaller than a client like NBC, but the audience size never mattered to me. What mattered was the opportunity to take on greater project-oriented responsibilities and roles that would challenge me to grow as a writer and producer.

Soon, through High Road Pictures, I was an executive producer on corporate projects for a growing list of clients, such as First Data Corp., Boston Market Restaurants, Einstein Brothers Bagels, and others. I was also creating and working on documentary programs for clients like Beavercreek Resorts, Jeep Corp., and Golden Gloves Boxing. I was able to branch out into this exciting new direction while still maintaining my long-established cameraman ties to NBC and the other news networks. By 1999, two and one-half years after moving to Denver, I had a healthy mix of network, corporate, and documentary clients, big and small, which kept me busy, engaged, and intellectually curious. All of these ventures and my involvement in Denver's network news coverage were far from over.

12

MORNING NIGHTMARE

On April 20, 1999, I had a morning meeting over coffee with a prospective real estate client in a nearby town. The client owned and managed large apartment holdings in and around Denver, and wanted to explore the use of video for marketing purposes. It was an introductory meeting. I talked about myself and background, High Road Pictures' capabilities, and what the client hoped to accomplish through video production. It was productive and wrapped up amicably with my promise to follow up.

I was fully immersed in High Road Pictures and the producing opportunities it provided me. But yet another tragedy was about to steal my focus back to network news and, sadly, reestablish Denver as the deserving focus of network news.

As I was traveling on the highway back to my office, I heard a siren quickly approaching from behind me. I pulled over to the right lane, allowing the police vehicle to pass. I could see in my rearview mirror that it was not a single emergency vehicle, but multiple vehicles approaching rapidly from behind me. I looked over my left shoulder and out my window to see a blur of vehicles fly past; one, two, three, four, five cars zoomed by me at top speed and in close order. As they disappeared down the highway, my news instincts kicked in. Two or three police cars meant there was a news event of local interest. But FIVE cars going over 120 miles per hour in close formation... that meant a news event of major importance. But what? My contemplation was interrupted by the ring of my cell phone. It was the New York desk for NBC.

"Tim, where are you and are you available right now?!"

"I'm in Denver, just heading to my office, and yes, I am available right now. I just saw five Sheriff's Deputy vehicles fly by. What's going on?"

"Grab your gear and soundman and get to Columbine High School as soon as you can. There's been a mass shooting. At this point, we believe the students are still inside the building. We're scrambling people as fast as we can. Call us once you're on site."

Mass shooting? Scramble? There would be no way to fly Steve in for an assignment of this nature. I phoned Eric, one of the handful of local Denver soundmen with whom I'd worked, and informed him of the assignment and its urgency. He was still available and I instructed him to meet me at Columbine. I then headed for my office to retrieve my camera equipment.

Within minutes, my phone rang again, this time from CBS in New York, and that call was followed by calls from ABC and CNN. I informed them all that I had already been booked by NBC and would be unavailable for the foreseeable future. It was already clear this would be "all hands on deck" breaking news coverage.

I drove a personal vehicle for personal use and a specially equipped Ford F-350 heavy-duty van as a crew vehicle. It had special shelving and storage for the gear, and TV monitors enabling videotape playback. It was always parked at my office and, like a fire truck at the fire department, it was always loaded and ready to go at a moment's notice, just in case of an emergency... like Columbine.

It's always horribly tragic whenever we hear the term "school shooting." Those two words should never be juxtaposed. Sadly, we hear if far too often today. Columbine was certainly not the first school shooting, but in 1999, it was something of a rarity.

I arrived at the school, parked the van, and grabbed my gear and met up with Eric. At that point, there was a small but quickly growing media presence outside the front of the school. The police had just established their police line facing the front doors of the school, behind which the camera crews had set up and begun taping. I saw Ray Farmer, the NBC staff cameraman and his soundman. We decided to divide our NBC presence and cover the scene from slightly different camera angles. In addition to the tape that we shot, I knew we would have access to material being shot by the many crews from our Denver affiliate, KUSA. They reported the news to their local Denver market. NBC reported the news to the national market. On stories like this, there's a great deal of sharing of resources, within limits.

There was a heavy presence of SWAT vehicles and what appeared to be a great deal of commotion and uncertainty among law enforcement. Word quickly spread through the assembled news media that both students and the shooters were still inside, and the shooters were continuing their bloody shooting spree. In an attempt to secure the exterior of the school, the police had prohibited coverage from all but the front of the school. As a result, news choppers hovered overhead and recorded fleeing students and police rescues from the other sides of the building.

We were close enough that we could clearly see the school through our zoom lenses. Yet, none of us knew what was going on inside. Reporters from both local and national organizations were desperately trying to get information, but details of the crime were sketchy at best. The absence of information made the wait seem endless. I wondered what was going on inside that school. What heart-pounding fear those students must be experiencing. And then my thoughts turned to the parents; what excruciating anxiety they must be going through.

Rumor spread through our ranks that there were still a number of students inside. Ray and I stayed at the high school, awaiting the emergence of more details and the possible safe rescue of more students. Some crews from our local affiliate had moved to a neighborhood adjacent to the school, where rescued students were being taken to reunite with their tearful parents. Once safely there, some of the students provided eye-witness accounts of the cold-blooded murders. There was also a make-shift triage area set up to assess wounded students before they were rushed to local hospitals.

The local stations were flooded with phone calls from frantic parents and relatives searching for any information. They also received phone calls from students still trapped inside the school. Those calls went on the air live, depicting live the minute-by-minute horror taking place inside the school. Some of those calls would also turn out to be pranks. While I was shooting tape, the choppers hovering above us were broadcasting live images. Those images showed the police activity on the ground. If the shooters were watching, they would know law enforcement's every move. In those first hours, what to put on the air was a minute-by-minute decision made by the local news staff.

After five hours, there suddenly appeared long lines of students hurriedly being ushered from the school. Like surrendering suspects, they were running in single-file with their hands behind their heads, a heavy police escort at their side. I had seen so many startling images in my decades as a network cameraman, but nothing like this. To see students, who had just endured such carnage and death, be treated as suspects in that carnage was mind-boggling. The police were justified in their actions because, at the time, they didn't know just how many shooters were involved. It was relieving to see those students safe, but shocking at the same time. The ordeal had ended, but the questions were just beginning.

Outside the school, late that afternoon, Jefferson County Sheriff John Stone gave an impromptu news conference. Grasping for details, he said the death toll inside the school could be as high as twenty-five. Eric and I looked at each other in shock. *Twenty-five!?* We knew it was a large school of about 2,000 students. But 25 was an incomprehensible number of murdered students. But then, one would have been too many. The two killers were identified as Dylan Klebold and Eric Harris, both of them Columbine Seniors who'd been found dead from apparently self-inflicted gunshot wounds.

The authorities would wait until the next day to reveal the exact number and identity of the dead, but some of the facts were beginning to appear. The actual killing lasted a little over an hour. After that, the shooters lay dead in the library with many of their victims. The SWAT teams entered the building within the first hour, but assumed the killers were still alive. Without the benefit of a map, the SWAT officers had to methodically clear every room they encountered. Along the way, they discovered students in locked rooms who were taking cover under their desks, and finally made their way to the library. In the process of their rampage, the two killers had detonated home-made bombs, hoping for even more devastation. Those bombs did explode, but aside from setting off alarms, they failed to cause any real destruction.

During their rampage, Klebold and Harris wore long black trench coats. It was reported there was a "Trench Coat Mafia" at the school, prompting concerns of a larger plot and hidden accomplices. There was so much to sift through, and still so much more to come. It was after midnight when I finally arrived home. Amy and Alexa were in bed and asleep... safe. I kissed them both and sat in my darkened living room contemplating the horrible story I had just covered. I was physically and emotionally exhausted, but it would be a restless night. I knew I had to get some sleep, however, as this dark story would go on for days, weeks. There was no visible light at the end of the tunnel.

Overnight, the national news media ramped up its coverage, with teams arriving in Denver from all over the country. NBC had brought in around 70 people for the extended coverage. That next morning, Katie Couric anchored the *TODAY* show from a park adjacent to the school. *Nightly News* and MSNBC created similar locations from which to broadcast their shows live. Jack and Roger had been on assignment in Sacramento, but they cut that assignment short and raced home.

On day two, the gruesome facts were confirmed. Twelve students and one teacher had been shot to death. The young students ranged in age from 14 to 18. So many young lives wiped out in a single act of violent hatred. Another 24 students and faculty had been injured in the massacre. Law enforcement would begin to follow the many twists and turns, the leads and misleads in the investigation, trying to understand the motives of the killers. It would turn out that they'd been two sick and angry kids who'd hated the world in which they lived, and were hellbent on destroying it.

That was one part of the story. The grieving families of the victims and the survivors had stories to tell, as well.

The news media can sometimes be callous when reaching out to victims' family members and survivors. At Columbine, given the ages of the victims, this was of particular concern. I did not witness any overt intrusion into the lives of those in mourning. Instead, I was surprised at how open the families were. They invited us into their homes, more than willing to share with us and celebrate the lives of their deceased loved ones. In the days following Columbine, there was so much emotion, so much sadness, and so many tears.

Being a messenger for the grieving is part of the job. The interaction with the families was heartbreaking, but necessary to show the devastation that resulted from the crime. That emotional wound and devastation reverberated throughout the community. There were so many memorial services held to remember the many whose lives were so abruptly ended prematurely. It is impossible, for even the most hardened news veteran, to isolate oneself from the pain and suffering of those whose stories are covered. You do your best to stay objective and removed from the story, even when it's impossible.

After a week of covering the tearful Columbine aftermath, I was spent. One evening at dusk, a candlelight vigil was held at a local park to remember the victims. I shot the crying mourners as the dim flicker of candlelight reflected off of their faces, illuminating the streaks of tears running down their cheeks. Afterward, Eric and I gathered our gear and slowly walked back to the van. I didn't make it. I was dizzy from exhaustion and lightheaded from the emotional drain. I began sobbing un-controllably as I walked through that park. I am not prone to those kinds of emotional breakdowns. But I had to stop and sit on a street-side curb, burying my chin in my chest and heaving with sorrow. Eric joined me on the curb and quietly empathized, staring at the street without saying a word.

Because this was early in our history of mass school shoot-ings, there was no established playbook for the media and law enforcement to consult when it came to a "School Siege." The investigation would continue for years. Unlike what had come from the errors reported during the Olympic Park bombing in Atlanta, most of the anger resulting from Columbine was even-tually aimed not at the news media, but law enforcement and the families of Harris and Klebold. In the early stages of the investigation, the Sheriff's department had released erroneous information while having failed to see tell-tale warnings of the pending attack. The young killers' families had been seemingly oblivious to the boys' death wishes, unaware of the stockpil-ing of weapons and bomb-making materials even though they'd been living at home.

Culturally, Columbine would teach us all something. Law en-forcement and the news media would both learn how to better react to and cover such terrible events, of which there would be many, many more. Sadly, Columbine has acted as a blueprint for copycat killers who have repeatedly mentioned Harris and Klebold in their deadly manifestos while planning their school massacres. Such events are news—great big, sad, tragic news—and must be covered. Yet, in doing so in our 24-hour, nonstop online news machine, that repeated coverage can seem like a glorification to twisted viewers who might be seeking recogni-tion through martyrdom. It's a delicate balancing act between the public's need to know and sensationalizing a horrendous act. We in the news media have yet to figure out that equilibrium.

Each year seems to bring another atrocity to another community. Columbine High School was followed by Red Lake High School, which was followed by Virginia Tech University, which was followed by Sandy Hook Elementary School, which was followed by Marjory Stoneman Douglas High School, which was followed by... the list goes on. I've listed only the major school shootings, which were interwoven with others. There had been other horrible mass shootings that occurred in nightclubs, concerts, movie theaters, and elsewhere.

The death toll for each sickening event differs. What they all share is the unforgettable suffering experienced by each community, survivor, and witness.

Only recently have we begun to diagnose some of the brave men and women in the armed forces as suffering from what the medical community refers to as Post-Traumatic Stress Disorder (PTSD). I have worked on news stories covering diagnosis and treatment for PTSD and can confirm it is a very real, very serious mental health condition triggered by the devastation these individuals have experienced.

There are journalists who have covered many and perhaps even all of those catastrophic mass shootings listed above. For those dedicated men and women, that work comes with a cost. I am not suggesting that the work done by those on the frontlines of news in any way, shape, or form mirrors the courageous dedication demonstrated by our military. What I am suggesting is that the mental toll paid by those who fight our battles can be similar to the mental toll paid by those who cover our tragedies.

Because Columbine was so painful to cover, there were members of the news media who requested to be assigned elsewhere. I did not. But I was already booked on another completely different NBC assignment that would take me far away from the death and sorrow of Columbine.

PHOTO ALBUM

The commute to work for *Where in The World is Matt Lauer* offered this view of the Himalayan mountains from our chopper.

The 'stage' for our Himalayan broadcast. Live television fell victim to Mother Nature as the dramatic backdrop of Mt. Everest suddenly disappeared when a major storm rolled in.

The challenging setup for another *Where in The World is Matt Lauer* from remote Machu Picchu, Peru.

Shooting among the mysterious and
ancient ruins in Machu Picchu

An impromptu press conference aboard Air
Force Two with then Vice President Al Gore
during the 1996 presidential campaign.

Steve and I, somewhere in the skies with
the accessible and friendly V.P.

Al Gore insisted on a photo with the traveling
press corps at the gates of Graceland after a late-
night campaign stop in Memphis, TN.

Steve and I with two of Hef's convivial
and dedicated employees.

Steve and I with Hugh Heffner, the legendary
founder of the Playboy empire; taken at the Playboy
Mansion 'Press Party' during the 2000 Democratic
National Convention in Los Angeles, CA

The NBC stage and crew on the rooftop of the Islamabad Marriott. Many networks constructed similar platforms as it proved to be a relatively safe and reliable location for live broadcasts as the war raged in neighboring Afghanistan.

The backward border town of Quetta, Pakistan.
Because of its proximity to Afghanistan, it has
always been seen as a Taliban stronghold.

Katie Couric broadcasting live from a very somber set for TODAY after the Columbine High School shooting.

Myself alongside colleagues Carl Filoreto (middle) and Ray Farmer right) as part of the NBC News team covering the Columbine High School shooting. The icy Spring temperatures coupled with the tragic news made for a very solemn atmosphere during those broadcasts.

Peter Freed/NBC News

As his crew set up, Tom Brokaw of NBC News prepared to interview patrons of a Des Moines diner yesterday about their presidential preferences.

The 2000 Presidential campaign kicked off with the Iowa caucuses. As part of that coverage, we conducted numerous multiple-camera interviews with candidates and voters; some in cozy main street diners. This photo appeared in the New York Times (photo reprinted with permission by photographer Peter Freed).

13

FOREIGN RETURN

The trials of the Oklahoma City bombers McVeigh and Nichols, the JonBenét Ramsey murder and investigation, and the Columbine school massacre were all major news events. Denver had suddenly morphed from cow-town into the epicenter of the 24-hour news cycle.

The domestic news cycle, that is. A mere seven years earlier, as a member of the foreign press corps, I'd been consumed with foreign news. Since then, I'd covered so many major domestic stories that international news seemed... foreign.

Living in Bonn and Rome for NBC News afforded me the opportunity to cover global news events, moving between exotic capitals and remote corners of the world. It was business travel that I loved. Moving to Chicago and subsequently, Denver offered me the chance to explore great U.S. cities while covering America's vast heartland. Criss-crossing the U.S. to reconnect with my homeland was also business travel that I loved. However, due to the all the years I'd spent abroad, I was keenly aware of the difference between, say, Frankfurt, GERMANY and Frankfort, KENTUCKY; or Paris, FRANCE and Paris, TEXAS; or Athens, GREECE and Athens, OHIO, or Geneva,

SWITZERLAND and Lake Geneva, WISCONSIN, or.... Well, you get the point.

I don't say this boastfully, but the truth is that I was worldly and aware of life beyond our American borders. I knew I was fortunate to have had that rare opportunity, and never assumed my fellow countrymen and women shared my global outlook, but there was no losing sight of my worldly perspective. I was, however, losing sight of international news coverage, because it was slowly vanishing from our airwaves.

Shortly after I returned to Chicago, NBC closed its Paris bureau, and that was just the tip of the iceberg. Except for London, every foreign bureau of every news network would experience a similar closure or "downsizing." All three broadcast networks had changed ownership, and the new masters pleaded poverty. They claimed the closures were in response to the "new realities" in viewership. Foreign operations were expensive to run, and as viewers declined (slowly turning to things like the internet), cuts had to be made. That was only partly true, and akin to selling snake oil to a gullible audience. The money was there, but it was being reallocated to things like skyrocketing compensation for executives and anchors and corporate acquisitions. So, the axe fell squarely on the foreign bureaus. No further justification was needed.

Some of the employees, particularly the Americans and the English, were relocated to London, which was the one place undergoing a mild expansion. The intent was to keep covering news in the eastern hemisphere, just in a reduced manner. And to do so, it was much cheaper to cover half the world from one bureau as opposed to twenty. A handful of American ex-pats returned home to jobs in the LA or New York bureaus. The vast majority of staffers in those foreign bureaus had been foreign.

When the American networks closed their offices, the foreign nationals were out of work. Many turned to freelancing. Leaving the network to embark on freelancing had been my choice, and one which had so far produced fruitful results. Once the network rug was pulled out from under them, most of those foreign nationals did not land on their feet.

Multinational corporations from tech to manufacturing see investment in foreign operations as mandatory, and the expense is simply the cost of doing business. That should be of particular significance for corporations in the business of news and information, and for decades that was the case. The slow but steady decline in news viewership that began in the late eighties gave the network owners an excuse to reexamine their operations. But instead of cutting costs across the board, the foreign side suffered the biggest cuts.

This flawed thinking and financial shell-game was made possible by some senior network news gurus in New York. They'd personally spent little time outside the U.S. and simply felt that viewers in America didn't give a damn about world news, so why pay to cover news around the world? Instead, they focused their cameras and reporters on domestic stories and saved millions of dollars in the process. From time to time, they could pretend to cover international news from Washington or London. They argued that the viewer would never notice, or even know the difference.

The issue with this thinking is two-fold. In some ways, news-gathering is similar to intelligence gathering; both are dependent upon having staff "on the ground" in foreign locations. I am not suggesting network reporters and cameramen engage in the same sort of vital national security work performed by CIA operatives. However, living and working within foreign cultures allows for the development of trusted sources as well as mutual awareness and understanding. Armed with this local knowledge, network bureaus in, say Rome or Tokyo would discover newsworthy foreign stories and "pitch" those stories to the ultimate decision-makers in New York. Devoid of that local interaction and the resulting knowledge, those stories aren't pitched. We are unaware of what's going on in the world around us. If our military is deployed, that is certainly news. But the U.S. Army and Special Ops should not be the only determining criterium of what constitutes world news.

Secondly, we're a nation that has always loved our cheeseburgers greasy and our steaks rare, but that's an unhealthy and unsustainable diet. There came a time when the medical community and the American Heart Association (those who know best) weighed in, advocating moderation, the occasion vegetable, and exercise (of both body and mind). Some of us listened, contributing to longer and healthier lives. In the same way, our news diet used to consist of a healthy mix of domestic and world news and information. The irony is that, when the networks (those who should know best) closed or curtailed foreign bureaus and international news coverage, they also reduced their viewers' mental exercise program. Watching and listening to foreign news stories made us aware, and made us all think about life beyond our local school districts. Not that local school districts aren't important—they are. But we are, as a society, able to comprehend and contemplate so much more if, or *when*, we were given the opportunity. Those overseas events aren't entirely isolated, and we don't reside in a vacuum here in the U.S. At some point, somewhere, events that happen halfway around the world impact us directly.

Obviously and sadly, today there is no better example of this global interaction than the Coronavirus. The deadly disease seemed to appear on our shores suddenly, getting through our airport customs and in our country with little advance notice. There were early warning signs voiced by brave foreign journalists, but almost everyone seemed to be caught off-guard and taken by surprise when the virus spread so rapidly. With less inward focus on our own backyard and more global focus around the world, we would have been far better prepared for the arrival and deadly spread of COVID-19.

＊ ＊ ＊ ＊ ＊

After returning to the U.S., I would regularly scan all of the network evening broadcasts in search of overseas stories. As a former staffer, I tended to land on NBC's *Nightly News* with Tom Brokaw. I respected, admired, and knew him. But I would (and still do) regularly tune in to the other networks' news programs. In the 90s, CNN was expanding its international coverage as the other networks were cutting back.

After our move to Denver, my morning news viewing continued to be mostly habitually driven. Turning on the *TODAY* show each morning at 7 a.m. was an almost Pavlovian response for me. That, too, was due in large part to my years of involvement with the program. The people behind that show had been pioneers in the live remote broadcast, having taken the show out of the studio and "on the road" years earlier. I was a cameraman on the production crew that, during the 80s, broadcasted anchors Jane Pauley, Bryant Gumbel, Willard Scott, and the entire two-hour television circus from places like Rome, Geneva, Paris, Zurich, Munich, Vienna, Venice, Beijing, Shanghai, and Seoul. Now, as I wrestled with the ongoing dearth of international news, I realized those kinds of expensive shows from foreign locations seemed to be a dying breed.

Early one April morning in 1998, dressed in my heavy, warm robe and Ugg slippers, I poured a cup of coffee, took a large gulp, and looked out my window. The bright morning sunlight reflecting off the vividly white, fresh snow combined with the caffeine rush made for a dizzying, half-awakened effect. As I routinely did, I grabbed the TV remote and turned on the *TO-DAY* show, which revealed another confusing image. Matt Lauer was reporting live from in front of the Sphinx, outside of Cairo, Egypt.

So much has been reported on and written about Matt Lauer's sexual misconduct and abuse of his anchorman power. Over the years, I worked with him and never witnessed any inappropriate interaction with *TODAY* staff members. So, like many, I was shocked when, in 2017, I learned of his concealed behavior and subsequent dismissal. As more details emerged and more women came forward, it became clear that his firing was certainly justified. But in 1998, he was barely a year into his new job as Bryant Gumbel's permanent replacement on *TODAY*. He was enthusiastic, uncorrupted by his newfound success, and keen for any assignment... like a broadcast from Egypt.

The next day, Matt was on the Grand Canal in Venice, Italy. And the next day, he reported from the Acropolis in Athens, Greece. That was followed by a trip to Agra, India and a live report from the Taj Mahal. On his fifth and final day from the road, Matt ended the week in front of the Sydney Opera House in Australia. *TODAY* producer Michael Bass was the brainchild behind *Where in the World is Matt Lauer?* It was programming gold. The idea borrowed heavily (okay, was shamelessly stolen) from the award-winning PBS children's show, *Where in the World is Carmen Sandiego?*, which had been created, in part, to address Americans' alarming ignorance of world geography.

If ordinary American viewers found it fascinating, I was mesmerized by it. I'd been to some of those locations before, and now I longed to revisit them as part of the production team. I was out of the New York loop and had missed out on an entire week of foreign assignments. That missed opportunity filled me with questions. Was this a one-off ratings grabber? And, how were those ratings? Would there be sequels? By now, I had established friendships with a number of people at NBC in New York. Some knew me as a reputable freelance cameraman based in Chicago and now Denver. Others knew me from my previous life as a staffer, dating back to my years overseas. I had options in seeking answers to my questions.

My first call was to longtime friend and *TODAY* producer Mary Alice O'Rourke. As her name might suggest, she was the product of a loving Catholic upbringing with impeccable manners and unwavering politeness. How she wandered into the circus of network news is beyond me, but it was a job at which she thrived. She was one of my friends from those overseas years. We first met in May of 1986 in Jakarta, Indonesia. I had just completed five months in the Philippines, covering the People Power Revolution that toppled strongman dictator Ferdinand Marcos and installed widowed housewife Corazon Aquino as president. That year, the 12th Group of Seven, or G7 summit, was held in Tokyo, Japan. On his way to the summit, President Ronald Reagan decided to stop off in Indonesia for some beach time and R&R, and NBC News sent us to Jakarta to report on what Indonesian life was like. It was Mary Alice's first international travel and first foreign story. I was instructed to "...meet the producer in the hotel lobby at 8 a.m."

As I was waiting, I watched from across the room as an American businesswoman wearing a neatly coifed page-boy hairdo and a freshly pressed Edie Bauer safari outfit anxiously approached small groups of international businessmen and asked, "I'm terribly sorry to interrupt, but are you my cameraman?"

"I apologize, but are you by chance with NBC... perhaps a cameraman?"

"Hi, there. I don't mean to be forward, but I'm supposed to meet an American cameraman by the name of Tim. Might that be you?"

For 8 a.m., it was all quite entertaining as she nervously migrated from group to group like a hummingbird in search of a rewarding flower. I caught up with her in the middle of the lobby and said, "Hi, I think I can help. I'm with NBC. My name is Tim, and if your name is Mary Alice, I believe we're going to be working together."

She exhaled a huge sigh of relief that brought a smile to her face. We found a quiet corner of the hotel lobby where we settled in as she began to brief me on the story she had uncovered. A Jakarta slum was being bulldozed—not as part of some urban renewal or affordable housing project, but to make room for a new highway. The cramped patchwork of corrugated tin shacks was the only housing option for a few thousand people. For them, it was home. And, soon, they would have a new highway... but no home. Eminent domain, Indonesian-style, would scatter them from their hovels to the streets and have them fend for themselves.

This was journalism 101, giving a voice to the voiceless and shining a light on injustice. A highway is progress, and progress is good, but at what cost? If that progress steamrolls over innocent, impoverished victims, then asking the question "Is this right and just?" is a vital role that journalism can and should play. These particular victims resided in a world, a third world, that was so remote and so poor, nobody at all gave a damn. That made our work there even more rewarding.

Mary Alice and I immediately bonded on that story, which would be followed by numerous other *TODAY* stories long after Indonesia and that G7 summit. We became lifelong friends, as our paths would intersect throughout the network news world for years to come.

When I called her inquiring about the inaugural *Where in the World is Matt Lauer?*, I wasn't surprised to find out she'd been instrumental in the show's logistical planning. Underlying her demure exterior was a meticulous attention to detail. It would take a relentless and almost military-like focus to successfully put together all the pieces of an international five-day, five-city live broadcast. Each location had its production team and technical facilities dedicated solely to that location's broadcast. That meant lights, cameras, microphones, monitors, satellite dishes, generators, cables, support equipment, and an entire crew had been sent to each of the five locations!

Additionally, there was a core team—a handful of New York staffers—who accompanied Matt throughout the entire trip. Mary Alice had not only been a key planner of the trip, but had also been along for the ride at every location, on every flight, for every grueling step of the journey. The taxing, week-long journey covered 27,000 miles and circled the globe. The tiny plane they charted was so small that the seats didn't recline. They slept sitting upright for a total of 12 hours... for the entire week! As she spoke, two things were made clear. First, it had been a demanding, exhausting, and punishing assignment that was groundbreaking and rewarding beyond belief. And, second, if there was to be a follow-up *Where in the World*, I wanted to be a part of it.

She was on the editorial side of the ledger where they dealt with "which" and "what" questions—which locations to visit and what stories would be covered as part of the broadcast. I found out from her that the "how" and "who" questions were decided by Field and Productions Operations, headed by another old friend dating back to my overseas days.

Stacy Brady, like Mary Alice, was a dear friend going back to my days as a staff cameraman overseas. We'd both been new to NBC when Stacy and I had first met in Geneva, Switzerland to cover the U.S. Soviet arms-control talks of the early Reagan years. There'd been a significant amount of hope and interest in East-West negotiations, which generated a significant amount of news coverage. Planeloads of broadcast equipment were flown from New York to Geneva as luxury hotel suites were ripped apart and temporarily converted into television studios. Stacy was part of the NBC team responsible for the transportation and installation of all of our technical facilities. Smart and engaging, she steadily rose through the ranks. She could quickly grasp the technology and the machines, but had a much deeper understanding of and appreciation for the men and women who operated them. As the role of technology in television increased, so did Stacy's importance and value. After a series of well-deserved promotions, she'd by now ascended to the position of Senior Vice President of Field Operations.

The technical needs and staffing of a behemoth international production the size of *Where in the World* would certainly be run by "Field Operations," so Stacy would be able to answer my questions. I called her and, after a few telephone pleasantries and a brief catch-up, I asked her, "So, what the hell was that?"

Pulling off that television feat was a huge tech accomplishment—one of many for her and her team. Full of pride, she could be heard smiling on the other end of the phone. "What? Oh, you mean that globe-circling week-long broadcast with Matt reporting from all over the world. That thing?"

"Yeah, that thing. What an undertaking. I'm a little out of the loop out here in Denver. I had no idea they... you guys were even doing a *Where in the World is Matt Lauer?* series. From the moment I saw Matt standing in front of the Sphinx, I was glued to the set for the entire week. What a great idea. How were the ratings?"

"The initial reports are great. I think it was a big hit."

"So, how does a former staffer turned freelancer sign up for any future installments?"

"Well, you have to ask, and I think you just did. I know you're busy out there, but had no idea you're interested in doing more international travel. It sounds like you are and I can certainly include you on the next one. I'd love to have you on the crew."

"That would be great. It's good out here in the Wild West and Rocky Mountains. I miss Chicago, but, as you mentioned, Denver's been a busy news town. It's also good to hear your voice. I'll do a better job of staying in touch. Please put me on the shortlist, should there be a 1999 version of *Where in the World*."

"Same here. You're at the top of the list."

Once all of the reviews and ratings were tallied, Stacy's belief that the week-long, far-flung experiment had been a "big hit" was confirmed. Almost immediately, *TODAY* show execs began planning for an even bigger and better 2.0 version of *Where in the World is Matt Lauer?*

In the early Spring of 1999, Stacy called to gauge and confirm my previously stated interest in traveling the globe... again. Because of the WOW factor when each hidden location was first revealed on the show, she was at first secretive when it came to the exact locations.

"So, you're still in; you still want to do this, right?"

"Absolutely. What, or I guess I should say, *where* are you thinking for this year?"

"At this point, I can't say exactly. We're still in the planning stage of potential locations. But we're getting pretty close to the final five locations from which Matt will be live. There's one place I think you'd be perfect for. It's pretty remote, as in really difficult to get to. Because you've traveled so much internationally, I don't think that would be an issue for you. It's also a pretty spectacular once-in-a-lifetime location. But at this point, I just wanted to confirm that you're in. I'll get back to you once all this gets finalized. Stay tuned."

As that date neared, my location was revealed to me. And, I was told only of *my* location and then sworn to secrecy. The other four locations for the week-long broadcast remained shrouded in mystery. Information was handed out on a "need to know" basis. Through hushed phone conversations, speaking in an almost clandestine code, Stacy eventually informed me that I would be traveling to Nepal. The first day of year two of *Where in the World is Matt Lauer?* would broadcast live from the base of Mount Everest.

My only response was, "Holy shit." Stacy was right. This was a once-in-a-lifetime destination. And yes, it would be really difficult to get to.

Travel arrangements were made. It's a circuitous path one must travel to go from the Rocky Mountains to the Himalayan Mountains. The first leg would require a full 24 hours for me to fly from Denver to LA to Hong Kong, finally overnighting into Bangkok. The second day would be a straight shot from Bangkok to the Nepalese capital of Katmandu, where the full crew would be assembled. After a few days in Katmandu, the crew would then travel into the mountains and set up for the show.

In some demented twist of fate, my departure for Nepal closely coincided with the Columbine mass shooting. I had been tingling with anticipation and excited to embark on a historic foreign news journey. My anticipation for one story was erased by the anguish and depression caused by another, and as I packed for the distant and dreamy Himalayas, I was haunted by the nightmarish acts of Harris and Klebold. The families who'd suffered the deepest and lost the most would never escape the horror of Columbine. It was another terrifying news event that would scar all of us in the news media who were there and covered it. But the journey to Mt. Everest would allow me a momentary pathway out; an escape from the inescapable.

With the horrible deaths of twelve students and a teacher vividly swirling around in my head, I packed my bags for Nepal. I shared long, emotional, and loving hugs and kisses with Amy and Alexa. We would miss each other dearly for the next ten days. They understood the emotional schizophrenia I was experiencing, filled with both anticipation and desolation. I was looking ahead to the Himalayas while carrying the baggage of having witnessed a school massacre.

It was a long couple of travel days, but well worth it once I arrived in Katmandu, a place that was foreign in every sense of the word—a sprawling town in a lush valley surrounded by mountains. The few tree-lined main boulevards were intersected by smaller streets that disintegrated into a maze of smaller alleys and crowded neighborhoods. It was a place shared by two main religions. Hindu and Buddhist temples seemed to be everywhere. Palaces were surrounded by poorer dwellings, but not overtly impoverished. The architecture was old and appeared to be an amalgamation of ancient civilizations reflecting a strong sense of culture or cultures. The Nepalese people were exotic looking, dutiful, and friendly. The Buddhists coexist with the Hindus there, which means the sacred cows coexist with everyone. Cows lounged unbothered on the sidewalks, in the streets, and on lawns.

Once at the hotel, I recognized the faces of many crew members with whom I had worked previously on other large assignments. There were some new faces, as well. Living in Colorado, I was used to the altitude and thin air, but many of my colleagues from Miami, New York, and Washington suffered from prolonged shortness of breath. Katmandu wasn't the end of our journey, either—merely the beginning. After a couple of days in the bustling capital, we would continue our trek into the mountains. At each stop, NBC scheduled time for us to do nothing but acclimate to the challenging environment brought on by the lack of oxygen. It was a news assignment at a much slower pace than usual.

After an earlier site survey, the producers had chosen a small mountain "guest house" used by climbers and trekkers to be the show's live location. It sat at 13,000 feet above sea level and stared out on a breathtaking panoramic view of Everest. But, getting there involved a couple of death-defying steps. First, we boarded a small twin-engine prop plane for the 30-minute flight from Katmandu to Lukla, a small mountain village and jumping-off point for the trek to Everest. The Tenzing-Hillary Airport in Lukla is widely regarded as the world's most dangerous for a variety of reasons. It's just plain dicey trying to land a plane at 9,300 ft. above sea level with strong mountain winds blowing in from all directions. The airport sits on a small mountain shelf and has one of the shortest runways at 1,780 feet (most are 10,000 feet). The approach end features a 2,000 ft. drop-off and the opposite end dead-ends into a sheer mountain face. The ever-changing, unpredictable weather is an added problem. Rain, fog, and snow often hide the runway from approaching aircraft. Because it's surrounded by mountains, there is no way to abort an attempted landing and "try again"—you get one shot at it. Once a plane begins its approach, it must land, or else, and there are many deadly examples of the "or else."

Because I've traveled so much, I am not *normally* a white-knuckle flyer. However, looking out the window on the approach into Lukla, I had a two-handed death grip on the flimsy armrest of my tiny seat. The packed cabin was tensely silent, no one uttering a word. We touched down safely, just past the ravine of death, and bounced *up* the runway (it is built uphill to avoid planes crashing into the mountain end) until we rumbled to a stop. The collective exhale from every passenger onboard could've filled a sailboat's mainsail.

When we stepped out of the prop plane and back onto Earth, we noticed two military helicopters standing by. We could've made the three-day trek from Lukla to our guest house on foot, but the thousands of pounds of equipment we carried with us made that an unattractive option. NBC had brought in the army to transport us to our final destination. The pilot responsible for the last leg of our commute was not just any pilot. Three years earlier, Nepal Army Pilot Lt. Col. Madan Khatri Chhetri had flown his chopper way beyond its limits on a lifesaving mission to rescue the injured American climber Beck Weathers and Sherpa Makalu Gau. It had been the stuff of legend, and is chronicled in the book *Into Thin Air* and the movie *Everest*. Our legendary pilot and his team safely dropped us off at our destination.

Given that the location was in the middle of nowhere... or in the middle of the Himalayas, rather, our guesthouse accommodations were what travel agents would call "rustic primitive with a medieval charm"; we had a small stone building void of running water or electricity. It was the ultimate fixer-upper. So, given that a television production crew had traveled from halfway around the world to create television history on this site, NBC had added some "improvements" that would make HGTV green with envy. Huge generators had the dual purpose of providing electricity for the live broadcast and improving the living conditions. A camping kitchen had been constructed to feed the crew. Temporary plywood "bedrooms" (resembling prison cells) had been added to the existing structure.

At this point, I must confess that I've peed in the forest and shit in the woods before. The thoughtful NBC advance team would have none of that on a shoot this epic, though. To address life's most basic needs, an environmentally friendly, ecologically engineered septic system had been built on a semi-level field near the guest house. Four full-sized porcelain toilets had been imported and placed atop the septic field. Privacy shelter or toilet tents had been built around the commodes. We had five-star bathroom facilities in the most remote rugged terrain on earth. I'm sure the locals thought we were mad, or at least pampered.

And speaking of the locals, they were an impressive people. Small in stature with great big hearts (and lungs), they possessed a will that could move mountains, which comes in handy in the Himalayas. They were hired to assist with some of the set-up-related heavy lifting and more. As I mentioned, we were given days for our bodies to adjust to the altitude. That adjustment period involved frequent hikes on which the local Sherpas were our guides.

Audrey Kolina was the Hong Kong Bureau Chief. She was a young and fit American thirty-something and a key member of both the advance team and our production team. Craig White was a New York-based staff cameraman, and one of the best. He was also a serious mountain climber, which made him perfect for the shoot. Shortly after landing in the mountains, the three of us decided to organize a hike for the following morning, and we asked the lead Sherpa if he would guide us. He happily nodded in agreement.

In the morning, we emerged from our plywood accommodations and entered the blindingly bright mountain sunlight and perfectly pure air. As veteran journalists, we knew how to battle the elements. Dressed from head to toe in the latest and greatest mixture of Gortex, down, fleece, and moisture-wicking waterproof membranes, we were a walking, talking, multilayered advertisement for North Face and Patagonia; prepared for the zombie apocalypse, so to speak.

Our Sherpa guide was waiting for us. His tanned skin was leathery from living in a wind-blown region closer to the sun than any other. He was dressed in a tee-shirt covered by a light windbreaker whose zipper closure was broken. He wore jeans ripped by hard work, not design. On his feet were sandals so worn that one of the toe straps was detached. He would lead us through mountain passes with a blown-out flip-flop. But the Nepalese were so strong in mind and body that I believe footwear of any kind was an afterthought. We three logo-adorned American fashionistas felt slightly overdressed. After he politely asked, "Ready?," we all followed his lead.

He continually peered over his shoulder to keep a close eye on us. Our pace was glacially slow, taking one step every few seconds while gasping for air. He patiently and watchfully waited for us. We were in no hurry. In every direction, the scenery was as dramatic as I have ever seen. Deep gorges disappeared into nowhere while jagged mountains touched the sky. We came to an impassable crevice in the earth, over which a bridge had been built. The sides of the bridge were made of rope and the flooring was wooden slats—old wooden slats. This was the kind of bridge only Indiana Jones or Tarzan would consider crossing, and it would take some thought... and courage before we proceeded on.

We had time to debate our next move. There was a sudden traffic jam on the one-lane mountain bridge. A local villager with a team of three cargo-carrying yaks approached from the other direction. We'd both arrived simultaneously at opposite ends of the bridge. Our guide kindly spoke on our behalf and invited the yak herder to proceed first. I was certain one of the heavily packed 800-lb. yaks would break through the wooden slats and hurl to its death. Nope. It was just an average Tuesday walk to work for the man and his beasts. Afterward, we navigated the bridge, over and then back again, to complete our sight-seeing and acclimating, breathing a little easier as we did.

On other hikes, similar Sherpa guides were eager to show us the Buddhist temples that were like spiritual rest-stops along the trekking routes. The orange-robed monks inside were always peaceful and serene. The hundreds of colorful prayer flags outside were always blowing in the stiff breeze.

The hiking exercises were a wonderful way to meet fascinating people and explore new and distant horizons in an almost fairytale-like land. At the same time, it allowed our bodies to adapt to the demanding climate. Not everyone adapted. A couple of engineers from D.C. and LA—cities at sea level—really struggled to adapt to the change in barometric pressure at

13,000 feet. Altitude sickness can be a mild illness or one that becomes life-threatening, causing a build-up of fluid in the lungs and brain. As their shortness of breath and fatigue worsened, NBC's proactive response was to immediately medevac out the two stricken techs. They were wrapped in pressurized, plastic "body bags," which helped to stabilize their worsening conditions. They were then loaded onto stretchers. But the chopper couldn't fly in the mountains at night, and the engineers needed to be in Lukla the next morning for a flight back to Katmandu.

Remember the yaks? A similar caravan with their Sherpa handlers was hired to hoof it down the mountain and descend in the dead of night. With all of the technology that we imported into those mountains, it was a centuries-old mode of transportation that ended up saving lives.

The stage was constructed and the outdoor studio assembled. We rehearsed, and then rehearsed some more. The generators, lighting, cameras, and audio and satellite transmission had been tested repeatedly and all performed flawlessly. Matt, Mary Alice, and the core New York crew arrived the day prior to the show. A pre-show celebration is a premature celebration and never done. But the fact that everyone and everything had safely arrived in the middle of the mountains for a shot at television history did create, at the very least, a sense of accomplishment within everyone. We had prepared for everything, it turned out, except Mother Nature.

Change is the only certainty with mountain weather. On the day of the show, the crystal clear, deep blue skies from the previous week were replaced by a thick and murky mist that caused everything to disappear, including Mount Everest. Everything in the Himalayas is exaggerated; the peaks are taller, the vistas longer. That also applies to the weather. The snow is deeper and the fog thicker. Because we were so high in the sky, when the fog rolled in, it was like trying to shoot television from inside a storm cloud. The show's dramatic mountain backdrop went invisible.

Fortunately, during the impeccable weather the week before, we had pre-taped breathtaking video from numerous angles of Mount Everest, neighboring Annapurna, and the many surrounding knife-like peaks. The show contained reports about life in Nepal, Buddhist spirituality, the history of the Himalayas, what it's like to climb to base camp, and more. Millions of viewers tuned in and learned about a place and people about which they'd previously known nothing.

The trip had an immense and lasting impact on my life, and for at least two hours, it did the same for *TODAY* viewers.

Where in the World is Matt Lauer? was an incredibly successful franchise because it provided a glimpse into other cultures, people, and places. Between 1998 and 2009, NBC News would send Matt as well as elaborate production teams on ten Earth-circling journeys, broadcasting from 49 different and challenging international locations. In subsequent years, I was fortunate to be on the production teams that broadcast live from the Piazzale Michelangelo with breathtaking views overlooking Florence, Italy; from the mysterious and ancient ruins of Machu Picchu, Peru; and from the deck of a 120-foot super-yacht anchored in the harbor of uber-exclusive Monte Carlo, Monaco. Every live program was a monumental undertaking and a testament to the limitless possibilities of broadcast news. While the assignments were sometimes dangerous, they did not require the kind of life-threatening commitment displayed by hard-nosed journalists who report on such events as the wars in Afghanistan and Iraq or the genocides in the Balkans and Rwanda.

Where in the World and the war in Afghanistan are at opposite ends of the foreign news spectrum, but they both share a common objective; instead of looking inward, the viewers look outward. This "global curiosity" is nothing new for our society, but our news media has allowed it to fade. Why?

Back in the day, the evil Soviet Union and their Communist allies posed a constant threat to our American way of life. The threat was real, omnipresent, and big news. We Americans felt the need to know the enemy to better understand the threat. That was at the same time that our American television networks had fully functioning news bureaus reporting from all over the world. When the Soviet Union and their allies collapsed, we as a nation breathed a long and victorious sigh of relief. We somehow perceived this new, post-communist world order as less threatening, too, and as a result, our world was suddenly less newsy. Veteran NBC News executive Reuven Frank commented, "Sunshine is a weather report, a raging storm is news."

But our need for international news and information didn't diminish with the demise of just one of our enemies (but by the way, the U.S.S.R. was renamed Russia and they continue to pose a very serious threat to our democracy). We vanquished one great big superpower rival. But, in the post 9-11 world, we face numerous other smaller terrorist menaces, all of them hellbent on doing us harm. Today, we face a long list of threats from around the globe, and Americans need to be aware of these threats. An aware society is an informed society, or more accurately, what we don't know can hurt us.

The aforementioned COVID-19 pandemic proves that some of the deadliest enemies we face are not armies or nations. When the disease first began inflicting damage and killing Chinese citizens in November and December of 2019, very little was reported in America. By early January of 2020, it was the news media who sounded the alarm and began informing the world of this mysterious and unforeseen danger. More journalists on the ground in China, in the form of fully staffed and functioning bureaus, would have meant an even louder and more urgent alarm. Even so, it was the mainstream broadcast, cable news, and print media who put reporters on the ground in Wuhan, China and first reported the news of the Coronavirus outbreak and the initial failure of the Chinese political and healthcare systems to identify and deal with its spread. And it was the same mainstream, international news media with camera crews in Italy, Spain, and elsewhere who showed us the shocking video and photographic images of locked-down cities to foreshadow the worst-case scenarios for the rest of the world.

The journalists there risked their health and safety to spread the truth about the disease. What the world desperately needed was to hear honest straight talk from the experts in the fields of virology and disease control to explain what "it" was and how best to confront "its" spread around the world. The much-needed, fact-based straight talk was delivered by the mainstream news media as journalists interviewed the experts and put them on camera to detail the deadly consequences of what we all collectively faced. And, even as I write this, the news media continues to report on the elusive search for better treatments and a vaccination.

Because honest reporting is sometimes an irritant to governments everywhere, it is worth noting that in March of 2020, the Chinese government expelled the American journalists working for *The New York Times*, *The Washington Post*, and *The Wall Street Journal*.

The globalization of the world means that we now have an

even greater need for global news than previous generations. Pandemics, immigration, trade, and global warming are all global in scope, the causes and effects stretching well beyond our domestic boundaries. They can only be fully understood and addressed if we as a society are informed beyond our local city councils and Washington, D.C.

Before the COVID-19 pandemic, the news regarding China was of a sudden trade war. The resulting tariffs have had a negative impact on American consumers, family farms, and manufacturing. In fact, there is nothing sudden about our trade war with China. It's been gradually building like a storm cloud on the horizon for the past 30 years. During that time, financial publications reported on China's meteoric rise and the looming crisis. Books were written on the subject, foreshadowing China's global assent and the resulting global impact. And in the late 80s, our mainstream broadcast news networks were expanding and staffing offices in places like Tokyo, Hong Kong, Beijing, and Manila. They were in place to report on Asia's economic transformation and the impact it would have on America's economy and workforce. The reporters, producers, and multi-ethnic staff there were just beginning to grasp and report on the financial explosion at that time. Ironically, just as the story began to unfold, those same bureaus were downsized or closed altogether as a cost-saving gesture. China became wealthier while America grew deeper in debt. With billions and billions in new income, China bought over a trillion dollars of America's debt load. They own more of us (I mean the U.S.) than any other country. But this was rarely covered by our network news.

It's impossible for American news networks to keep Americans informed on developments in Asia if the reporters, producers, editors, cameramen, and soundmen responsible for that reporting are removed from Asia. As a result, the Chinese economic success story, which had been 30 years in the making, "snuck up" on most of us.

Similarly, immigration is another hot-button news story. *Suddenly*, we have an invasion of immigrants at our southern border. Who are these immigrants, where are they coming from, and why are they here? These are all perplexing questions to many Americans. Whether you view this as a security or economic issue, the answers to these questions could be found through accurate news reporting. But the network of news bureaus in Central America, which we once relied upon, has long been closed.

Our airwaves used to be filled with reports from Nicaragua, on the Communist Sandinistas there, and the Iran-Contra scandal, and from El Salvador regarding the war with leftist guerillas there, and from Panama on, we heard of Colonel Manuel Noriega's corruption and money laundering. When the bureaus in those counties were curtailed, so also was our ability to report on the growing immigration problem... until, one day, we had a sudden immigration crisis on our southern border. Ongoing news reporting could have alerted both U.S. citizens and our legislators to what was coming. Awareness of the news is a first step in developing policies meant to deal with such events' impacts. Developing lasting immigration solutions, beyond simply building a wall, requires more than a strictly domestic perspective.

World news coverage hasn't disappeared from our television screens. It can still be seen, albeit packaged differently. There are still many courageous reporters reporting from the dangerous frontlines of news from all over the globe. Increasingly, coverage of far-way stories originates from central locations like New York, Los Angeles, or London. This in no way reflects a lack of daring on the part of the reporters, who would much rather be on the frontlines. Rather, it's too costly or time-consuming (or both) to scramble a crew from Los Angeles to Honduras. Because of that, far more is lost than saved.

The true value of having foreign correspondents on the ground is their ability to contextualize the news. Putting the facts in context illustrates a story's importance in two ways. First, a correspondent can show the importance or impact of the news locally, on the ground from where he or she is reporting. It also demonstrates the importance or impact of the same news story back in America, where the viewer is watching from. This helps to get stories into the minds of the viewers and show why a story is important in both China and the U.S. Sometimes, the context or consequences of a story can be more important than the news itself. This type of reporting, though, is only made possible via the factual storytelling of a skillful foreign correspondent. Sadly, this valuable breed of reporter is becoming rare.

Journalism should always strive to inform and serve the public interest with news that is both domestic and foreign. Covering foreign news is a more costly endeavor than doing so domestically. In the past, those costs were always justified as part of the public interest function of network news. When foreign bureaus and budgets are slashed, it is safe to ask if the networks are abdicating their civic obligation in favor of the bottom line.

14

ELECTION REJECTION

As the last millennium came to an end, the world wondered what digitally generated havoc would be created by computers' inability to transition from 1999 to 2000. No computer had ever actually processed a date with three zeros. The flames of public fear were fanned by numerous experts as well as the media, who wrote about disturbing scenarios affecting everything from the financial and telecommunications industries to public utilities. Even the Department of Defense worried about doomsday situations. Then United States Deputy Secretary of Defense John Hamre stated, "The Y2K problem is the electronic equivalent of the El Niño and there will be nasty surprises around the globe."[1]

Entire niche industries were created to reprogram, test, and guard against computer failure catastrophes. A presidential commission was formed to study the possibly dire consequences. Programing giants like Microsoft tried to allay the public hysteria by predicting there would only be minor glitches. Still,

---

1 Verton, D. "Y2K Failures Abroad Threaten U.S. Security." (1999, February 26). Retrieved May 15,2020 from http://www.cnn.com/TECH/computing/9903/01/y2ksecurity.idg/

people wondered... what if?

Y2K disasters or not, the news media was going to cover that particular New Year's celebration like a blanket. Some networks began their day-long coverage in Sidney, Australia and followed the New Year as it swept west across the globe.

Stacy Brady would be supervising the technical staffing for NBC's global coverage. Jack, as the Denver Bureau Chief, reached out to me first to gauge my interest in working on the Y2K story. I had no interest in covering a bunch of drunken partyers in the streets of Denver—or New York City, for that matter. I told him I'd much rather stay at home and raise a glass with Amy and friends. But he had planned a different angle on the Y2K story for December 31, 1999.

The headquarters for our nation's air defense system was buried inside a mountain in Colorado Springs. Cheyenne Mountain was the top-secret subterranean home to North American Aerospace Defense Command (NORAD). This was the location from which our military monitored the heavens, watching for and warning against incoming ballistic missile and air attacks on North America. It was a highly secure, almost secretive facility hidden deep inside a granite mountain. If there was going to be a glitch with major implications, it would occur at Cheyenne Mountain. The government, confident that this would not be the case, invited us to observe.

It's not the kind of place that offers regular tours. It is the kind of place that makes for interesting news coverage and the kind of once in a lifetime assignment that I'd happily accept.

Instead of simply watching and reporting on the inevitable nothing happening on New Year's Eve, Jack pitched NORAD on the idea of showing the valuable mission performed *inside* Cheyenne Mountain. Astonishingly, the military agreed.

Once our credentials were approved, we traveled to Colorado Springs the day before New Year's Eve. Outside the mountain, our team of Jack, Roger, Steve, and I cleared an extremely rigorous checkpoint, including inspections of both gear and personnel. We then boarded a military vehicle that took us through a seemingly endless mile-long tunnel and to our final destination. There was a small military village that looked and operated like any other small military village, except this one sat 2,000 feet underneath a mountain. It was comprised of 13 different buildings that operated 24/7. To go from the tunnel to the buildings, we passed through two 23-ton blast doors designed to withstand a nuclear blast.

Because it's a top-secret location, our shooting inside the mountain was limited. The base commander did agree to give us an extensive interview. For the location of that conversation, we chose a glass conference room in the center of the operations monitoring room. Lined with windows, the conference room looked in every direction, out onto enormous video screens. The screens monitored all of the military aerospace movement around the world. At one point during the interview, metal blinds suddenly lowered, completely sealing us in and blinding our view of something classified on the video screens. I asked if we were under attack. The commander only smiled and said, "If we were, you would certainly know."

Once we finished our shoot, we packed up and made our way back to the earth's surface and daylight. Shooting the day before New Year's Eve had allowed us a day to write and edit the story on Cheyenne Mountain. It would play New Year's Eve on *Nightly News*. The story reminded me of the positive power of the press and the special, value-added perspective it afforded me. A report about the dedicated men and women who man the operations and perform the daily missions ensuring the rest of us remain safe was informative and worthwhile. And, covering the news once again allowed me privileged and rare insight.

NORAD and the Cheyenne Mountain Complex are part of the much larger Peterson Air Force Base. It was there that we spent New Year's Eve. We joined other news media members outside their command center and watched and waited as the clock ticked close to the witching hour of midnight. As was the case in other time zones, nothing happened when the clock struck 2000. The build-up and media hype had been all for naught.

Having survived the Y2K apocalypse, the news media's attention turned to the 2000 presidential election. Stacy had booked Steve and me months in advance as part of NBC's coverage of both the Republican and Democratic National Conventions. The Republicans nominated George Bush and Dick Cheney in Philadelphia in late July. The Democrats nominated Al Gore and Joe Lieberman in Los Angeles ten days later. Our assignment required us to spend a week in each city. We were also booked to cover the November Election night coverage, although our exact location for that shoot was "To Be Determined."

Having worked on the Democratic Convention in Chicago four years earlier, we were familiar with the routine. National political conventions seem to draw two predominant groups: demonstrators protesting the party in town and politicians supporting the party in town. Our roving news crew would be utilized to cover the many opposing demonstrations and shoot interviews with the many supporting politicians. Most of the coverage from inside the convention centers would be done by large "hard cameras" shooting from fixed positions with long zoom lenses. Occasionally, portable roving cameras would add an up-close and personal perspective from the convention floor.

There was and is no NBC bureau in Philadelphia. The site for the Republican National Convention was the First Union Center, a professional sports arena that would later be renamed the Wells Fargo Center. Our workspace was a small village of GE trailers—the kind that populate construction sites. They were randomly thrown together and intermingled with several large satellite dishes. The other networks operated out of the same temporary housing. The parking lots that surrounded the arena with all of the temporary trailers and rental trucks made it look like the circus had come to town.

The gathering of so many troops for one event was always an excuse to get together with friends after work and strengthen the bonds of camaraderie... or at least relive and embellish familiar war stories. Both Bush and Gore had easily won their party's nominations, securing the required delegates six months before the conventions. Both conventions were flawlessly choreographed and perfectly produced spectacles, void of any drama... and void of real news. The real news would occur three months later on election night.

After Philadelphia, we headed to Los Angeles. There was and is a large NBC bureau in Los Angeles. The sprawling NBC complex in Burbank occupied a great big piece of television history. Everyone from Bob Hope to Johnny Carson to Jay Leno and many others have passed through its security gates. It was home to *The TONIGHT Show*, soap operas, and specials as well as local and network newscasts. The "lot" was made up of a series of studios and offices, of which the Burbank News Bureau occupied a sizable chunk. Heather Allen was the well-respected and well-liked bureau chief at this time. She hailed from South Africa and had spent the previous decade running the Johannesburg bureau, covering everything from Apartheid to Nelson Mandela's election. Our paths had crossed in Beirut and elsewhere. It was good to see her familiar face once again.

The site for the Democratic Convention was the Staples Center, home of the Lakers, Clippers, and Kings. Because of the bureau in LA, the temporary workspace around the Staples Center involved a smaller presence. Steve and I were in the bureau awaiting work one morning when Heather approached.

With her strong South African accent, she informed us, "I have something for you gents later on today. You're going to a party."

"You mean like the Democratic party?" I asked.

"Not exactly. It is an official function, but a little less stuffy than the Democratic Party. You're going to attend the press party... at the Playboy Mansion."

"They allow cameras into the Playboy Mansion? I mean, we are going there to work, right?"

"Yes, of course. You're representing NBC News. But work only loosely applies here. Spray the event, and if you should see Hef, by all means, shoot him. Otherwise, my advice is to enjoy yourselves."

By "spray," she meant we should shoot general B-roll to show the party at the Playboy Mansion. And by "Hef," she was referring to the one and only founder of *Playboy*, Hugh Heffner.

There were parties thrown at each convention in both Philly and LA. The one thrown by the LA Democratic Party at the Department of Water and Power in downtown LA had to be a far cry from the bash we attended.

Most invitees boarded buses at the nearby UCLA campus and were dropped off at the party. Due to our TV equipment, we were allowed to park at the mansion. With our gear, we walked down a long, stone driveway and through a side gate where our credentials were checked. Once inside the gate, we were on the grounds of what looked like a make-believe land. A large meandering lawn was enclosed by tall, manicured hedges and Eucalyptus trees reaching up to the starlit sky. We followed a walkway that took us by an outdoor bar populated with celebrities. There, we saw a rocky, manmade structure that partially covered a sprawling pool. This was the famous grotto. Welcoming lounge chairs with striped beach towels were both poolside and inside the cave-like grotto. We meandered through as I thought, "If these rock walls could only talk."

I noticed tubes of massage oils, lotions, and lube strewn about side tables and chairs in the grotto. I wondered if those had been forgotten from the previous night's debauchery or were intended for us.

It was early and the press was too uptight (this including Steve and me) to take full advantage of the grotto, so we made our way across the lawn and towards the backside of the gigantic mansion. I saw a tall, silver-haired man in a dark suit and salmon-colored shirt surrounded by and engaging with attendees—*Hef*. Steve and I shouldered our camera and audio gear, joined the group, and began taping the conversation.

It was an interesting mix. Hef with two beautiful Playboy Bunnies at his sides, a handful of print reporters, and us. He was extremely at ease chatting with us press. Why shouldn't he be? It was his house and he was Hugh Heffner. He took umbrage with the righteous moral majority and seemed to side with the Dems and Gore.

After the interview, we shot some video and "sprayed" the party, and then we shut off our equipment. If, say, Dick Cheney crashed the party and skinny-dipped in the grotto, we were ready to shoot. But in the absence of any breaking news, we followed Heather's orders and enjoyed ourselves. The Bunnies were extremely approachable and conversant, although not necessarily deep political thinkers. *Playboy* had hired still photographers to capture the evening's moments. Steve and I posed with some, actually many, of the Bunnies so that... well, so that they would have some keepsakes of us to cherish from that memorable press night!

In addition to talking to the many Bunnies, Steve and I struck up a conversation with a guy who was the head of security for the place. He was a former detective for the LAPD. Transitioning from the police to the Playboy Mansion had put a half-concealed but permanent smile on his face. We talked to him for about half an hour, at which point he asked if we'd like a tour. The party was taking place in the backyard, which featured different luxury tents for food and drink. But the mansion was off-limits. At least until our new friend offered his tour.

With our camera gear secured and drinks in hand, we strolled with our new friend around the grounds of the mansion. On even more sprawling manicured grounds, Hef had built a small, enclosed zoo that featured exotic birds and monkeys. Our guide then took us inside to get a glimpse of what it was like to live there. We did not tour the entire mansion and the private living quarters. What we did see was palatial, with a blend of old-world aristocracy and new-world mogul who'd built a famous empire on sex.

We made our way back to the party in the backyard. Those members of the press fortunate enough to attend were thoroughly enjoying themselves. This was my first and only time at the Playboy Mansion, so I had no sample size by which to compare this *Playboy* Press Party against other Playboy parties.

I imagined a more unrestrained and less-clothed type of fun occurring at other *Playboy* events.

I asked a bartender who looked like he'd seen more than a few of those other events, "How does this party compare to others?"

Shaking his head from side to side, he smiled and said, "It doesn't. But you press people do like to drink. I'll give you that."

I loved covering politics. And after my assignment at the Playboy Mansion, I REALLY loved covering politics... and all it entailed.

My final stop on the 2000 presidential campaign was for election night. We received word from Stacy that we'd be part of the team covering the Bush campaign in Austin, Texas. Steve and I arrived a couple of days early for set-up and rehearsal. The real set-up work had been done by a commercial construction crew. To accommodate all of the credentialed local, network, and international news media, a heavily reinforced, five-story metal scaffolding structure had been constructed. This was the camera platform for all of the still and video news cameras. The platform looked out across a small grass quadrangle where the supporters gathered and directly towards the State Capitol Building, in front of which a stage and podium had been erected. It was the place from which the anticipated speakers were supposed to give their speeches to the mass of onlooking supports and news media.

On the morning of Tuesday, November 7th, we arrived at work anticipating a long election day, not unlike most. NBC and others had already rented the same kind of temporary workplace trailers used at the conventions. The "news village" was just off to the side of the capitol and scaffolding structure. The rain started early in the day and picked up intensity, becoming a pounding and windy storm in the late afternoon and throughout the evening.

Steve and I spent most of our time at our camera position on the scaffolding. We were in constant contact with our many bosses; walkie-talkie communication with the producers in the trailers and headset communication with the master control room in New York, where Tom Brokaw was anchoring the live election night coverage. We shot live updates with our correspondent David Gregory while waiting for speakers to appear at the podium. During lulls, we sought shelter and nourishment in the warm, dry trailers.

We knew going into that day that the polling showed Bush and Gore locked in a tight race. Bush carried his home state of Texas by more than 20 points and was projected to be the early winner there. As the nationwide race tightened, the reporters and anchors focused on other states.

The late moderator of *Meet the Press*, Tim Russert was a political genius and gifted communicator. In an age of digital wizardry, that night he employed the most basic analog tools to explain the key to the presidential race. When asked his opinion, he pulled out a small white dry erase board, and on it wrote, "FLORIDA FLORIDA FLORIDA."

Around 8 p.m. EST/7 CST, the giant video screens erected around the capitol and our scaffolding structure flashed a major headline. The networks had almost simultaneously projected three crucial toss-up states—Michigan, Pennsylvania, and Florida for Gore. With one more state, he would have enough electoral votes to declare victory. The New York mothership came to David and our live location for reaction. He reported that the mood in Austin, of the 20,000 drenched Bush supports, had turned somber.

Steve and I stayed at our camera position waiting for an announcement. By then, the frigid and stinging rain was blowing from side to side. Still, there was no word from the Bush campaign.

What we didn't know was that the conservative western panhandle portion of Florida was on a different time zone than the rest of Florida—central time. The polls had *still been open* there when the networks had made those projections. That is a journalistic no-no. Bush campaign strategist Karl Rove was livid, and he called the networks complaining that they had made the call too early and, in doing so, negatively influenced the Bush vote.

As more votes were counted in those conservative panhandle counties, the results started to swing in favor of Bush. Two hours after declaring Florida for Bush, the networks backpedaled and called it "too close to call."

Both candidates hovered at around 245 electoral votes each (with 270 needed for victory). As all eyes fixated on Florida, the networks announced that Bush had suddenly taken a 20,000-vote lead there. Steve and I, along with everyone else outside of the Texas Capitol, had grown numb from the freezing rain. But when the giant screens flashed that announcement, the tired crowd began to stir.

Around 1:15 a.m. Austin time, Fox News was the first to call Florida for Bush. The other networks soon followed and announced George W. Bush as the 43rd President of the United States. The loudspeakers at the Texas capitol cranked out the tune "Signed, Sealed, Delivered."

Every soaked and frozen member of the news media stood by, expecting an acceptance speech from the Bush campaign. There were rumors that Vice President Gore had conceded on a call to Governor Bush. Then, at 2 a.m., the Associated Press reported that Bush's lead, which had ballooned to 29,000 votes, had shrunk to less than 6,000 votes, triggering an automatic recount in the state of Florida.

In the following days after that election night, details of those calls between Bush and Gore were made public. When Gore phoned Bush a second time to withdraw his concession, Bush became irritated. Gore responded with, "Well, you don't have to get snippy."

Clutching his victory speech, Bush replied, "Let me make sure I understand. You're calling me back to retract your concession?" Bush's younger brother, Florida's Governor Jeb Bush, had assured him Florida was a done deal and in the Bush column.

Gore fired back, "Let me explain something—your *younger* brother is not the ultimate authority on this."[2]

The 2000 election was unchartered territory. As Tuesday became Wednesday, confusion reigned with both campaigns in Texas and Tennessee as well as throughout the state of Florida. It was especially confusing in the network headquarters in New York. They had all called Gore the winner in Florida, and then Bush... and then no one.

Tom Brokaw finally went on the air and confessed to the world, "We don't just have egg on our face... we have an omelet."

Because of both the long hours and the elements, Steve and I were more exhausted than confused. Finally, at about 3 a.m., we packed up, dried off, thawed out, and officially hit the wall. When we woke up on Wednesday morning (late), the entirety of the news media was gearing up to follow the story on to its next stop, Florida, and cover a statewide recount to determine

2   Sobierai, S. (2000, November 8). "The Story Behind the Near-Concession." *The Washington Post*. Retrieved from https://www.washingtonpost.com/wp-srv/aponline/20001108/aponline180633_000.htm

the 43rd president.

I knew this was a historic time. NBC asked if we could continue to Florida and remain indefinitely. Unfortunately, I could not. I had a firm commitment to a major corporate project whose wheels were already in motion. I had to return to Denver, and Steve returned home to Chicago. We joined the vast majority of Americans who followed the hanging chads and Florida recount from afar via television and print media.

The Supreme Court ultimately decided the outcome, and on December 12, 2000, George W. Bush was awarded Florida's 25 electoral votes and named the next U.S. president.

For an industry that prides itself on getting it right, most of us got it wrong—and did so more than once that election night. Some online and print news media outlets did not make the same mistake, but they were a tiny minority. After the 2000 election, there was much soul-searching done, most of it focused on the polling methods used for that and previous elections. Exit polls were revamped after 2000. Today, there are "decision desks" at each network that are employed to sift through and interpret the exit polling data that is fed to the on-air pundits. It's a safeguard against repeating the mistakes of our past. It is not foolproof.

The late Curtis Gans, who was Founder and Director of the Committee for the Study of the American Electorate, wrote, "In almost every election, there's this rush to judgment, and there's something inaccurate reported. Networks are creating the news by projecting winners, not reporting it. No data is as accurate as tabulated results."[3]

We learned a valuable lesson in 2000. Yet, as the competition in our news world increases, so also does the urge to rush to

3 Shepard, A. C. (2001, January/February). "How They Blew It." *American Journalism Review*. Retrieved from https://ajrarchive.org/article.asp?id=519&id=519

judgment.

15

Fate at 30,000 Feet

As I mentioned in earlier chapters, the added news magazine programs were a boon to television journalism and, pragmatically speaking, freelance news crews with network credentials. The shooting would often last multiple days or even weeks to gather all of the story elements. Instead of shooting one or two interviews, the magazine stories could allow for and involve seven or eight different interviews, showing different perspectives or angles on any one story. Those different interviews could involve travel to and from different locations. And, much more B-roll (supporting non-interview video) would need to be shot to explain the story and visually cover the lengthy script. The days were frequently 14 hours long and followed by ensuing 14-hour days. The accumulated overtime translated into increased income, which was a sure-fire way to rejuvenate an exhausted crew.

The cornerstone of the magazine story is the lengthy and determinedly probing interview, which involves two camera crews—one camera trained on the correspondent and the other on the interview subject or subjects. It wasn't even uncommon to employ additional cameras for alternative visual perspectives. As the crew size increased, so, too, did the challenges. It's a more challenging process, for instance, to record flawless audio from three mics placed on three people as opposed to one mic on one person.

Lighting numerous subjects for numerous cameras proved especially challenging since everything had to be hidden. Not a single light or cable could be visible in the shot. On most shoots, the objective was to bathe both interviewer and interviewee in unblemished, flattering "soft" light, getting them looking their best for the inevitable TV close-up. To play up dramatic elements of a story, "hard" shadows could be cast on both the subjects and the backgrounds to create an eerie, dramatic mood. Since we (the crews) were supplying the equipment (which we owned), the magazine shoots with their added equipment demands and long hours were particularly prized assignments. The more specialty lights we hung or microphones we used, the greater the rental invoice billed to the network, which again translated into more income for the crew. These elaborate interview set-ups would, at times, resemble mini movie sets—except we weren't shooting on a Hollywood soundstage. We were often shooting in someone's mobile home or a tiny apartment.

Any cameraman worth his salt has mastered the basics of lighting. But these complicated lighting schemes went well beyond Lighting 101. While living and working overseas for NBC, I had been a part of numerous on-location "multi-camera" shoots, so the format was nothing new to me. But those foreign productions had always employed lighting directors with their grips and gaffers to deal with the rigors of lighting. Even when I moved back to Chicago, it was common to have a network lighting director supervise the interview lighting for a magazine show. But with so many magazine shows scheduling and booking so many multi-camera shoots, that staffing equation simply wasn't feasible. The lighting tasks for those complicated shoots fell into the hands of the cameraman who was now in charge of both shooting and lighting. To keep up with the ever-increasing lighting demands, I (and many of my fellow cameramen) invested in sophisticated yet portable lighting gear we could transport to any location. I was constantly purchasing the latest soft lights, diffusers, grids, gels, flags, dimmers, stands, and clamps to facilitate a greater mastery of lighting. As my lighting arsenal grew, so also did the rental invoice I submitted to the client at the end of each shoot. The more equipment we bought and used, the more we charged. And as long as the correspondent looked radiant and lovely or handsome on camera, there was never a charge questioned.

In the early to mid-nineties, studio cameramen who manned the massive studio cameras for the evening newscasts were being replaced by robotic cameras. Freelance news cameramen, like me, could not be replaced by robots. And, with our freelance soundmen partners, we became the trusted crews who made up the very privileged labor pool from which the networks drew upon to staff the vast majority of magazine shoots. The trusting bond between network producer or "booker" and freelance crew had to be forged not by a single shoot or show, but over years of shoots and shows. That bond was another form of camaraderie. The person on the other end of the phone in New York knew I was a reliable choice with no risk to them or the network. They knew that my talent, and that of my sound partner, would visually and audibly enhance the finished product—the story. And, in return, I knew they would be happy to put money in my pocket.

Email was not yet the go-to communication choice, so the

first point of contact was always the phone. For instance...

"Hi Tim, this is Susan at NBC in New York. I'm calling about a Dateline *shoot in Denver. It's a four-day shoot. You'll need to be there on the morning of September 1st and should be wrapped on the 4th. They're doing a follow-up story on the JonBenét Ramsey case. It's a two-camera shoot and you would be the A camera. I hope you're available."*

"I am available. Sounds good. Who am I working with?"

After she informed me of the correspondent and producer who'd be brought in, she concluded, "We haven't booked the B camera yet, but I'll let you know who that is once we've confirmed them. They've noted on the Crew Request some special equipment requests like a track dolly and HMI lighting for the outdoors. I'm sure they'll go over those specifics when they call you directly to discuss the shoot."

"We can certainly take care of those special requests. I'll talk with the correspondent and producer regarding their travel plans, where and when exactly they want to meet up, and if they plan to ride with us or have their own vehicle. Let me have the producer's number, please."

And with that, we'd be hired. Given that it's the news business we're talking about, where very little is predictable, we never knew when or with how much advance notice these calls would come. But, these kinds of news stories involved much more advanced planning and pre-production legwork on the part of the producer than your average breaking news story. To receive a call two weeks in advance of a magazine shoot was a luxury, but not all that rare.

That scenario would repeat itself week after week, month after month, year after year. My six years in Denver became the heyday of the freelance crew; the pinnacle of the relationship between busy network news divisions and their independent contractors. Their cost analysis and budget projections justified outsourcing the work, and we were thrilled to be their recipients at the right place and time.

For the bookers in New York or LA, trying to fill all of the Crew Requests with available crews in all of the cities and locations across America was an endless task. At its height, *Dateline* was on FIVE nights a week. And that was one show on one network. The same process was being repeated for all of the news magazine shows on all of the networks. Because it's the news business, at times, the pace could be frenzied, and that pace would be evident in the initial booking call...

"Hi Tim, its Susan at NBC. I've got a two-camera shoot that was just dropped in my lap. Please tell me you're available Tuesday, October 10th for three days."

Checking my calendar, and then: "Hey, good to hear from you. October 10th... three days... yep, I'm available"

"EXCELLENT. Look, details to follow and I don't have time to find the second crew. I know you have talented cameramen friends in Denver. Can you take care of the second crew, same days? Just let me know who you book. I'll have the producer call you shortly. Gotta run."

"Can you take care of the second crew?" meant both "I'm in a hurry" as well as "I have faith in you to hire the most talented crew available." The bottom line was that my ass was on the line not only for my work, but also for that of my colleagues. If, as the second crew, the people I found for the shoot produced lacking, inferior, or just plain shitty video and audio, I would shoulder the responsibility because they'd been hired on my recommendation. If they were technically sound but acted inattentive, aloof, or abrasive towards to rest of the crew, I would also hear about it.

Who I selected as a second crew was a big decision. On those occasions, there was a shortlist of cameramen upon whom I would rely, and Gordon "Gordy" McClean always topped that list.

Our friendship had only deepened since meeting during the Timothy McVeigh and Terry Nichols trials. His primary client was CBS; mine was NBC. There was never even a hint of competition, only mutual respect. As neighbors with similar interests, we saw a lot of each other outside of the news business. Amy and I had eventually joined the Hiwan Golf Club, where he and his wife Heidi were members, which sounds more prestigious than it was because... it's the only course in town. As he and I spent more and more time together, that time often involved golf clubs and wine glasses, not video cameras.

Two-camera magazine shoots were the place where our work paths would occasionally converge. When needed, Gordy and his soundman would be my second crew on NBC shoots and he returned the favor by calling me for any of his CBS shoots needing a second crew. These shoots always seemed to take place in some spectacularly dreamy location....

I was booked to shoot a profile on Buck Brannaman, the real-life "Horse Whisperer" upon whom the 1998 Robert Redford film of the same name was based. Buck would be training, or whispering, to wild stallions on a majestic 4,000-acre ranch in the Montana wilderness. But this wasn't just any sprawling, drop-dead gorgeous, Big Sky ranch. This was Tom and Meredith Brokaw's ranch with a guest list that would include their friends and neighbors Ted Turner and Jane Fonda.

And I was the B camera to Gordy's A camera on a CBS shoot for 48 hours when we met up in Aspen, Colorado. We were in the exclusive playground for the rich and famous to shoot a story on the "Children of Billionaires." Our Aspen profile was focused on young Eric Trump, who was just finishing high school at the time. No one knew he would eventually be spending time at the White House. However, under those bright Aspen skies, it was crystal clear that it's good to be Donald Trump's kid. And, it was also good to be on assignment in Aspen. We made certain to wrap the shoot in a leisurely fashion, adding a ski day on the back-side of the shoot; lift passes courtesy of the resort, thank you very much.

Gordy and I worked together on numerous other shoots. One in particular had lasting implications.

In August of '01, CBS asked Gordy to assemble a four-man crew (two cameramen and two soundmen) for an unmemorable assignment regarding a relatively forgettable *60 Minutes* story in Kansas City, Missouri. Not every location was Aspen or Montana. I expected that the most notable aspect of the Kansas City story would be the authentic barbeque we'd savor while there. I was wrong.

I was the sole crew member who upgraded to first-class for the 90-minute flight. This might seem excessive or even bourgeoisie, but it offered me the rare opportunity for an unfettered examination of the *USA TODAY* sports section. I settled into my aisle seat and sifted between the dashed hopes of the Colorado Rockies and the promising hopes of the pre-season Broncos. Suddenly, two smartly dressed but harried businesswomen hurried through the plane door as it was about to close. Both the women and their designer carry-ons appeared in disarray, presumably from a mad dash through DIA. They graciously thanked the flight attendant for holding the flight for them as they tried in vain to reorganize the contents of their many bags.

One woman then turned her attention to the passenger sitting across the aisle from me. She bent down to softly ask, "Excuse me, sir, I'm sorry to bother you, but my colleague and I were put in different rows in first class and we were hoping to get some work done. May I interest you in the aisle seat in row three so that she and I might sit together?"

From my periphery, I could see that the male passenger was bothered by the inquiry. Without looking up from his *Wall Street Journal*, he dismissed her, "Look, lady, I don't give a damn where you or your *colleague* are sitting 'cause I'm sitting right here. I ain't movin.'"

The woman stood straight up and, without missing a beat, turned to the entire first-class cabin, all ten of us, and, pointing to her shoulder blades, asked, "Excuse me, but do I have a KICK ME sign on my back?"

Everyone, having witnessed the exchange, burst out into simultaneous laughter. The emasculated and embarrassed asshole hiding behind his *Wall Street Journal* was as red as a beet.

I turned to the stranger in the window seat to my left and asked, "Hey, pal, do you have any burning desire to sit next to me for the next 90 minutes?"

"I don't care where I sit."

At which point I then turned to the two businesswomen still standing in the aisle and offered, "Excuse me, I think we have a solution. Why don't you guys take these seats and we'll take yours?"

"That's very kind. Thank you."

By then, the flight attendants were instructing everyone to take their seats so the flight could take off on schedule. I had barely completed the sports section when we touched down in KC. Gordy and the rest of the crew were still fighting their way out of coach when I arrived at the luggage carousel with the other first-class passengers. I spotted one of the women with whom I'd exchanged seats. Dressed in an expensive-looking, well-tailored, dark pantsuit with her long black hair pulled tightly into a ponytail, she slowly approached me with the confident air of an Ivy League law professor or Fortune 500 corporate exec.

Poised and professional, she said, "I want to thank you again. That was very nice of you, especially given the first response I received."

"That guy was an idiot. No, that guy was a *rude* idiot. And your comeback was a perfect foil. He didn't know what hit him. After that, I think everyone in first class wanted to accommodate you and your coworker."

By now, some of my crew's 40 metal equipment cases had begun tumbling onto the carousel. I reached for a couple of cases and, as I grabbed them, she asked, "What do you do? I mean, what line of work are you in?"

"I have a television production company. I'm here in Kansas City as part of a *60 Minutes* shoot for CBS."

"Wow. How exciting."

"Well, it often sounds more exciting than it actually is."

"Do you ever do corporate work? I'm sure I could introduce you to someone at the company where I work who could use your production services...."

Aha! Corporate exec, not a law professor.

By now, Gordy had reached baggage claim and begun grabbing cases of TV equipment. Upon landing, the soundmen had made a bee-line for the rental cars to procure our SUVs, which were now parked curbside.

I continued chatting with the attractive exec, mindful that my crew-mates were doing most of the heavy lifting. "Well, that is very kind of *you*. Yes, I have worked for a number of corporate clients in Denver and Chicago. But I don't want you to think I gave up my seat so I could pitch you or solicit work. It just seemed like the right thing to do. And now, I'm afraid I'm going to sound a little rude. I've got to join up with the rest of our crew. We need to finish loading everything and go set up this TV shoot. I really don't mean to be brief but, look… take care."

"Of course, and good luck with your shoot."

It had ended up being a hurried exchange. We did not trade business cards, and I left without knowing anything about that woman.

Gordy and I finalized directions to the location before getting behind the wheels of our respective SUVs. The soundmen collected the last remaining cases of equipment. Once all of the gear had been accounted for, our two-Suburban caravan streaked off to connect with the correspondent and producer for the first of many interviews.

As is often the case, a long day's shoot was capped off with a late-night meal. The four of us gathered at one of KC's finest steakhouses, the Plaza Three, for a meal that was more memorable than the shoot. With dueling cellars, Gordy and I had packed a few rare bottles of Napa Cabernet Sauvignon and French Bordeaux. After we agreed to pay a modest corkage fee, the restaurant was happy to open our stellar wines, which paired perfectly with their equally stellar steaks. As the wine flowed, so did the conversation.

We were the last group left in the place when my sound partner Eric suddenly remembered, "Oh yeah, I almost forgot. That lady was really appreciative."

Confused, I asked, "What lady? What are you talking about?"

"You gave up your seat for some lady, right?"

"How did you know that sitting all the way in the back of

coach? I thought what happens in First Class stays in First Class."

"Well, you should tell her that. As I was getting the last of the gear, she came up to me and gave me some restaurant gift certificates and her business card. She said to tell you 'Thanks again.'"

"Restaurant gift certificates... what restaurant?"

"Applebee's—I think that's where she works. I think her card said 'president' or something."

"*President!?* She was the freaking *president* of Applebee's?! How is that possible? I thought company presidents flew in Gulfstreams and Net Jets!"

Now Gordy chimed in, "Looks like, with a little corporate ass-kissing, Timmy could have a new corporate client."

Gesturing to Eric, I insisted, "He's out of his mind. Let me see her card."

"I don't have it with me. I left the gift certificates and her card in my room. I could be wrong."

"Okay. Just make sure I get everything before we leave KC."

Countless interviews and two 15-hour days later, we were wrapped and all on a flight back to Denver. This time, I was sitting in coach next to Eric and going over expense receipts when I came across a copy of the bill for the Plaza Three dinner. Recalling that dinner, I could almost taste the buttery sirloin and mature Napa Cab when, BOOM, it hit me. The gift certificates.

I turned to Eric and inquired, "Hey, buddy, I think you have something for me."

"Huh?"

"Gift certificates. Restaurant gift certificates and an executive's business card?"

After a long pondering pause, he erupted with, "Shit! I left

263

them in the hotel room. Oh man, I'm…"

"What? You left them? Where are you working tomorrow, then, because it sure as shit isn't with me!"

"I'm sorry. I'm sorry. I just forgot. I was packing all my gear and clothes, and I didn't even think to check the desk drawer. I can call the front desk and see if they were turned in."

"So, you find free money in the form of gift certificates, not made out to anyone specific, just sitting in a drawer. You going to walk those down to the front desk or walk to the nearest Applebee's for a free lunch?"

"You make a good point… human nature being what it is and all."

"Another part of human nature is forgetfulness."

"And let's not forget guilt. I feel terrible."

"Don't worry about it. My problem is that the right thing to do is to reach out to this woman with a show of gratitude."

"For what it's worth, I'm almost positive her business card did say President of Applebee's."

"That's helpful. Now all I have to do is call a number I don't have and reach a woman I don't know to thank her for something I never received. Let me get right on that."

I returned to Denver and resumed freelance life, all the while procrastinating the bothersome little task atop of my to-do list, which was eating away at the "do-the-right-thing" part of my brain. When I couldn't take it anymore, I looked up the 1-800 number for the Applebee's headquarters in Kansas City, Missouri.

The call was promptly answered by an efficient female voice. I nervously began my pitch, "Hi. I'm wondering if you might help me. You see, I was on a flight recently and met this woman whom I am now trying to locate and…"

The efficient voice immediately interrupted, complete with a disciplinary overtone. "Sir, I must interrupt you, as we don't engage in that sort of activity here at Applebee's."

No good deed goes unpunished. I'd called to say thanks, but missed the mark entirely. I quickly realized that, in the eyes and ears of the Applebee's receptionist, I looked like some kind of perverted stalker. Trying to redeem myself to the switchboard gatekeeper, I pleaded, "Wait a second. Hold on here. You've got it all wrong. I gave up my seat in first class on a connection from Denver to Kansas City so two female business colleagues could sit together. I believe one of them was the president of Applebee's. She provided me with Applebee's gift certificates and I was just calling to say thank you because... well, it's the right thing to do."

The phone went silent for what felt like an hour as the receptionist evaluated this new wrinkle. The silence was broken by her gum-snapping as she pondered the question, "Could there actually be an ounce of truth to the far-fetched fairytale?"

"Ummmm... one moment."

I was placed on hold, and the next voice I heard was that of a different woman.

"Hi, this is Donna."

Okay. I seemed to be making progress. Worried I'd once again be dismissed as some creepy Peeping Tom, I proceeded cautiously. "Hi, Donna. My name is Tim Ortman. This might sound unbelievable, but please bear with me. A month or so ago, I was traveling from Denver to KC and traded seats with a woman so she could sit with her colleague. And then—"

"I remember you! I was on that flight. I'm one of the women with whom you traded seats."

Salvation, at last! "Wow. I can't believe I finally caught up with you. I just wanted to say thank you for your business card and gift certificates. It was a generous gesture, but I never actually received either, so I didn't know exactly who to thank."

"Gift certificates? Umm, that wasn't me. That would've been the other woman, my boss. Let me put you on hold for just a second."

It seemed that perseverance paid off. The third and final female voice I heard was the one for whom this entire search had been aimed at. "Hi, this is Julia."

There it was. Finally, a NAME. "Julia, this is Tim. Tim Ortman. We met on a plane from Denver to KC a while back."

"Yes, of course. I remember you. How's it going?"

"Things are good. Thanks for asking. You know, we exchanged seats but nothing else. Do you mind if I ask, I mean, I don't want to appear forward but, what do you do at Applebee's?"

"I was the president. I thought I left someone a business card."

"Yes, you did leave a business card with one of the soundmen on the crew. And, very generously, some gift certificates, too. I can speak for all of us working in television news that a free meal is a highly cherished thing. But my absent-minded coworker left all of it in the desk of his hotel room. So, without a card, you've been this sort of mystery woman. He, the sound guy, thought you had a lofty title at Applebee's, but couldn't be certain. Wait, did you say you *were* the president?"

"It's a long story, but I handed in my resignation a couple of weeks ago. You're not going to believe this, but I just came in today to pick up a few personal things."

I had been procrastinating making this call. The one day I'd summoned the fortitude to dial 1-800-WHO-R-U had turned out to be the last day she was reachable.

"I guess timing is everything. So, where do you go from here? What's next?"

"I have a number of interesting options I'm looking at. It seems there's a lot of people in the restaurant industry that would like to talk to me."

"I have to believe the president of Applebee's has both an impressive resume and an extensive contacts list."

Suddenly, the minuscule portion of my brain responsible for business development fired a synapse. "I remember, as I was racing away from baggage claim for my *60 Minutes* shoot, you asked if I had any corporate clients. I absolutely do. I don't know what happened at Applebee's—I think that begs a longer conversation—but, please keep me posted on your job search. Whatever company is lucky enough to land you, let me know if they have any television production needs I could fill."

"Well, Tim, you've got a deal. Why don't you give me your cell phone and email? At the very least, I promise to get you some gift certificates from my next stop."

After some searching, I discovered that Julia, formerly of Applebee's, was something of a heralded superstar in the C-level suites of the bigtime corporate restaurant world. Why she would leave Applebee's was a mystery to me, but my conscience was clear. I'd done the right thing and found the hard-to-find, enigmatic exec, and thanked her for that which I had not received. My obligation was complete. I thought that would be the end of it.

It was not the end, but rather just the beginning.

Gordy was right. Eventually, I would have a new corporate client—one involving extensive opportunities.

16

THE ALARM

On the morning of Sept 11, 2001, like most mornings, I habitually turned on the *TODAY* show. With live video of a smoking skyscraper, Katie Couric and Bryant Gumbel were already reporting that a plane had flown into one of the World Trade Center towers. For a moment, I allowed myself to believe we were watching one of the deadliest airline accidents in history. And then, a second commercial jet slammed into the other tower and erased any thoughts I'd had about an accidental disaster.

For three days, all commercial air traffic in the U.S. ceased while our nation mourned, began to investigate the terror, and prepared for what was certain to be a massive and deadly retaliation against those found responsible. The attacks accounted for one of the darkest hours in our nation's history. The ensuing reporting was determined and illuminating as the world's attention focused on the stories coming out of New York and Washington, D.C. One simply couldn't *not* be moved to tears as we all learned more about the 2,977 innocent victims who'd died and the heroic efforts of the courageous first responders. After so many years spent working in network news, I was experiencing an added emotion that compounded the sadness and anger I felt as an American. I was empathetic for the newsmen and women covering the attacks and aftermath. I had covered many different stories, but nothing like this; no one had.

The work of covering 9/11 must have been horrific, gut-wrenching, grueling, and devastatingly sorrowful. I wanted to be there on the ground to see things firsthand, to be part of the network teams reporting the news. But as a freelancer based in Denver, I was geographically isolated from the story. Instead of joining in on the coverage as a participant, I tuned into the coverage as a viewer, which made it even tougher for me to watch as I sat on my hands, helpless to contribute to the coverage. I called old network news friends in New York who had witnessed and lived through the horror to check in on their mental states and general state of exhaustion from the round-the-clock reporting. These were confident and seasoned pros with years and even decades of news experience. Yet, when they spoke of the attacks and the prevailing atmosphere in New York, their voices seemed to waver and crack at times. Fear and uncertainty were everywhere.

With so many people missing and presumed dead, the search for survivors was a race against time. The story unfolded and the networks reported on it from myriad angles. It was a national tragedy of epic proportions—something that we as a nation had not experienced since the Japanese attack on Pearl Harbor in 1941. The modern-day, 24-hour network news machines kicked into overdrive, keeping a mournful and anxious nation well informed.

Once commercial air travel resumed, my knee-jerk reaction was to call those same New York colleagues, offer my cameraman services, and race off to New York or Washington and join the growing network coverage. But I could not.

I was already committed to and deeply involved in a large and expensive international project for one of my corporate clients. In terms of overall importance, the project paled in comparison to the largest terrorist attack in our nation's history, so I was so much more than merely conflicted. I desperately wanted to be part of the news team following the developing 9/11 story. I had worked and was well-aquatinted with many of the executives who I knew would be directing the coverage, as well as the journalists and photojournalists laboring on the ground. They were my peers and I longed to be back on the street with them. But as the executive producer for the corporate project, I felt obligated to see it through, even if that role excluded me from joining the coverage of the biggest news story of my life. That desire would have to be an unfulfilled one, at least initially.

At that time, First Data Corporation was a multi-billion-dollar, multi-national corporation based in the Denver area... and a client of mine. When I'd been a cameraman in Chicago, corporate videos had allowed me to shoot events other than news—an opportunity I'd enjoyed, embraced, and built upon. In Denver, that opportunity had blossomed, vastly expanding my role to one of executive producer (EP). My company was now contracted to produce entire and massive projects commissioned by multinational corporations. Such projects required that I build teams, hiring cameramen, soundmen, lighting directors, editors, and on-camera talent for each specific project, then oversee the entire process from start to finish. These projects were profitable ventures which I found personally rewarding.

One of First Data's wholly-owned subsidiaries was the money order and money transfer company, Western Union, which was experiencing enormous growth, particularly throughout the eastern hemisphere. Both the brain and the beating heart of this overseas corporate success were located in Paris. Months before 9/11, I had been engaged by First Data to produce a video project detailing and hailing these highly profitable Western Union developments. That September, I had already begun production in Denver, and it was not a commitment from which I could simply walk.

As the Western Union project EP, I had arranged for travel, accommodations, schedules, and crew needs well in advance. Given that this was an international production, I double and triple-checked my pre-production work. The cameraman I had booked for the shoot was an old friend from my days in the foreign press corps. Andre Morize had been a longtime staff soundman and, for years, had been based out of the Paris bureau. He and his American cameraman partner, Brian Prentke, made for a solid American-Franco team and, like me, had been part of the backbone of NBC's European operations. We had worked together on stories from Beirut to China and most everything in between. Whether on or off the clock, working or relaxing, Brian and Andre enjoyed each other's company. With Paris as their home, they had developed an appreciation for the finer things in life, so that an unforgettable meal or great bottle of wine were daily occurrences. But even while on assignment in some of the most remote corners of the third world, they were able to discover a palatable meal with passable wine. They had their priorities right.

Both Brian and Andre had been affected by the closure of the NBC Paris bureau in 1990. Brian had been transferred to the London Bureau; Andre had been out of a job. But with the help of Brian's talented and watchful eye, he'd learned the nuances of shooting and had stayed in his beloved Paris, setting up shop as a freelance cameraman. He was my first call when I was hired for the Western Union project, and I was thrilled that he was available for the shoot dates. Working with a reliable friend helped reduce the inherent stress level of a foreign shoot, and he filled out the rest of the crew needs, from sound to lighting, with local hires from his Parisian network of production personnel.

I flew to Paris roughly a week after 9/11. During the lengthy flight, I scoured the newspapers from front to back for news regarding the attacks. The many pieces of the puzzle were just beginning to come into view as details of the suspected team of hijackers began to emerge. The press was anxious to report on it, but this story more than any other demanded accurate and responsible reporting.

I may not have been involved in the coverage, but I was following its every detail.

The shooting schedule for the Western Union project that I had created was almost leisurely by network news standards. We would spend a day interviewing the president of Western Union's European operations. Then, we'd do the same with a couple of supporting senior managers. That initial day would be followed by a couple of days videotaping the day-to-day activity at the corporate offices before finally venturing out to the actual agent locations where hundreds of millions of dollars were being transferred around the globe. I had allowed for an extra day on the front end to help adjust to the time difference and battle jet lag. On schedule, I checked into my luxurious Parisian hotel, where I was greeted, as expected, by a haughty receptionist and shown to my room. After unpacking, I sat in an elegant Louis XVI chair at an elegant Louis XVI desk and phoned Andre to confirm the schedule. *All good.*

I then did the same with the Western Union office. *Not all good.*

The Western Union President had developed some reservations, and he began with, "I've been reading through the script and interview questions for tomorrow's shoot and... I think we should probably talk about this a little before actually shooting."

"Sure. Sure. No problem. We'll have plenty of time to go over everything before we tape anything. I want you to be completely comfortable before putting you on camera."

"Well, that's just it. I don't feel comfortable saying... any of it."

"Huh?"

"You know what, let's talk about this tomorrow at the office. You just got in from the States. And I don't want to do this over the phone. Get some rest and I'll see you in the morning."

"Sounds good. See you at 10 a.m." Alone in my room, I thought, *What was that all about? Do what over the phone?* The script had been approved by the First Data headquarters in Denver. I'd written it weeks before my arrival in Paris, which meant they'd had weeks to become familiar with its content.

Then, I realized: weeks ago meant the script predated 9/11.

The time difference between Denver and Paris, alongside the phone conversation, made for a restless evening. I rebounded the next morning thanks, in part, to a flawless *pain au chocolat* paired with a couple of a textbook *café au laits*. Savoring my breakfast in a street-side Parisian café helped put me at ease before I had to navigate the uncertain waters that lay ahead at Western Union.

After breakfast, I arrived at a five-story Haussmannian-style building that looked more like an urban mansion than an office. I met Andre and his production crew in front of the building. They were eager to begin loading in camera, audio, and lighting equipment and get the ball rolling. Because I was uncertain how exactly my pre-production "chat" with the boss would go, I mentioned it might be best if perhaps they chilled at a nearby café. Telling a Frenchman to have a coffee and croissant while getting paid will never start an argument, and Andre and his team happily embraced my suggestion.

Once I was inside, I found that the structure's classic exterior belied the glass and steel interior of the modern-looking Western Union offices. I guess if you're in the business of electronically transferring billions of dollars around the globe, hi-tech is a good look. They were expecting me and I was led through an expansive, active office floor to the president's corner office. He was warm and welcoming, and looked every bit the successful corporate executive dressed in a perfectly tailored suit. I sat across from him at his desk as he asked about my trip and accommodations—how I liked Paris. It was your standard routine, door-opening small talk; the kind of banter that on any other day I'd be happy to exchange. On this day, I was less interested in small talk and more anxious to gauge his comfort level, or lack thereof, with the video we were about to shoot.

"You mentioned on the phone yesterday that you're not comfortable with the script. How so?"

Holding up the script and referencing it, he said, "Everything in here is accurate. The sales data, the reported revenue... everything's correct. But going forward, everything's changed. Any projections or forecasts that we may have had are out the window. I, *we*, have no idea what the future holds. I spoke with my superiors back in Denver last night. We all agree, we just can't go on camera, on the record, talking about future sales numbers and earnings data because we just don't know. No one does."

America was reeling, and sending aftershocks around the globe in places like… Paris.

The entire project was canceled; not postponed. *Canceled*. To borrow from a production metaphor, my total production would go "dark" in the City of Light.

At that time, my immediate world was focused on producing a corporate video. The much greater world in which I resided was preoccupied with uncertainty and pondering whether the pre-9/11 life we had all known would be irrevocably changed. This man was right. It would have been foolish and reckless to talk about business forecasts and past successes so soon after 9/11. However, that reasoning did not erase the considerable pre-production time and money which I had already committed to the project.

From my work on previous First Data projects, I knew them to be a highly ethical, stand-up company. But I needed to address the elephant in the room. So, I continued with, "I completely understand. You're totally right. I would never want you or anyone at First Data to go on camera and state anything that you don't 100% steadfastly believe. I only wish we could have decided this before I arrived in Paris. We have a five-member production team standing by at a nearby café, ready to begin the shoot."

"Look, don't give that a second thought. You and your team have done a tremendous job up to this point and this certainly isn't your fault. We'll take care of all of your expenses and make sure everyone's paid in full. I hope at some point we can resurrect this project and actually work together."

It was comforting to know that company management was empathetic to my dilemma and was agreeing to pay in full for a project that would never be realized. I expressed my gratitude for the company's understanding. Since I no longer needed a week in Paris to produce a canceled project, their travel department helped change my hotel and airline reservations. I then called Andre and the team, who by now were on their third cup of coffee and second pack of Gauloise cigarettes.

"Andre, thanks for waiting. Change of plans."

In his thick French accent, he responded, "What do you mean... shaunz of plonz? We are not shooting here?"

"No, bud, we are not shooting here. We are not shooting anywhere. They pulled the plug. The shoot is... how you say... *fini*."

Alarmed, Andre responded with, *"FINI?!* How can be *fini*? We are booked for zee next shree days."

"Not to worry, *mon ami*. I'm disappointed, but it's okay... everyone gets paid." Yes, I was disappointed—or, maybe more disillusioned—with the morning's outcome. Given that these were the scary and uncertain days following 9/11, though, there was plenty of disillusionment to go around; mine was but a small and insignificant piece of the whole. But the company had agreed to compensate everyone. And, I realized, I was in Paris with newfound spare time on my hands. Perhaps there was a better reaction than wallowing in disillusionment.

"Andre, I have an idea. What's the best restaurant in the area? Instead of shooting today, I'd like to buy the crew a nice long lunch. Or, I mean, First Data would like to buy us a nice long lunch."

As any true Parisian would, Andre knew the city like the back of his hand. After he made a brief call from his cell phone, we were soon seated around a large table draped with a white linen tablecloth, ensconced in an elegant Parisian dining room. It was an impeccably served, four-hour affair. When one plate was finished, a new and deliciously differently one followed; when a wine glass was emptied, it was immediately refilled. The conversation flowed as seamlessly as the Burgundy as Andre and I got caught up and relived the glory days from our network news past. We had both spent numerous tours in Beirut during the war, and in particular in the days before the 1983 Marine barracks bombing. We'd been to Bali on presidential summits. We'd recounted the D-Day invasion in Normandy with WWII veterans. We'd beamed live *TODAY* show coverage from places like the Roman Colosseum, the Great Wall of China, the Notre Dame Cathedral, and the Grand Canal in Venice, to name but a few of the locations. In that four-hour lunch, we managed only to scratch the surface of all the news stories we'd been a part of. But we also managed to momentarily escape the inescapable aftermath of 9/11.

After I paid the not so inconsequential bill, I said adieu to Andre and his team, promising to keep in touch. Outside, it was a lovely afternoon. With its wide, tree-lined boulevards, omnipresent ornate lampposts, and magnificent architecture, I have always found Paris to be one of the most walkable cities on Earth, so I decided to forego a taxi and stroll back to my hotel. The walk offered me a chance to reset from the morning meeting and reflect. The rush hour traffic was building. Pedestrians stopped off at their markets and bakeries en route home. On the surface, it all appeared normal. But below the surface, there was a sea of anxiety being felt around the world. My little corporate cancellation was a mere drop in the bucket. Returning to normalcy was a long way off.

When I arrived back at my hotel, I called Denver to inform Amy of the developments. I'd be returning home early. Under normal circumstances, that would have been good news, but these were not normal circumstances, and even a wine-infused lunch couldn't conceal my unease.

When she asked how it was going, I could only respond truthfully, "They had reservations about doing the video 'at this time' and canceled the entire project."

"The whole thing? You were supposed to be in Paris for a week. And then come home and edit for weeks back here! They're not doing any of it?"

"Nada. Zilch. Nothing, which is what I'm likely to have in the near future. At least First Data agreed to cover the production costs. But I had cleared my calendar to shoot and edit what I thought was going to be a major, time-consuming video. And it's not just First Data. I have a feeling the entire business world will be on edge for the foreseeable future and cutting way back on any corporate videos. That office at Western Union was full of uncertainty and fear. I think execs everywhere are feeling the same way." She knew my alarm was real and justified, and I was not in the mood to be consoled. "Look, I'll see you when I get home tomorrow. Give Alexa a kiss for me."

"Okay, safe travels."

The next morning, after navigating my way through passport control in Charles de Gaulle Airport, I was perusing the international papers at a newsstand before boarding my flight to Denver. Suddenly, police began swarming the gate area, urgently questioning passengers about a single unattended black leather briefcase. The loudspeakers soon blared warnings in French and English, all urging the absentee owner of said briefcase to come forth and claim it. *No takers.* All of us anxious international travelers were then herded up and ordered to hurriedly evacuate the gate area. The bomb squad entered to encase the briefcase in an indestructible, bomb-proof housing, and, after three ear-piercing whistle shrieks, we heard a muffled but loud thud resonate throughout the terminal. Some absent-minded businessman had misplaced his stylish attaché, which was now a thing of the past... just like the comfortable halcyon pre-9/11 life so many of us had led. The world was now living on a razor-sharp edge. A forgotten briefcase that would previously have been viewed innocuously was now seen as a ticking timebomb.

The familiarity of being back in Denver and the comfort of reuniting with Amy and Alexa helped put things in perspective, somewhat. My family was safe and well. I hugged them both with an embrace that lasted much longer than usual. It was a chance to exhale and be thankful. I shared with them the story of the controlled explosion at Charles du Gaulle—controlled, but disturbing nonetheless. They were shocked, as well, as this was something we'd never experienced, or even heard of before.

It had been a long travel day. After a while, I poured a glass of Cabernet Sauvignon from a prestigious Napa Valley winery and retreated to our backyard deck, which looked straight into the Rocky Mountains; a majestic vista that, coupled with the wine, offered me another chance to exhale and be thankful. It was the kind of late September warm afternoon in Colorado that can change in an instant. The 80-degree temperatures and deep blue skies vanished as ominous, lightning-filled thunder clouds rolled in over the Continental Divide. I had seen it on many occasions before this one, but this time I viewed it as a disturbing metaphor for the menacing climate of the times. 9/11 had darkened the once sun-filled skies, and no one knew how or when the darkness would end.

My trip to Paris had, for me, reinforced the intensified level of uncertainty in which we were living. The only certainty was that the U.S. would pursue, to death, the perpetrators of 9/11. It was also certain that the U.S. news networks would report on every step of that pursuit. Devoid of my Western Union commitment, I was suddenly and indefinitely available. The time was right to offer up my services to those same news networks.

Throughout my television career, I've worn many different hats. In September of 2001, I'd departed Paris as an executive producer, but NBC knew me best as a cameraman. A dependable, world-traveled, network cameraman who didn't mind the dirt that so often accustoms news coverage. As I sipped my Cab and watched the developing storm, it appeared the time was right to exchange my producer's blue blazer for my cameraman's Velcro vest and join the news teams following the story of the 9/11 attacks.

Each day brought news about the attacks and the terrorists who'd perpetrated them. Behind the scenes, the Bush White House was working around the clock to develop a retaliatory strategy. Osama bin Laden, al-Qaeda, and the Taliban were emerging as key players. America had been attacked, but this was much more than just an American story. President Bush reassured a nervous nation by saying, "We will not tire, we will not falter, and we will not fail." He simultaneously put the world on notice. "Every nation in every region now has a decision to make. Either you are with us, or you are with the terrorists."[4]

Stacy Brady had facilitated my involvement with *Where in the World*. She would be the best person to contact regarding joining the 9/11 news coverage. As Senior Vice President of Field Operations, she was "in the know." But she was also a dear friend of twenty years, and I was concerned about how she might be holding up. I'd spoken to her right after the attacks to verify her safety, but I needed an update.

As a veteran news pro, she had her emotions in check, but

4   Bush, George W. (2001, September 20). Live Television Address to Joint meeting of Congress.

she was moved by the many stories of insufferable loss and death-defying courage that had been reported.

"How are you guys holding up?" I asked.

"It's been tough. It seems like everybody at NBC knew someone who either worked at the World Trade Center or with the NYFD. It's like... collective suffering, and it's really difficult to remove yourself from the story."

"I can't imagine. This changes everything. We don't even know yet how much our lives will be changed."

"You're right. There's no going back. And, this thing, this story is just beginning to unfold."

"For instance?"

"We have no idea what's next. We're just basing people all over the world, trying to prepare for what might happen next. I mean, people are standing by in places like Cairo and Istanbul just in case. Everyone believes there will be a response. Obviously, the White House is being pretty tight-lipped about everything and we need to be very careful about what we report. But no one knows for sure."

"Well, if you had to guess, and yours would be a very... educated guess, where would you go?"

"Wait a second. Why are you asking me? I mean, are you available and interested in going overseas again? Can I put you in the mix?!"

"I just returned from overseas, although it wasn't exactly combat duty." I explained the whole ordeal of the Western Union shoot cancellation. I also explained that I was absolutely available and eager to be a part of "the mix" covering this historic story. I had no desire to sit by and simply read about it in *The Denver Post* or watch as others filed reports from abroad.

I pressed her a little further, "I know you can't say too much and I don't want you to divulge national secrets here, but I'm not that interested in twiddling my thumbs in Cairo if the story is elsewhere. Soooo, I know you can't say, but... talk to me."

Her response was almost whispered into the phone, as if we were discussing highly classified intel.

"Pakistan. There are a lot of hushed conversations going on right now about Afghanistan, but it's a closed country. You can't get there. We might be positioning people both to the north and south, poised on both borders... protectively, should something happen."

"What kind of time commitment are you looking at?"

"You should be prepared to be gone at least two months."

"Something tells me there aren't direct connections between Denver and Pakistan."

"*Ha*. I think you're probably right. Those movements are being coordinated by the London Bureau. That would be your first stop. They'll work with you on getting a visa and everything else you'll need. Are you good with this? You, uh... want to run this by your family?"

"I'm a yes. But you're absolutely correct. I'll run this by the home front and get back to you tomorrow."

I had talked, at length, with Amy about the 9/11 attacks and what a horrible tragedy they were. But I had not shared with her my thoughts about joining the coverage team. Working on the story in New York and Washington had been irrelevant, as my Western Union project had looked to monopolize my time for quite some time. Once I had returned to Denver with time on my hands, things had changed—and I needed to share with her my thoughts on those changes, in-depth.

Eighteen years before this, we were a young married couple when my big break with NBC News moved us to Europe. At that time, the biggest story of my career was the war in Lebanon. I lobbied my bosses incessantly to be a part of that story. They eventually acquiesced and I spent numerous tours covering the Lebanese conflict. I became consumed with the headline-making war coverage that was Beirut. It was an intoxicating experience for a malleable, 25-year-old cameraman. My infatuation with that war story was a major distraction, but one of many that distracted my focus from my marriage to my career, and ultimately led to the break-up of our first marriage.

I never saw myself as a "combat cameraman," although covering conflicts was very much an adrenaline-producing and intense part of my job as an overseas staff cameraman during the 80s. There were and always will be plenty of wars and "conflicts" for international journalists to cover. But as I've noted before, Alexa was a newborn when Desert Storm erupted, and I was happy to sit that one out with her in my arms.

I had been on assignment in the former Yugoslavia in the mid-80s. The ethnic hatred between the various inhabiting clans was seething just below the surface then, but kept in check by the Communist regime. When the Serbo-Croatian war blew up in '91(and lasted until 1995), I found it to be a complexly interesting and yet gruesome story. And, it was yet another opportunity for me to cover yet another international crisis. But with a wife, pre-school daughter, and budding production company, I chose to pass on covering ethnic cleansing and genocide in the Balkans. With years of network experience and solid contacts in New York, those were the types of stories I could have covered if I'd chosen to. I had not. The attack on America was a story I was choosing to cover. I just needed to break it to Amy.

Amy was still a highly paid attorney and very much in demand, just no longer for Boston Market. The company's mismanagement and over-expansion had caused the stock price to collapse, so much so that it had eventually led to a bankruptcy filing. McDonald's bought the company for pennies on the dollar. At that point, Amy decided to leave the corporate restaurant business and take a position at a prestigious Denver law firm, where her future was bankable. I had built up a solid business with my production company, but Amy and I both knew my freelancing future was never going to be guaranteed—and certainly not solid—in the uncertain weeks and months after 9/11.

My desire to cover the U.S. response to 9/11 was far more about journalism than income jitters, however. My news roots began to sprout as a cameraman in the local markets of Dayton, Ohio and Chicago, Illinois. They then became intractably entrenched in 1983 when I joined the network and shouldered an NBC News camera in West Germany. As for so many others who came up in the news business, those roots of mine run deep and true. To follow the perpetrators of 9/11 with the news media was something I had to do.

Amy and I had known each other for too long. I saw no need to sugarcoat my intent. "This cancellation of the whole Western Union thing has me thinking of the immediate future. I suddenly find myself with a lot of… availability on my hands. So, I called 30 Rock just to check in. It looks like they're starting to follow the international implication, post-9/11."

"Just to 'check in,' huh?"

"C'mon. I go way back with many of those people; covered a lot of ground with them. I'm *still* covering ground with them."

"And so, what did they mean by… how did you put it… international implications?"

"They'll be going through the wreckage at the Trade Center for a long time. But the next phase of this story is somewhere out there, well beyond New York and Washington. The government is certain to go after whoever is behind this, wherever it leads. That's the international part."

She immediately sensed where this conversation was leading, and it was headed in a direction she wasn't fond of.

"Okay, well, who did you talk to in New York? What did they say?"

A few years earlier, we had attended Stacy's wedding in the posh Long Island suburb of Glen Cove, New York. As two bright and successful career women, the mutual respect they'd felt had been genuine, so Amy and Stacy had immediately hit it off. They'd both ascended to positions of power in the male-dominated worlds of law and network news, admiring each other's drive to get there. So, when I revealed to Amy that the "who" in New York was Stacy, it added weight and substance to my aforementioned NBC conversation.

"I talked with Stacy Brady. I'm sure you remember her from the wedding. As V.P. for Field Ops, she's in charge of covering NBC's ass when it comes to global news coverage, which means getting the right people and equipment into all of the right places. Afghanistan looks like it's the bull's eye, but you can't just waltz into Kabul these days."

"Afghanistan!? You're seriously thinking about going to Af-fucking-ganistan? Well, I'm glad you shared this with me. Jesus. You're not twenty-five anymore, and this isn't Beirut. I hope this isn't about you trying to relive some of your crazy, impetuous youth."

"Of course not. I have no desire to relive my youth. It was exhausting in my 20s. I can't imagine keeping that pace in my 40s. I'm quite content "maturing" comfortably. I just don't want to grow... complacent. Look, this is a major news story. 9/11!

And I have a chance to be a part of it, to witness it firsthand."

"I get it. And, I know that you're a little freaked out over the cancellation of the Western Union thing in Paris. I just don't want you picking up and racing into a warzone again. Look around you. You have a family now. There's a beautiful loving daughter to think about. It's not just work and your career anymore."

"I'm aware, trust me. And, I'm not going into Afghanistan... at least not initially. It would be Pakistan... initially. And, I'm not 'racing into a warzone.'"

"You don't know that! You can't say that!"

She was right. I had no idea what I would encounter, should I go. I was trying to reassure her of something I was uncertain about. And, in the process, I overreached.

"What I meant is that it's unlikely I'll be on the frontlines. And, it's not like I'm going it alone. This is with NBC News. I used to work for them full-time. They are a great big international company and this is what they, *we*, do. It's what I *used* to do regularly when I lived overseas all those years, remember?"

"Yes, it was your dream job and I became a casualty of your work. We separated and I moved back to the states. Then we eventually divorced. Oh, I remember it vividly."

"Okay, I deserve that. But my point is, I'll be part of a much larger team of seasoned pros. Hell, you probably know most of the people I'll be working with."

"How long would you be gone?"

"Two months, tops."

"That's a long time to be gone. Well, clearly, you've given this some thought and this is something you want to do. I know what motivates you... the reasons why you need to be there. I get it. But I also remember sitting in our apartment in Bonn,

Germany while you were covering the war in Beirut, wondering if you were okay; if you were dead or alive. I'm not relishing sitting here in our beautiful home being a single parent to our beautiful daughter and reliving that same emotional roller coaster ride... again."

She was right, again. There was no way she could block out and forget about the fears and worries she had experienced 18 years prior. We were both older and wiser. But this was still a perilous assignment. As much as I would think about my family and call home, I couldn't empathize with what Amy and Alexa would be going through while I was away on assignment in Pakistan. And there would be no way for them to empathize with what I was about to experience, or even know if I was safe or not. I was asking a lot. Understanding was the best I could hope for—Amy's understanding that this was something I needed to do. And, in turn, I needed to understand that my absence would be arduous for her and Alexa back home.

She didn't like the idea I was proposing for a variety of reasons. It was understandable for her to be upset. But knowing the importance of the assignment and how it weighed on me, she wouldn't stand in my way when it came to joining the developing post-9/11 story. How much this would conjure up painful memories from the past and what toll this would extract on our relationship was unknown.

The next morning, I phoned Stacy regarding next steps. She was thrilled to have me on board and confirmed that London would be my first stop on this international news story.

17

Two Months Inside

While the assignment carried with it the possibility of serious peril, I was looking forward to spending a few danger-free days in London with old friends. Since returning to the States in 1990, I had covered international stories and traveled through Europe on assignment. Those trips had been opportunities to reconnect with former colleagues. But I had not visited the London bureau for 11 years. It was always a place that kept buzzing with activity. NBC had relocated it to a more affordable location on the outskirts of London, but with the closure of the bureaus in Paris, Frankfurt, and Rome, London had become an even busier hub. Post-9/11, the London bureau controlled the movement of the "pieces" on the international chessboard of news coverage—beefing up staff and facilities where needed while trying to anticipate the next moves of a very secretive U.S. military. London was where I would get briefed on what our coverage, our *ever-changing* coverage, might look like. It was also where I would be inoculated for the myriad diseases awaiting in Pakistan. Thus, I received shots. Lots and lots of shots. Of course, not all maladies or threats can be prevented by inoculation.

The staff at the London bureau had remained amazingly consistent, with a few new faces but very little turnover during my 11-year absence. There were numerous cameramen, soundmen, editors, engineers, reporters, and producers with whom I reconnected and briefly caught up. Some of my old "mates" had already made their way to Pakistan, where they were setting up shop in Islamabad. I would be joining their growing team.

The NBC international team was one I felt at ease with joining, or more accurately rejoining. Since returning to the States, I had carved out my path with a healthy mixture of freelance shooting and producing. I was proud to have built a diverse client list that reflected that mixture, and it was a list that I hoped to continually expand. I was also enjoying the new and added responsibilities and creativity that producing afforded me. I suppose, to some, jumping from Denver corporate producer to overseas news cameraman might be a jarring transition. It was not difficult for me, though, as I felt comfortable in both roles. I had seen so much of the world through the viewfinder of a network news camera that it always felt familiar, no matter how foreign the land might be.

The London bureau chief introduced me to Mark, a young freelance soundman. He had proven himself as a reliable sound engineer on assignments in and around the UK. Although he had never previously covered any conflicts, he had voiced an interest in working in Pakistan and he would be my soundman/partner for the next two months. At times, the news business can resemble a military operation. You do what you're told, go where you're told, and perform to the best of your ability. I had requested this assignment, so I wasn't about to question whether this partnership made sense... at least not at this early stage.

We were booked on PIA, Pakistan International Airlines, for

the London to Islamabad flight. With our 20 plus cases of equipment, we proceeded to the PIA check-in counter at Heathrow Airport, which was a madhouse. Most of the passengers were dressed in the traditional Muslim hijabs and tunics, and appeared to be in a frantic hurry to get back home. Heated conversations between harried passengers and overwhelmed desk agents seemed to be the norm. I'd thought, with an impending U.S. military invasion of neighboring Afghanistan, people would be fleeing like refugees to get *out* of Islamabad. Not so. Our flight was oversold; every seat was taken and then some. We finally made it through security and I headed straight to an airport bar for a few stiff drinks. Once on the aircraft, I settled into my business class seat for the eight-hour flight. I knew this would differ from other business class flights. PIA is the official airline for Pakistan, which is more accurately known as the Islamic Republic of Pakistan. Any country whose official title begins with, "The Islamic Republic of..." is going to strictly prohibit the consumption of alcohol. That was the regulation on my PIA flight, on all PIA flights, and it was the law throughout the entire country of Pakistan. I wasn't going there for a vacation or a wine tasting. This was going to be an endurance test of news coverage on foreign turf. However, that would likely intensify my longing for the unattainable glass (or bottle) of wine at the end of each long news day.

Mark and I landed in Islamabad. While Karachi was and is, by far, the largest city in Pakistan, Islamabad is the capital city and power base for this important central Asian nation. Baggage claim at the Islamabad airport was total confusion—a madhouse that made the madhouse at Heathrow check-in look like an organized military parade. People were everywhere trying to force themselves through the crowd to the conveyer, wrestling with their oversized belongings and, in the process, their fellow passengers. It was a mosh pit of people, baggage, and commotion that produced a prevalent and pungent aroma of international body odor. After fighting and grappling with our fellow passengers, we eventually claimed all of our extended belongings and proceeded through customs, which was surprisingly uneventful. The customs officials were more preoccupied with the sheer volume of people than our couple of carts of TV equipment, and we cleared customs without any hassle, after which we were met by our NBC driver.

We snaked our way through the sprawling city. I'd traveled to and seen all sorts of foreign capitals from London to Manilla, but found Islamabad to be an odd mixture. Of course, the landscape was dotted with the ubiquitous mosques and minarets of the Islamic world. Mixed in with the religious structures were enormous, palatial government buildings framed by manicured lawns and super-wide boulevards. This was a capital city on display. After a couple of turns, we'd transitioned to crowded business districts looking as though they had just "popped up," complete with make-shift power lines run to the various tenants. Islamabad was a community planned to showcase the glorious seat of government and its illustrious political leaders. But the fresh-coat-of-paint façade the Pakistani planners had applied to their capital belied the reality of the neighboring towns and villages, where overcrowded inhabitants resided in dilapidated dwellings.

We arrived at the Islamabad Marriot Hotel, the epicenter for most western visitors to the capital and the place where NBC had set up its operations. The hotel compound was surrounded by the standard concrete barriers meant to deter terrorist activity. I had first seen these kinds of barriers in Beirut, where car bombs exploded frequently, destroying buildings and killing and maiming civilians. Sadly, they were not unique to Beirut or even Lebanon. They were common in many countries where suicide bombers had previously identified an easy target. Before 9/11, America had been mostly sheltered from such bombings, which was one of the reasons we'd been so ill-prepared for those attacks.

I recognized the impenetrable barriers at the Marriot and knew they'd been put in place to safeguard those inside. Even so, I had an eerie feeling checking in. With so many Westerners housed in a single location, it would be like shooting fish in a barrel for any dedicated suicide bomber. A successful attack would surely be followed by a VIP reception in Allah's martyrdom for the responsible jihadist. Thankfully, the hotel would not be targeted during my two-month stay. However, seven years later, suicide bombers would somehow navigate a dump truck filled with explosives and detonate it at the front of the hotel, killing 54 people and wounding 266.

After check-in, I stowed my bag and camera equipment in my room and met up with Mark in the NBC "Islamabad bureau." On the hotel's third floor, three adjacent rooms had been converted into a makeshift office space. The beds had been removed and replaced with desks. Added phone lines, faxes, printers, computer cables, and terminals were strewn everywhere. Three clocks on the wall displayed the time zones of Islamabad, London, and New York. An old producer friend was running the show.

Charlie Ryan had been a London-based staff producer. We'd first met in Beirut in 1983 on my first trip there. We'd worked together on many stories since. Like me, he had moved back to the States and had been living in Atlanta when the world was shocked by 9/11. Now, 18 years after our first meeting in Lebanon, we both felt the need to connect to yet another major story with hazardous implications.

I introduced Mark to the NBC News team, almost all of whom I'd known for years. Keith Miller was a longtime friend. He was a Rome-based correspondent and I had been a Rome-based cameraman. Craig White was the most renowned cameraman in the New York bureau. In addition to the *Where in the World is Matt Lauer?*, we had also covered political campaigns and conventions together. He had witnessed the attack on and collapse of the World Trade Center, and felt compelled to follow the story to Pakistan. Meanwhile, I worked the room, getting caught up with those I knew and getting to know those I didn't.

Charlie approached me. "It's been a while. How ya doing? You look good. Life's treating you well. How was the flight in?"

"Thanks. Yeah, life's good. No complaints. The flight was... crowded, and about what you'd expect from Pakistan Airlines. Most of the toilets backed up. No booze. Terrible food. Couldn't wait to get off the damn plane."

"Ah, sounds like a fun ride. Well, we have another one for you. I mean, not right now. Decompress, spend a couple of days getting over your jetlag. But don't get too comfortable. You're heading west. We want you to hook up with our correspondent Mike Taibbi—I think you know Mike. He's in a town called Quetta on the Afghanistan border. It's not too far from Kandahar."

I had an immediate flashback to those mountains in Lebanon. I reminded myself I'd asked for this assignment.

"The Afghanistan border, eh? Kandahar. Sounds... strategic?"

"That's a good way to put it. Things are very... fluid. We need to have that part of the country covered, just in case. Once you get there, it could be a "wait and see" kind of news coverage. It's a completely different place from Islamabad. Here, things are all neat and orderly—well, for this part of the world. But out there, it's more like the wild west. We just need to try and be prepared for whatever happens."

"Whatever happens" referred to the many possible scenarios for the invasion of Afghanistan by U.S. forces. Kandahar was the Taliban stronghold; their headquarters. Quetta was only a hop-skip-and-jump away. It was the closest Pakistani position from which to base coverage of an attack on Kandahar. Any U.S. mission would be targeted to defeat and decimate Osama bin Laden and his al-Qaeda terrorists responsible for the 9/11 attacks. But the Taliban ruled Afghanistan with a brutal Muslim fist and had provided a haven to bin Laden when it came to training and planning the attacks. The two groups were Islamic partners in crime.

Having just arrived in Islamabad and with a quick turn-around to Quetta in my future, it was time to phone Colorado and update the home front on my travel plans. Fighting jetlag, I was up early, which worked in my favor. There was an 11-hour time difference between home and work; 6 a.m. in Islamabad is 7 a.m. in Denver. I figured this was an ideal time to call, as Alexa would relish a break from homework and Amy would be home from work, already enjoying a glass of Pinot Grigio.

Fighting through the international phone delay, there was a pause after Amy's hello. I followed up with, "Greetings from the Islamabad Marriott. Can you hear me okay?"

"Yes, I can hear you fine, except for the lovely delay that I remember so fondly from Germany. Marriott, eh? Just like being in America."

"Just, except for the minarets, mosques, hourly call to prayers, turbans, robes, and oh, lack of a hotel bar... as in the whole damn country. That little wrinkle of their society might take some gettin' used to."

"I do feel for you. I almost feel guilty pouring this second glass of Pinot Grigio."

"Ouch. You know how to hurt a guy."

"Just know there is a fully stocked wine cellar here waiting for you upon your return. I'll check on it regularly. Can I change the subject? How are you?"

"I'm good. NBC's taken over a few rooms on the third floor and turned them into a makeshift bureau. That will be our headquarters for the foreseeable future. Most of the people I've met, I've already worked with before."

There was still a slight edge to her voice, showing her upset with my sudden departure. But she was trying to be positive and supportive. "Well, that's got to be comforting. And, over time, I'll bet the Marriott might even feel like a home away from home."

"Perhaps. But I won't be here long enough to find out. In a day or two, my soundman and I are joining a correspondent and producer in Quetta; some remote town near the Afghanistan border, close to Kandahar. It's a precautionary move, a 'wait and see' approach in case something develops in that region. At any rate, it looks like the Islamabad Marriott is only going to be a brief stop on the way to somewhere or something else."

I sensed this added information and the uncertainty it conveyed had put her even more on edge. I wanted her to be informed of my whereabouts, but it seemed as if this had been too much too quickly. As the wife of a news guy, she was far more informed on world events than your average corporate attorney. She knew buzz words like "Afghanistan border" and "Kandahar" could be interpreted as "dangerous." She paused and, sounding somewhat startled, she resumed, "Okay, well, uhm… Alexa is upstairs doing homework. I know she wants to talk to you. Just let her know you're safe in Pakistan. It might be too much for a 5th grader to follow your every move all over Pakistan and Afghanistan."

I would never intentionally alarm my daughter, but Amy's point was well taken. Keep it simple. Exciting, not dangerous.

I could hear her call up the stairs, "Alexa, your dad's on the phone." Which was followed by the sound of rapid footsteps bouncing down the stairs, the last three of which were taken in one giant leap and the landing of which caused a loud thud.

Alexa grabbed the phone from her mom. "Dad, are you in Pakistan now?"

"Hey, kiddo! Yes, I am. I flew in from London, just like we talked about."

"I looked at it on a map. You're like way far away, like half-way around the world in the middle of nowhere. What's it like?"

"Well, remember when we went to Europe and the buildings and stuff looked different from home? And the people spoke different languages?"

"Yeah, so it's like being in Europe?"

"Not exactly. But it's different like that. Way different from home. They wear different clothes and speak a different language and eat different foods."

"What do they eat there?"

"I'm not exactly sure because I just got here. But they probably don't eat a lot of hamburgers and pizzas like we do."

"Too bad for them. Well, what time is it there?"

She was an inquisitive, curious, wonderous little nine-year-old sponge, soaking up as much information as she could. I always wanted her to be aware and knowledgeable of other countries and cultures, and felt fortunate that my work could help expand her horizons. We had only just scratched the surface, but our enlightening back-and-forth had brought a huge smile to my face.

"That's cool, Dad. Mom says I gotta get ready for bed. Here she is. I miss you. Love you!"

"I miss you and love you, too, Sugar. Night."

Amy came back on the phone to say, "It's getting late here. I'm glad you called. Keep us posted once you get to wherever you're going. We miss you."

"I sure will and I miss you guys, too. Talk soon. Bye."

It was still early morning when I hung up, and I had plenty of time to reflect on the call. I had traveled extensively and knew those calls home could be a double-edged sword. They could foster a closeness between the participants, if even momentarily. Or, they could be a depressing reminder of the distance between you and the ones you loved. But my assignment had just begun. I would be gone for at least two months, so it made little sense to turn melancholy or depressed.

There was another feeling that ran through me; one which created a conflict within me. I should not have been so forthright about my movements. Amy was well-aware of all the scrapes I'd been in while covering the news. Perhaps I didn't need to share with her more of the same. Perhaps she didn't need to know I was relocating to the border. But if I'd been candid with her in the past about all that, it would feel odd to begin to conceal things now. If I couldn't share with her what I was experiencing, I would be closing off a part of our long relationship, even if my actions were well-intended. Maybe it was best to keep things to myself. Maybe she would benefit from not knowing. But curtailing or "closing off" communication on one topic could lead to a general decline in communication. When people stop talking to one another, the distance between them can grow. In the worst cases, they become isolated from one another. I'd seen it happen to other married couples. I didn't want it to happen to us.

As I prepared for my trip to Quetta, I referenced a well-written book on the region. During my stay over in London, I had purchased *Taliban: Islam, Oil and the New Great Game in Central Asia* by Ahmed Rashid. I'd devoured it from cover to cover during the eight-hour flight to Islamabad. The Pakistani journalist and author Ahmed Rashid began covering Afghanistan in 1979 and watched the first Russian tanks roll into the country. He was a frequent visitor to Afghanistan as the CIA-backed Mujahidin battled and eventually defeated the Red Army. And, he continued to cover the country during the Taliban's bloody ascent to power. His book offered an in-depth analysis of a complicated situation and was an indispensable read for me or anyone trying to make sense of the entire region. The book explained that Kandahar was the base of the Taliban and home of its leader, Mullah Omar. Furthermore, Kandahar and Quetta shared a closeness running much deeper than the mere proximity of the two towns.

Much of the world connects to a national identity. At the Olympics, U.S. athletes are wrapped in the stars and stripes. At World Cup soccer matches, entire stadiums are filled with flag-waving, rabid fans gathered in enthusiastic support of their national team. But, in many remote parts of the world that I visited, I found that nationalism takes a backseat to tribalism. Regardless of whether you're a citizen of, say, Afghanistan or Pakistan, you are first a member of a tribe, and on both sides of that international border, that tribe was and is Pashtun. It's a bond grown over centuries and one that's sealed in blood. I knew from reading *Taliban* that the Taliban was made up of Pashtuns, just the same as most of Quetta's residents. The fact that the two were located on opposite sides of an international border was meaningless. It seemed medieval to me, but this is the way that that region, and others like it, exist and operate even today.

It was a brief hour-and-30-minute flight from Islamabad to Quetta. I soon realized Western Pakistan was a barren, isolated, sparsely populated, and dusty area. We piled our gear and ourselves into a small taxi and made our way to the hotel to connect with our NBC News colleagues.

Upon arriving at our hotel, it was evident Quetta was on edge. The hotel was inside a walled compound of sorts and offered the "best" accommodations in town—and by "best," I mean reliable electricity with generators as back-up and running water. NBC and other news organizations were staying there. As a result, for added security, a moveable yet impenetrable barrier had been installed at the entrance. This was not done for decorative effect, but rather to discourage suicide bombers hellbent on either disrupting Western news reporting or grabbing a few headlines for themselves. Heavily armed Pakistani guards toting AK-47s manned the gate and roamed the grounds. They'd been hired to provide an added sense of security, but that wasn't exactly the sense I was feeling. I just didn't know exactly whose team they were on—whose allegiance they were sworn to. This was not the sort of hospitality you'd find at an American or European hotel, but we weren't pulling into Paris. The hotel staff did their best to extended a cordial greeting at check-in, but there was nothing about this place that said, "WELCOME."

I walked the grounds and realized that, at four stories, the hotel towered above most of the city's one-story mud and plaster structures. Its rooftop provided a prime perspective from which to photograph the sprawl of this third world city. It was also the optimum place from which to broadcast updates or live shots. We met up with correspondent Mike Taibbi and Ara, a freelance producer from the States, to discuss the timing and frequency of these live shots.

Technology tends to shrink (see *cell phones*, *hard drives*, and *calculators*). In 2001, the hardware required to pack into the field and set up on location to broadcast live TV signals had already shrunk considerably. That was a double-edged sword. The most reliable way to broadcast the strongest, cleanest signal was to pair a skilled tech with a massive satellite dish pointed into the heavens. But much smaller, laptop-sized devices had been created as a means to make a live transmission more portable and... streamlined. Forget about the skilled engineer who's knowledgeable in things like electromagnetic spectrum and bandwidth. A producer or crew could unpack one of these suitcases, dial a cell number, and voila. Live TV. But the first generation of these smaller, suitcase-sized devices was fraught with issues. At best, they were capable of delivering herky-jerky, grainy live video of a correspondent on camera. There were bothersome delays in the video and audio, and often as not, the transmission unexpectedly "dropped out" or died altogether.

The rooftop live shots were only a part of our day and night routines. We would take our gear into town and report on what life was like in Quetta and that part of the world. Islam played (and plays) a major role in that life, and the various Muslim clerics are like powerful priests whose word is gold. The only problem is, while they read from the same book, the Koran, they all have many different viewpoints. I certainly don't speak Pashto, the language of the region, and we were never allowed to record in their most sacred place, inside a mosque. But through our translators, it was evident some preached a moderate interpretation of the Koran as well as those who preached a more extreme and violent interpretation, full of hatred for the West and anti-American rhetoric.

And this anti-American venom was coming on the heels of the 9/11 attacks. Around the world, there had been an outpouring of compassion for America and her loss. That compassion was not on display in Quetta.

I found that religion there went well beyond what we know as Sunday services. Before my travel to Pakistan, I had never heard the term *madrassa*. A simple translation is "religious school." While focused on learning Islam, the curriculum at a madrassa *could* also include things like science, world history, literature, and poetry and at many *madrassas,* the courses reflect a balance of subjects. Or, the school could focus solely on Islamic studies, and to hell with science and literature. It all depended on the whims or leanings of the headmaster. In a madrassa, the headmaster is a Muslim cleric who *could* be teaching moderation or *could* be brainwashing his impressionable students by screaming "Death to the infidels!" These clerics are the sole force in molding these young minds into whatever they wish. There is no oversight. No one monitors who is teaching what. The students attending these schools come from impoverished families with no other education options, and very little or no means. Yet, they continue to have kids who they ship off to the... you guessed it, madrassas. It's a steady, even growing stream of students or recruits. If the cleric is teaching that Jihad (Holy War) is good (and many are), then you have a steady stream of young, malleable candidates willing to strap on a vest full of C4 explosives and blow something or someone up. It is an uninterrupted supply chain for terror. To be certain, not all *madrassas* preach Muslim extremism. But the often-penniless parents don't have the means of choosing which type of *madrassa* their children will attend.

Another shocking revelation that became apparent as we drove the streets of Quetta was the prevalence of drugs. This seemed so out of step for a region that was so tightly bound to Islam, which preaches: *Absolutely NO alcohol or drugs*. On a filthy creek turned open sewer on the edge of town, there was a large homeless camp where drug addicts existed. The Taliban realized there was money, lots of it, in the cultivation of opium poppy fields. That was their cash crop and they used it (even more so today) to fund everything from their terrorist operations within Afghanistan to the spread of terrorism outside their border. So much heroin produced nearby and so readily available made it an easy "score" in the slums of Quetta. It has grown to be a major problem that plagues all of Pakistan, which today has been called "…the most heroin-addicted country, per capita, in the world."[5]

Since we were in Quetta as a protective measure for a possible U.S. attack on Kandahar, we decided that to truly get the lay of the land, we needed to take a dive north and scope out the Pakistan-Afghanistan border. Afghanistan was a closed country. There was no way we were just going to stroll into the place in advance of U.S. troops. And any attempt by an American TV crew at crossing the border and wandering into Kandahar would mean certain death, or worse. But we weren't going *into* the country. We just wanted to take a peek at what lay between Quetta and the border.

---

5   Browne, David. "How Pakistan Succumbed to a Hard-Drug Epidemic." *The Telegraph*. March 2014.

With our local driver at the wheel, we drove two hours north on a paved, two-lane road running through endless and barren brown ground. We arrived at the border town of Chaman, the last stop before the Afghanistan border. I had traveled from the Himalayas to tiny uninhabited islands in the South Pacific, from the deserts of Africa to the jungles of Asia, and in the process, seen a lot of the diversity the world has to offer. This part of Pakistan was a remote outpost as far removed from anything Western than I had seen in my previous 18 years of international travel. Take away the tangle of power lines and few motorcycles and vehicles, and it could have looked the same as it might have a thousand years ago. The place and the people in their robes and headwear had a feudal "sense" about them. I knew, at least physically, that we were in Pakistan, but it felt eerily like no man's land.

As journalists, no matter where we go, we're supposed to maintain an open mind and avoid preconceived notions and judgments. That's the only way to remain unbiased, to simply report what we see, hear, and witness. It's also important to stay on our toes and be aware of our surroundings, and in that place, I was extremely leery of those around me. This was Pashtun country. The residents were Pashtun. The Taliban were Pashtun, as well, and we were intruding outsiders. Just driving through the dusty town, I could feel the icy looks of the locals peering through our car windows, suspicious of our very presence.

We drove out of town and made our way to the northern outskirts of Chaman, where we pulled over to stretch our legs. Safely out of sight of the dubious townspeople, Mark and I pulled out our equipment. I set up my camera and tripod to shoot some video of the area and zoomed into the farthest end of my lens to shoot down the straight and narrow road in front of me. The heat from the uninterrupted sunlight caused the pavement to shimmer, creating a mirage-like effect in my lens. I could barely make out the Afghanistan border off in the distance. As international borders go, it didn't look like much, consisting of some reinforced barbed wire fencing and a checkpoint. It didn't require militarization to keep out terrorists. The terrorists already resided *within* the border. And since they were all the same people, Pashtun traveling back and forth, there was no threat from either side. If the U.S. chose to hit Kandahar, they were not going to line up their heavily armored military caravans at a border crossing like this and present their military IDs.

As I looked through my lens, I wondered what life was like on the other side of that border. If the U.S. was going to attack Kandahar, we would certainly find out since we would be summoned to cover that attack, possibly embedding ourselves with those U.S. forces. But, at the time, I could only imagine what Kandahar life was like, and I envisioned a life of fear ruthlessly ruled by true evil. Those are the kind of speculative thoughts you try not to succumb to while working on news stories.

Years later, it would be revealed that Osama bin Laden summoned his second in command, Khalid Sheikh Mohammed, to Kandahar in 1999 or 2000, at which point plans for the 9/11 attacks were given the final approval there.

Having seen what we came to see, we drove back to Quetta. Our "wait and see" approach from there on meant that most of our reporting was done via low-quality, rooftop live shots, using the imperfect cell phone and suitcase dish for transmission. We did the best we could with that early-stage technology.

From what I'd seen, venturing into Quetta for a night on the town was not an option. The hotel's one restaurant was our only real dining option. The bland menu looked like a Pakistani version of Denny's—omelet, hamburger, or spaghetti with meatballs, with a couple of mandatory curry dishes thrown in. On certain evenings, the hotel's kitchen staff prepared a banquet, showcasing the region's finest delicacies. It wasn't a nightly occurrence. The first time I encountered it, it appeared to offer a departure from the normally limited menu. The banquet was more like a buffet. Long tables were draped in colorful local cloths. Ornate chaffing dishes offered up a variety of local fare and Pashtun delicacies, none of which were identifiable to me. I grabbed a plate and stepped into line at the buffet, joining other diners who were helping themselves. It was almost exclusively robe-wearing locals I stood among in the line. I didn't think much of the absence of other westerners or journalists in that line.

Years and years and years of international travel had taught me to eat sparingly and cautiously when first entering a remote foreign country like this one. Between Islamabad and Quetta, I'd been in Pakistan for over a week. My only gastrointestinal issue had been the complete lack of wine that regularly coursed through my system. But that was more of a psychological issue and less an intestinal one. My experienced digestive tract had had ample time to adjust to the local bacteria, though, so I carefully surveyed the prepared specialties and confidently enjoyed a plateful.

It didn't take long for me to regret my culinary courage. Less than an hour after the meal, I was in my room and realizing my mistake. The initial violent vomiting was immediately followed by uncontrollable diarrhea. That first evening was a constant race between the bed and the toilet. Once my system was purged of anything and everything, I experienced gut-wrenching dry heaves over the toilet, being unable to expel anything because there was nothing left in my stomach. I knew from previous food-borne illnesses that dehydration could become an issue, so I forced down bottled water... which was immediately rejected. The food poisoning that I had experienced years earlier in Manila and Damascus had been a walk in the park compared to what I was suffering in Quetta.

After a painful and horrible sleepless night, I phoned the producer Ara to inform him that I had contracted something and needed a day off.

"Hey Ara, it's Tim. I'm not feeling 100%. Spent the night in and on the toilet. Didn't get much sleep and feel like shit. I don't think I'm going to be very helpful today. I just need to get whatever this is out of my system."

"Sure. Sure. We've got you covered. Don't worry about work. Just try and get some rest. Why don't I get a doctor and bring him by your room to figure out what you've got?"

"No need. I just ate something I shouldn't have. Been here before. I'm not having any fun, but I'm also not too sure I trust the local medicine man in town. I don't know how advanced medical science is in this part of the world. Let me see how I feel tomorrow."

"Alright. I'll let everyone know you're down for a day or so. I'll check back in on you to see how you're doing."

"Give me a day. Let's talk tomorrow morning."

There wasn't much to report and not much work to be done. The few live shots that were scheduled could be handled by Ara, Mike, and my soundman.

My condition worsened over the rest of that day and night. My stomach and intestinal tract clenched in a steady pattern of excruciating spasms. When my body wasn't constricted in bed in the fetal position, I was convulsing with the dry heaves over the toilet. Every muscle in my body ached as I spent another night with only brief intervals of "shit sleep." It was in a state of constant and inescapable misery, and I wanted to die.

I soon realized my body was not going to let me "wait" this out. When Ara called to check on my condition, I raised the white flag of surrender and requested medical help… any medical help.

Later that morning, I was visited by a local physician whom the hotel had contacted. I'd been expecting a rustic, bearded man adorned in the turban and robe costume prevalent in that region, and carrying a bag of homeopathic local herbs. Instead, a clean-shaven MD in western clothing, toting a doctor's black bag and stethoscope, showed up at my door. My spirits rose ever so slightly. He could see I was in trouble and his thorough examination focused mainly on my abdomen.

He continued with a medical diagnosis that sounded straight out of the Mayo Clinic, recited in English learned from Oxford, and delivered with a rapid cadence and heavy Pakistani accent.

"My dear sir, it appears that you have an inflammation in your colon that is called colitis. Most likely, this is due to an infectious etiology. It is caused by toxigenic E. coli. You may also be suffering from a parasite known as Giardia lamblia. It is unfortunate that I must acknowledge your illness is somewhat common here in this portion of Pakistan. You should have called me earlier when you first noticed this condition. It is only going to deteriorate. The good news is we can treat this."

He was right—I'd been foolish to wait. And my initial suspicion of the local medical practices had been even more foolish. Instead of a voodoo doctor, I now saw a Western-trained savior.

"Whatever you say, Doctor. Anything, any treatment, is better than this."

He administered a massive injection of what I presumed to be antibiotics and provided me pill vials full of enough ciprofloxacin to kill off anything and everything in my system. He recommended a strict diet of clear liquid to which I'd thankfully adhere. I was relatively certain my HMO back in Denver didn't cover Quetta, so I happily paid him in cash for his services and medicine. I made sure to get a receipt, too, as this was a charge that would most definitely be included in my NBC expense report. I thanked him, hoping I'd never again need to see the good doctor.

I was in no condition to contribute to the newsgathering efforts of our news team. Thankfully, we were still in our wait-and-see mode and I could wait just fine from my hotel bed. I was also in no condition to check in with the home front. As a result of the infection, I had gone radio silent with phone calls to Denver. Finally, I mustered the strength to phone home and provide Amy and Alexa with updates.

"Hello. How are things in Pakistan? You are still in Pakistan, right?"

"Still in lovely Quetta, Pakistan."

"We were wondering if we were ever going to hear from you again. It's been almost a week."

"Ah, well, I sort of lost track of the days here in paradise. I may have eaten something I shouldn't have, and it took me out of action for a few days."

"Food poisoning?"

"More like full-body, head to toe, front to back poisoning."

"I am sorry. Sounds horrible. What did you eat?"

"Not sure exactly. Whatever it was, it didn't stay with me for long. They must have some super-killer bacteria over here that just wreaks havoc on the human body. I was hurting for a few days, but saw a doctor today and I'll be fine."

"I'm sure you're still hurting. Don't be in any hurry and take your time to get well. What's next once you're back on your feet?"

"Not sure. I feel like we're on an international stakeout, waiting to see if anything happens in Kandahar. If so, we're poised to cover it."

"Be careful. Please. We miss you."

By the fourth day, my condition improved enough to where I was out of bed and back in action, albeit moving slower than usual. Our undefined mission at this remote outpost was still lacking definition. We were still in a holding pattern and awaiting some sort of military action in Southern Afghanistan. That all changed and, after about ten days in Quetta, our crew was ordered back to Islamabad. It seemed that the military action would commence somewhere else and not in or around this Pashtun territory.

We made our way to and through the small, rural, dirty Quetta airport and checked our gear. I strapped myself into the cramped commercial prop-plane for the 90-minute domestic flight back to the capital. It meant I had time to reflect on my first stop of this story. Turned out, there hadn't been much news to be had. Aside from a tribal mentality, Islamic terrorism, suspicion, hatred, poverty, drug addiction, and dysentery, there didn't appear to be much to speak of in the whole damn region. I knew I was wrong to generalize, but couldn't help thinking, "If the world were to receive an enema, this is where it would be inserted."

We returned to the Islamabad Marriott and once again checked into our respective rooms. We then made our way to the third floor and the NBC News bureau to check in there. We talked with the producers and correspondents regarding the strategy behind leaving Quetta and rebasing to Islamabad, and where this dynamic, everchanging story was headed next. I moved to log in to an available computer terminal and spotted a stack of brown cardboard boxes in a corner all labeled "MREs"; **M**eals **R**eady to **E**at. I had first discovered MREs while covering stories with the Marines in Lebanon during the 80s. These were the military-issued meals in a pouch served in combat situations when kitchens weren't available. The first version was the canned "C-rations" distributed to U.S. troops in WII. They were updated for use in Vietnam and in 1981 became the MRE.

Stacy Brady and the Field Operations team back in New York had been responsible for packing up and shipping all of the news-gathering equipment required for remote foreign assignments; everything from satellite dishes to 9-volt batteries. Decades of experience had produced the kind of foresight in them to include things like MREs on the packing list. The meals were bland, filling, and safe, and after my gastrointestinal battle in Quetta, they were just what the doctor ordered. I grabbed an armload to stash in my room. While the vomiting and diarrhea of Quetta had recently passed through my body, the memory of that suffering was still intense. Back in the States, I fancied myself a bit of a "foodie." But in Pakistan, I happily traded taste-worthiness for trustworthiness. Night after night in my drab hotel room, I would savor a pouch full of Meatloaf with Gravy or Chicken Tettrazini or Beef Stew. It was a routine that offered the convenience of room service garnished with the confidence of knowing an American-made MRE was the safest food in the country. That peace of mind made an MRE taste like a three-starred Michelin meal.

Much of news coverage is inherently unpredictable; you don't know what's going to happen next. So, you cover your ass. Such was the case post-9/11 in that part of the world. Being in the capital of Islamabad, with the prevalence of Pakistani government offices and officials, there were plenty of asses to cover. The Ministry of Foreign Affairs, the Ministry of Defense, and occasionally the Prime Minister's office would all hold press conferences to update the world on developments within Pakistan. There was a regular stream of information on which to report. As this was my first visit to Pakistan, I was beginning to form my impression of Pakistan; one not meant for public consumption, but my edification. And it was becoming clear there was much which we could *not* report.

On paper and in front of the cameras, Pakistan was a staunch U.S. alley, standing side-by-side with them to combat the evil terrorists who threatened the security of both nations. But just below the surface was a complicated international spiderweb. The Pakistani version of the CIA is ISI, or Inter-Services Intelligence. It was and is a hugely powerful and sometimes rogue spy agency, which is so secretive and shadowy that the late Prime Minister Benazir Bhutto called it "a state within a state."[6]

In the 80s, the U.S. and Saudis channeled billions of dollars into Afghanistan to support the Mujahedeen in their war with the Russians. The covert aid had to be channeled through Pakistan, and the ISI became the delivery boys for all of that cash, intel, and weaponry. It was the ISI, along with then Prime Minister Zia ul-Haq, who decided who got what in Afghanistan. It was the ISI, not the CIA, who formed the tight relationships with the "freedom fighters," the Mujahedeen, which was a de-

---

6 "A Conversation with Benazir Bhutto." (2007, August 15). *Council on Foreign Relations*. Retrieved from *https://www.cfr.org/event/conversation-benazir-bhutto-0*

velopment unforeseen by the CIA, and one which would have disastrous consequences later. After the Russians headed home, the Mujahedeen splintered into many different groups, one of them being the Taliban. But their relationship with ISI never splintered—it only grew stronger. Some within the ISI saw the Taliban as a brutal group of terrorists that could be used to wreak havoc on Pakistan's true enemy, India. But the Taliban and Bin Laden's al-Qaeda had their sights on a different enemy. Even as U.S. forces were preparing for a war in Afghanistan with the Taliban and al-Qaeda, the ISI was channeling intel to old Taliban buddies.

That war was looking imminent, and the news media began gearing up by adding staff. But, at that time, the "where and when" were still unknown variables. NBC sent a small team to Afghanistan's northern neighbor, Tajikistan. Correspondent Tom Aspell and cameraman Steve O'Neill had traveled with a soundman and producer to set up camp in the Tajik capital of Dushanbe, awaiting further instructions from London. I had met both Tom and Steve in Lebanon when covering the war there from 1983-1985, and I'd worked with them both elsewhere, as well. They were two of the most ballsy, seasoned combat veterans in the business. They were smart and fearless and dedicated journalists.

Our staff in Islamabad was also growing. Kiko Itasaka was a well-traveled veteran producer. She had first worked in the Tokyo bureau, but with its closing, had been relocated to the London bureau. She was a welcome addition to the Islamabad team. I'd never worked with her before, but had heard only great things about her. As part of the NBC unit in Pakistan, I would find out first-hand what a talented journalist and team player she was and is. Never boastful, she had an extensive resume of news coverage that included numerous conflicts, beginning with the first Iraq war of Bush 41. And to that vast experience, she added a sharp, almost wicked sense of humor. The seriousness of the post-9/11 coverage and impending war was inescapable, but amid that focus, the ability to step back and have a rare laugh with your colleagues is a valuable commodity to bring to the table.

National capitals have foreign embassies, and Islamabad is no exception. The U.S. embassy there is a fortress-like building (for good reason) with an extensive maze of security to get in and out through. Other western countries have similarly constructed embassies. Even Afghanistan had an embassy in Islamabad, and while the U.S. never recognized the Taliban as a legitimate government (and nor would any other Western government), they set up shop in Islamabad. And they did what governments do from time to time... they held press conferences to address the international press corps that Kiko and I were assigned to cover with the aid of a local translator. We were both intrigued to see what exactly a Taliban news conference looked like. And, interested in getting our first firsthand glimpse of the "diplomats" from Afghanistan.

The embassy wasn't much of an embassy. It was housed in a small, nondescript residential compound in a basic residential neighborhood. It was walled with a small gate at the driveway, which was where we and other news teams entered. The ragtag security guards led us to a small living room that had been converted into the "Press Center." There was a large woven carpet on the floor and the Taliban flag was draped on the wall as a background for the cameras.

Two robed men with long beards and black turbans walked in, sat on the carpet, and crossed their legs like kindergarten-ers at school. On 9/11, a Taliban spokesman had appeared on Al Jazeera television and stated, "We denounce this terrorist attack, whoever is behind it."[7] The two Taliban men in front of us continued with the same rhetoric. It didn't matter what they had to say. Part of the Bush doctrine translated into, "You are either with us or against us. If you harbor terrorists, you are with the terrorists." Since the FBI and CIA had long ago connected the dots, linking the Taliban and Osama bin Laden, the Taliban's goose was already cooked. Knowing their home country and fellow Taliban members would soon experience an American-led onslaught, they took a predictable, Islamic militant posture and began a broken English rant. "We will wish to warn the Americans and the world, any invasion of Afghanistan, you will lose. The blood of the invaders will run like a river in the streets. The God, Allah is ours. He is with us."[8] They boasted that they were firmly in control of the country, going so far as to suggest that the Western news media would be invited into the capital of Kabul to witness for ourselves just how stable and secure the place truly was.

We in the news media were highly skeptical of their claim about control in Afghanistan. Anti-Taliban forces, known as the Northern Alliance, had already begun attacks. But if we were invited into Afghanistan, that was an invitation we would accept.

One thing we were all certain of was the Taliban's notorious policies against women. They had put their policies in writing and publicized their version of Islam.

Women were forbidden to work or attend school.

7   CNN. (2001, September 12). "Officials: New Information Points to bin Laden." Retrieved from http://edition.cnn.com/2001/US/09/11/investigation.terrorism/index.html

8   Tim Ortman. Personal notes/records from press conference attended on behalf of NBC. (September 2001).

Women were forbidden to be seen on television or in newspapers, or even be seen at public gatherings.

Women were forbidden to be treated by male doctors unless accompanied by a male family member.

Women were to be covered from head to toe, forced to wear a burka.

This was all to be done so that Islamic men wouldn't be tempted by females. Forced marriages were the norm, frequently involving girls under 16.

We interviewed some courageous women who had endured the Taliban's oppression, then escaped from their "prison" in Afghanistan to the relatively looser (yet still very much Islamic) standards in Islamabad. In very emotional and often tearful fashion, they recounted what life was like for a woman in the Taliban's Afghanistan. They all described a similar life of horrible oppression and fear. Life in Afghanistan under Taliban rule was a living hell for women. It was tough to hear of the humiliation and violence against women, but this was an important story to report to the world. It was particularly difficult for a strong, independent, and successful woman like Kiko to listen to.

After one such interview, Kiko and I were strolling through a shopping bazaar in neighboring Rawalpindi. It was a huge, open-air market where small stores or stalls displayed vividly colored garments and fabrics as crowded shoppers dodged motor scooters in the packed narrow streets. It was not the kind of enclosed, airconditioned mall prevalent in the U.S. But, as in the U.S., there were occasional second-hand or "thrift stores" selling used goods. I stumbled upon a small stall selling, or more accurately re-selling, women's apparel. Hanging on one of the racks, right in front of me, was an authentic blue burka;

the real deal, imported directly from the dirty streets of Kabul. It was head to toe concealment, like moveable solitary confinement with a tiny little screen at the eyes through which the imprisoned wearer could barely see.

I turned to Kiko and said, "Check it out. This is the real deal. I have to have this. My wife and her girlfriends won't believe this."

She looked closely and examined it. "I think you're right— that looks like an authentic burka, not that I would know for sure. The Taliban's treatment of women is repulsive, but the odor coming from that garment is almost as bad."

I hadn't thought to look, or smell, that closely, but she was right. There was no such thing as women's rights in Afghanistan. Similarly, dry cleaners and personal hygiene must have been in short supply, too. Afghan women could only do their chores and manual labor, silently, all the while sweating through their burkas, and the garment in my hand omitted the obnoxious stench as evidence.

"Good catch," I said. "I'll have it dry-cleaned when I get back to Denver." With my newly acquired, old burka in hand, Kiko and I continued our stroll through the shopping bazaar.

The suffering of those poor Afghan women was in sharp contrast to the many successful women I had known and admired in my life. Amy's drive, intellect, and cunning had made her a successful attorney. Years before in Lebanon, I'd met and fallen in love with Francoise Demulder, a courageous, passionate, and world-renowned war photographer. There were many other women with whom I had worked and admired. Unlike the women under Taliban rule, they'd all had opportunities (albeit not enough of them). And, while embracing those opportunities, they'd resolutely maintained their independence without losing sight of and while retaining their femininity; not easy to do in our male-dominated world. Again, not to be compared to the horrible plight of the women in Afghanistan, but thanks to Amy, I was intimately aware of her struggle to carve out a name for herself in the legal and corporate world. I was less aware of the similar struggles endured by my female news colleagues, and I would never fully understand exactly what those women in Afghanistan had endured. But, perhaps I could better understand what it was like for women covering conflicts, like Kiko.

In network news, I'd worked with affected divas, both male and female. Kiko was the antithesis of a diva, hardworking and loathsome to complain about an assignment. I had gotten to know her and felt at ease talking with her. As we strolled through the crowded bazaar with my burka in hand, I asked, "So, what's a nice girl like you doing in a place like this?"

"I came here for the women's fashions. And, that sounds like a pick-up line from the 80s."

"One of my best. Coupled with my cameraman charm, it worked a good ten percent of the time. Damn near foolproof."

"Well, you might want to work on some new material."

"It wouldn't help anyway. So, Pakistan. You mentioned you covered the Iraq war and other conflicts. I'm curious if you have a penchant for these kinds of stories."

"I wouldn't say *penchant*. This is a big story, so, yeah, I was interested in covering it. But it's also... kinda what we do. As a staff producer, we don't really have beats that we cover. We cover the news. All of it. You know how it works. On top of that, it's a job I love and one I share with a lot of colleagues, some of whom are dear friends. If I said *no* to a story, or started picking and choosing assignments, what would that say? What kind of message would that send to them? But enough about me.

What about you? I know you used to be staff, but now you're a freelancer. That means you had to *ask* to be here. Do *you* have a penchant for war stories?"

I was enjoying the honest dialogue as we meandered through the maze-like streets, not knowing where the next turn or comment would lead. We passed a stall selling handmade copper and brass wares, and then passed tables of exotic spices that filled the air with pungently foreign aromas.

"I'm like you. This is a big story and one that I'm interested in covering. But, I'm also *not* like you, in that I'm a guy. These big stories usually occur in shitty places with a higher than normal ratio of unsavory characters."

"Right, and because we're the 'weaker sex'…"

"That's not at all where I was going. I'm really not some Neanderthal. Bear with me. I think us guys are too often driven by bravado and testosterone, where you guys employ more thought and reasoning. So, in that regard, you're probably the stronger of the sexes."

"I tend to agree. Keep talking. You're beginning to make sense."

"The colleagues you mentioned; I've had the good fortune to work with Michelle Neubert and Carol Grisanti out of the London bureau on many stories."

"Both dear friends."

"Not surprising. You guys are all pros. Top-notch journalists. And I think it takes more guts and courage for a woman to come into a place like this, particularly in the Islamic world, and cover a story like this, than it does for a man."

"I don't know if it's more or less. Maybe it's a different kind of courage, or… resolution."

"The point I'm belaboring to make is that, it seems no matter how much machismo bullshit you guys have to deal with, you never get caught up in it and never lose sight of your female side. I don't mean to imply that you guys flaunt it. You don't. But you always maintain your femininity. That can't be easy in places like this."

"La Perla."

"Who's La Perla?"

"Jesus. I thought you said you're married."

"I am. What's that got to do with this La Perla dude?"

"Everything. All of a sudden, I feel sorry for your wife. La Perla is not a person. It's a thing, or in this case, it's more of a state of mind."

"Maybe it's the spice market we just walked through, but I'm a little hazy here. What the hell are you talking about?"

"La Perla is the finest, sexiest, handmade Italian lingerie on the planet. I pack it whenever I'm working in… what did you call it, 'shitty places like this.' Many of us do. You're never going to forget you're a woman when you slip on La Perla, no matter where you are."

"So, you wore this… La Perla when you covered… the Gulf War."

"Absolutely."

"And during the Balkans?"

"That's right."

"And here in Islamabad, like… right now?"

"Yep."

I had been in the Islamic Republic of Pakistan for almost a month, devoid of sex, or even a drink. The imagery that immediately burst into my brain was that of the attractive Asian co-worker next to me, dressed in revealing and lacey, erotic lingerie. It was completely distracting and almost too much to bear.

BANG! With my mind adrift and not focused on the crowded shops and stalls before me, I slammed directly into a table piled high with men's sandals. The impact caused boxes and footwear to be strewn all over the street. As I picked myself up from the pile of flip-flops, an angry shopkeeper berated me in an intensely loud Pashto voice... that was growing louder.

"OH MY GOD!" Trying to fight back her laughter, Kiko extended a hand to help extricate me from both the shoes and the shopkeeper.

To make amends for my collision, I made a half-assed clean-up attempt, grabbing an armful of sandals from the street and handing them to the irate shopkeeper. I accompanied the gesture with the only Arabic phrase I knew, "Allah Akbar"—'God is Great.' That did little to calm him. He was still flailing his arms and screaming as Kiko and I made a quick exit from the scene of the crime.

Disheveled, disoriented, and still reeling with the racy imagery of Kiko's semi-undressed body in my brain, I tried to compose myself. "I did not see *that* coming, and I'm not just talking about the shoe store."

"Yeah, you really took your eye off the ball there. Didn't mean to ruin your day."

"Yeah, I guess my mind was elsewhere. No, no, quite the opposite. Your revelation didn't ruin my day; it made my day. I, uh, sometimes fool myself into thinking I have a clue into what makes women tick. And then I realize just how clueless I truly am. You guys are wonderfully complex creatures... and thank God you are."

Kiko smiled confidently. While my acknowledgment may have been a news flash for me, it was a long-held truth for her; the gospel according to womanhood. We made our way out of the bazaar and retraced our steps back to where we had left our driver. Our shopping mall conversation was just one of the many lively and honest discussions we would share. During the drive back to the Marriott, I thought about how much I enjoyed working with her, and the newly enhanced mental imagery I had of her only heightened that appreciation.

* * * * *

By mid-October, there were substantiated reports of fighting inside Afghanistan between the Taliban and the U.S.-backed Northern Alliance, who were launching attacks from the north. The Aspell/O'Neill team had been stationed in Dushanbe, Tajikistan to cover exactly this sort of scenario. However, in the early stages of the battle, and given the extremely remote nature of the battlefields, those early reports were sometimes difficult to confirm.

By early November, there was a noticeable increase in activity in and around the Afghanistan embassy in Islamabad. This commotion was a departure from the normal stonewalling we got in what the Taliban were keen to call press conferences. Something was developing inside the embassy (and perhaps their country, as well); we just didn't know what, exactly. Armed men wearing Taliban black turbans were coming and going in and out of their residential compound. November 7th was a Wednesday, and an impromptu press conference was called. We were sent to cover it. Camera crews and reporters with cell phones jostled for position, engulfing the Taliban spokesman as he spoke.

"There are rumors of fighting in Afghanistan. This is lies. We, the Taliban, are rulers of Afghanistan. The Taliban is control of all the country. We take you Kabul. We show you Kabul is safe and Taliban control all."

A flurry of questions ensured from the press scrum. "*You* are going to escort the press into Kabul?!"

"Yes, we escort to Kabul."

"When will this trip take place? How large will the convoy be and how will it be organized? Who is in charge of security during the route?"

The spokesman was slow to fill in the details after his initially brazen statement. We were told specifics of this press "junket" would soon follow, and we returned to the bureau with the tape of the press conference.

This was quite the offer from the super-secretive and adversarial Taliban. A guided tour of their capital for the news media and the whole world to see, complete with a military escort?! That escort was a key component of the offer. There was only one route to get from Point A, Islamabad to Point B, Kabul. The drive would be a grueling, 12-hour trek over seriously formidable mountain terrain. It would switchback through barely passable mountain roads, eventually leading through the Khyber Pass, which sits in a border region known for its complete and utter lawlessness. Having been used by invading hordes dating back to Genghis Khan, the pass was now ruled by roving bandits and thieves whose only allegiance was to themselves. An armed Taliban escort through this no-man's land would help ensure we reached Kabul alive. What would happen after that was anyone's guess.

All of us in the news media were slightly skeptical, but anxiously awaited details of this Taliban *journey*.

The next morning, we were all in the bureau discussing this assignment with Charlie Ryan. He had spoken with the same Taliban spokesman regarding specifics of the proposed trip to Kabul. Things were coming together rapidly. Because of space restrictions, not every TV news network would be permitted to make the trip. One network would be chosen as the "pool" to represent all of the American TV news organizations, sharing their footage with everyone else. This sort of pool arrangement was common and it didn't apply to just the television networks. A reporter and a photographer would be the pool for U.S. print media, the same for radio and European and Asian outlets who would each have their own pool. Charlie informed us that NBC News had been selected as the pool for American TV. Our crew consisted of Mark, myself, and correspondent Ron Allen. The convoy to Afghanistan would leave that evening. We immediately began packing that afternoon for a long journey... and an uncertain future.

The plan was for a late evening departure from Islamabad, which would have us navigating the Khyber Pass at sunrise, with an eventual mid-day arrival in Kabul. As instructed, we arrived at the consulate shortly after sunset to begin preparations for the long haul to Kabul.

There was a large and dirty cargo truck parked in front, presumably for the equipment and luggage. It was accompanied by a few dusty old minivans, presumably for the passengers. There were about a dozen or so of us journalists and photojournalists, all milling about and awaiting instructions for loading and departing. The few scattered streetlights provided very little illumination. A handful of Taliban commanders appeared to be gathered on the street and frantically yelling Pashto into phones and walkie talkies. Through the darkness of that evening, the only thing visible was the total confusion of our organizing party. When we approached them for clarification, we were waved off and told to be silent. Some members of our party began loading luggage into the dilapidated cargo truck and were suddenly stopped in their tracks. After a couple of hours of this communications tumult, we were approached by a commander who addressed our perplexed group.

"Nobody leaves tonight. Tomorrow night, we leave. We *aaaaall* go Kabul tomorrow night."

This change in scheduling prompted a flurry of questions from our group of postponed and somewhat pissed-off passengers. The Taliban would provide no further information. As press, it was our job to ask why. Why weren't we leaving that night? Why was tomorrow a better option? Why the change of plans? We soon reached a point of diminishing returns. They had no desire to explain the finer points and nuances behind their change of heart. And, with them being our official guides on this guided tour to Kabul, it was fruitless to antagonize them further. It was now late in the evening, and I phoned Charlie with the update that we had not left and would not be leaving that night. The whole mess was pushed back a day... at best.

That evening, sleep was hard to come by. My mind drifted, wondering what the trip would be like with our Taliban bodyguards. The U.S. and Taliban weren't exactly allies. And, what would Kabul be like? It had been isolated from most of the world for five years, ever since the Taliban had seized control of the country.

Our equipment and few personal belongings were already packed. After conferring with the bureau personnel, we decided to arrive at the Afghanistan embassy earlier than instructed. Arriving in the afternoon would allow us to get a better glimpse of our convoy and the overall operation in the daylight.

We drove down the same dusty street and arrived at the same small, residential embassy as the previous evening. Yet, there was one major difference. The armed men, the cargo truck, and the old minivans were *gone*. The turban-wearing armed embassy guards were gone, too. The place looked like a ghost town, all locked up with nobody home. My initial reaction was, "We missed it! There was some communications screw-up and the fucking Taliban left without us!" Ron urgently relayed our discovery back to the bureau to see what they could find out. We stayed put, staking out the embassy to see if, miraculously, a Taliban convoy would materialize and drive us into Kabul as planned.

But there would be no convoy from Islamabad to Kabul.

The Taliban were not forthcoming about what had happened or why the convoy, along with its confidently verbose planners, had been vaporized. The details from within Afghanistan were becoming clearer, however. The war there between the Northern Alliance and the Taliban had intensified. Beginning in the north, the two longtime adversaries were locked in fierce and bloody fighting. Thanks to some major help in the form of U.S. and British aerial bombardments on Taliban positions, the Northern Alliance had gained the upper hand, winning battles in key cities like Mazari Sharif. They were heading south towards Kabul, slicing through the rest of the country and the Taliban like a hot knife through butter.

The whole convoy to Kabul idea had been little more than a public relations stunt by a desperate Taliban government who knew their army was on the verge of defeat. Escorting news cameras and reporters into the country to record that defeat might contradict the image of a strong and unwavering Taliban rule, which they had previously so loudly proclaimed. And, well, that just might be bad for morale. So, at the last minute, they pulled the plug on the entire, hopeless "show-and-tell" scheme. Four days later, on November 13th, the defeated Taliban would abandon Kabul, and Northern Alliance forces would take control of the capital. Within a week, the Afghanistan embassy in Islamabad would be closed entirely.

The real appeal of the plan was the guarantee of an armed escort, which would have helped us to navigate through the "badlands" on the border and perhaps increased the odds for a safe arrival into Kabul. A week after the fall of Kabul and with the Taliban on the run, Afghanistan was a country with no central authority, no laws, and no police force. It was also a closed and war-ravaged country in dire need of international reporting.

Against that backdrop, a group of journalists formed their own eight-vehicle convoy and attempted to make it into Kabul on their own, without the support of an armed escort. Just inside the Afghanistan border, driving through the empty, windblown, boulder-strewn landscape, the convey came upon a small concrete bridge manned by six heavily armed men. Initially, it was unclear if they were run-of-the-mill Pashtun thieves or Taliban militia. The first car sped through without stopping. The next two cars were stopped at gunpoint, and the occupants ordered to get out.

Inside those two cars were two Afghan drivers and four international journalists: Maria Grazia Cutuli of the Italian newspaper *Corriere Della Sera*, Julio Fuentes of the Spanish newspaper *El Mundo*, and Australian cameraman Harry Burton and Afghan photographer Azizullah Haidari, both of the Reuters News Agency.

The four journalists were brutally beaten with stones and rifle butts, and then shot to death. The drivers were told to leave the area and never return with foreigners headed to Kabul. One driver was quoted as saying that the gunman had said, "This is not the end of the Taliban. The Taliban is still in power and can do anything it wants."[9]

In November of 2001, that sounded like a bold statement by an Islamic regime whose strict government was collapsing and whose army was on the run. The U.S. war in Afghanistan, code-named "Operation Enduring Freedom," would decimate the al Qaeda fighters in Afghanistan as well as their leadership, culminating with the death of Osama bin Laden in May of 2011. But, over the years, the Taliban proved their resiliency. While their leadership scattered and relocated to Pakistan, the Taliban insurgents who remained in Afghanistan have used violence and terror to continually inflict casualties on the U.S.-led coalition forces and the Afghan people. At 19 years and counting, it is America's longest war. For ten years, negotiations to find a non-military resolution to the conflict have started and stopped. At each junction, the Taliban have been part of the process. Like a resistant viral strain, they have adapted to stymy an enormous and international military coalition. Today, they occupy as much of Afghanistan as they did prior to the 2001 invasion. In 2018, in Doha, Qatar, official peace talks began between the U.S. and the Taliban, proving there will be no lasting peace in Afghanistan without Taliban involvement and endorsement.

In November of 2001, the fall of Kabul was *the* story. The Tom Aspell and Steve O'Neill team was one of the first on the ground. The journey from Tajikistan to Kabul was a death-defying ride like few others. Once they arrived in the capital, they found a neglected city in a backward country, lacking even basic staples like clean food and water, sanitation, housing, reli-

9 Tempest, R. (2001, November 20). "4 Journalists Feared Dead in Ambush." *Los Angeles Times.* Retrieved from https://www.latimes.com/archives/la-xpm-2001-nov-20-mn-6291-story.html

able electricity, and communications. As part of their limited equipment, they had brought with them the same portable video phones that had proven challenging for us in Quetta. Yet, any video is better than no video. The herky-jerky, grainy video and underwater-sounding audio were the only pictures and sounds they could transmit of the fighting during their journey through Northern Afghanistan. As the Taliban retreated from the capital, the videophone was the only way to report live from the scene. To be on the ground as eyewitnesses, shining an international light on the darkness that was Kabul, their presence and reporting offered invaluable information to the outside world. Eventually, permanent satellite facilities would be shipped in and installed for more technically reliable transmission. But as the tip of the spear, their early live reports from the capital were sporadic due to the many technical hurdles they had to overcome. Because of their courage and dedication to journalism, however, they were our eyes and ears.

Islamabad became a more reliable place from which to report on the developments and machinations inside Afghanistan. With its unobstructed vista overlooking all of Islamabad (and its stable electrical grid) the rooftop of the Marriott hotel, our home away from home, became the prime position for round-the-clock live updates from an arsenal of live correspondents. Massive, rock-solid satellite dishes had been shipped in and were manned by rock-solid engineers who ensured that the live reports from Islamabad looked and sounded just like the live reports from, say... Chicago.

Of course, the U.S. military response to the attacks of 9/11 was a huge story, and it would remain so for quite some time, until the search for weapons of mass destruction (WMDs) in Saddam Hussein's Iraq would divert both media attention and military troops to Iraq. But in November of 2001, the build-up of both was in Afghanistan and Pakistan. The proliferation of news cameras and correspondents on the Marriott rooftop was head-spinning. A decade earlier, there would have been four camera positions occupied by ABC, CBS, NBC, and CNN. There were now three times that number. And the same expansion of news outlets applied to the foreign news networks; the BBC was now squeezed between ITN, SkyNews, and others. It seemed as if everyone was covering the news.

The vastly expanded landscape for broadcast news was on full display on top of that crowded Marriott rooftop. Side-by-side with each other, each network had its own dedicated, four-foot position that was shared with a camera, tripod, lights, stands, boom microphone, cameraman, soundman, and correspondent. It looked like the official starting line for the network news version of the Boston Marathon. As I took note and surveyed how the coverage of news had expanded three-fold, I wondered if the audience for news had expanded by the same multiple, or if it had merely been fractured and divided up.

The U.S. Operation Enduring Freedom was supported by forces from the United Kingdom, with many additional nations soon joining the coalition. This was a global story that would only grow in both size and scope. All of the news networks beefed up their presence in Islamabad with increased staff. We quickly outgrew our third-floor converted office in the Marriott. The local Pakistani staffers, who became invaluable as we learned the many nuances of their culture and government, found a safe and spacious house in which to relocate the bureau. We continued to use the Marriott rooftop location for live shots and stand-ups. But the residential location with its small, walled courtyard and tree-lined streets provided a more relaxed and less cramped workspace from which we would write, edit, and transmit stories.

Reporting from Islamabad, the Pakistani government stressed their support for the U.S. invasion in Afghanistan and the hunt for Osama bin Laden. That was a predictable official stance from a government that was about to receive over $2 billion from the U.S. in military and humanitarian aid. But outside the corridors of the ministries, outside the governmental press conferences, in the cauldron of the impoverished surrounding towns, there was a different fervor brewing among the locals. With our cameras and mics, we ventured into the streets, outside the mosques and madrassas, to gauge the unofficial response from the people. It was on these assignments that we increasingly encountered protests—anti-American protests opposed to the U.S. invasion of Afghanistan.

As a world-traveled international cameraman, I had spent decades covering countless anti-American protests. There'd been the rabid German protestors opposed to the deployment of American cruise missiles on European soil during the early 80s. There'd been the angry Lebanese protestors opposed to the American-led multinational peacekeeping force deployed to keep the peace in that bullet-riddled country.

Each time I was assigned to these kinds of stories, as an American citizen shouldering a camera for an American news network, I knew I needed to remove myself from the story or protest. Hell, at times, I might even have empathized with the protesters' argument. Regardless, I was there to record the event, and only that. No matter how vile the rhetoric or agitated the demonstrators became, a journalist couldn't take the bait. Never take it personally. Additionally, by voicing their opposition to American policy and/or actions, such protestors were demonstrating their freedom of expression, their right to free speech. I wasn't intimately familiar with the Pakistani constitution, but I was damned certain that freedom of speech was one of the most important of the inalienable rights guaranteed us as Americans by Thomas Jefferson and company. It was also the rudimentary tenant upon which the entire news business was based. So, it would be hypocritical of me as a newsman to take issue with a band of angry Pakistani protestors chanting anti-American slogans.

Call me a hypocrite.

We encountered about 500 black-bearded men somewhere in their 20s and 30s, all of them marching in a dusty, dirty, squalid neighborhood of mostly one-story dilapidated housing. There were a handful of uniformed police watching from the fringes. Like so many marchers before them, they carried similar homemade signs proclaiming "Death to America" and "Go Home American Invaders." They burned similar U.S. flags and stomped on the hot ashes; they suspended similar Uncle Sam dummies (resembling George W. Bush) from a pole with a hangman's noose around each dummy's neck. As they marched, one of the organizers approached my camera lens and pointed his bullhorn inches from my camera. His scream into the bullhorn was so deafening that Mark ripped off his earphones to avoid hearing loss. As his verbose remarks were in Pashto, we had no idea what he was screaming, but the intent was clear. Hatred. From the perspective of a veteran cameraman, it all looked so familiar, almost boring. At the same time, it felt different. I felt anger as a reciprocal hatred grew inside me.

It had only been two months since 2,977 innocent men, women, and children had been murdered by al Qaeda via those hijacking terrorists, and like every American, I still retained those memories, fresh and vivid (as they still are today). The video I was recording of the protestors was being blended in my mind with the video of planes slamming into the World Trade Center and the smoking buildings collapsing to the ground.

Focus. Cover the event. Do your job. Don't take the bait.

Mark and I continued to backpedal with our camera and mic trained on the protestors, who were all chanting in unison and thrusting their fists in the air. The chants became louder, the thrusting fists more violent, and the hatred more resolute. Again, the bullhorn-toting leader appeared before my camera, just inches from my lens. His delivery was so shrill, the veins in his neck popped out as the spit from his screaming mouth peppered both his bullhorn and my camera lens. "Personal space" was non-existent, but he was now trampling like a Sherman tank through my comfort zone.

Whether pushed by the riotous followers behind him or in an act of over-zealous leadership, he rammed into my camera lens with his increasingly bothersome bullhorn. I held the camera lens in my right hand, but my left hand was free, and I used it to retaliate, pushing his bullhorn away from my lens... and squarely into his mouth. This brought about shock, bewilderment, and a bloody mouth in my protesting antagonist. He was momentarily dazed, but quickly recovered, rallying his "troops" by pointing and screaming in our direction. We were soon engulfed by protestors and quickly became the focus of the anti-American protest. It was like being in the eye of a hurricane, surrounded by tumultuous yelling from rabid fanatics. In that instance, the demonstrators disregarded their anger for the American military and replaced it with anger for American TV... specifically, *us*.

Mark and I had our backs to one another, defending ourselves in opposite directions as the "noose" around us tightened. I did not envision a way out. Given the language barrier and the rising temperature of the collective group, it seemed unlikely we were going to be able to talk our way out of this predicament.

Suddenly, from my left periphery vision, I saw an angry protestor disappear as if he'd been catapulted away from me. Then, I witnessed another angry young man grabbed by the collar and ripped out of the group. Baton-wielding men had appeared to disperse the angry mob around us. The cavalry had arrived! The police, who had surreptitiously observed the entire protest march, had come to our rescue. Amid the dusty pushing and shoving and club thumping, there was little time to thank our saviors. The mob ran for cover and we ran in the opposite direction.

Once we caught our collective breath, Mark and I retraced our steps back to the place the march had begun in the hopes of finding our car and driver, ever-leery of encountering the remnants of our adversarial mob. We talked about how quickly things had turned ugly and how fortunate we were that the police had been monitoring the whole thing.

For me, the irony of what had happened here in comparison to the aforementioned 1989 protest in Prague was an unavoidable consideration. That march had also been accompanied by police supervision; military police. In those other picturesque, narrow cobblestone streets, things had taken a gruesome turn for the worse. Without provocation, the military police had violently and indiscriminately beaten the protestors—all of them. Instead of ensuring our safety, the Communist police had taken particular pleasure in pounding the press and destroying our camera. Because we'd managed to broadcast video of the brutal event on *NBC Nightly News*, the brutality had been seen and heard by millions, and ultimately had a negative impact on the already weakened Communist government, which was then toppled and replaced with democratic elections.

The motivation of the police in Pakistan and Czechoslovakia was strikingly different. Opposite. On the one hand, the Pakistani protestors were attacked to protect the press. On the other, the Czech protestors were attacked in the process of attacking the press.

The motivation of the two protestor groups was also strikingly different, and to me, this was particularly bothersome. Again, I wasn't assigned to either march to judge, just to cover the events. Yet, in Prague, the students, in rebelling against their Communist oppressors, had been yearning for freedom; the stuff of which America is made and for which it so proudly stands. Outside of Islamabad, the protestors were rebelling against America and were protesting against our ability to defend ourselves. We as a country had just been attacked, and our retaliatory invasion of their neighbor to the north had been made in response to those attacks. Of course, this sort of rationale was not popular in that part of the Muslim world where extremists like the Taliban had so much grassroots support.

A key part of our job is to accurately report on varied or differing viewpoints within our society. Those Pakistani protestors, who so vociferously believed the U.S. invasion in Afghanistan was unjust, were voicing their viewpoint. While I may not have agreed with what they were saying (and I absolutely did not), it was our job to report it. But coming so quickly on the heels of 9/11 made that job a bitter pill to swallow.

After 20 years of network news coverage, such bitter pills were beginning to leave a bad taste lingering in my mouth.

I spent Thanksgiving of 2001 in Islamabad. It was not the

first and nor would it be the last American holiday I would spend on assignment away from home. Some of those holidays, like the Christmas spent in Ethiopia during the horrible famine, passed without merriment. At least, this time, there was a celebratory atmosphere among the international staff, who all created and shared an international feast. Our bureau/house included a full kitchen whose ovens, stovetops, and counters were overstuffed with American and Pakistani holiday dishes. Somehow, someone somewhere had found us a turkey in Pakistan, which was the centerpiece around which all of the other delicacies were served. There were a couple of versions of stuffing. In keeping with local culinary customs, grilled lamb, lentil stew, yogurt and vegetable salads, and plenty of roti (bread) accompanied the turkey and dressing. Through some friend of a friend of a friend's connection at the U.S. Embassy, we were even able to scrounge up a few cases of beer in the Islamic Republic of Pakistan. After such a long dry spell, the sudsy hops tasted like Dom Perignon and, for a wine-drinker like me, slid down my throat with astonishing ease, one after another. The camaraderie and coworker fun (and beer) helped rinse away the bad taste left in my mouth from the anti-American protestors.

It's a rare occurrence when on assignment, to get everyone under the same roof and have them collectively pause their cell phones, computers, cameras, and editing software. Some of us at that gathering were nearing the end of our assignments, while others had just arrived as part of the staff build-up for the long haul. As I strolled through that house and partied with my colleagues, I thought, regardless of arrival or departure date, this was a tight and cohesive team. Its members had come from America, Europe, and Asia, from vastly different backgrounds with widely varying skill sets, uniting for a common goal: to truthfully and accurately report on the international events following 9/11. This was unspoken… just a thought of mine I kept to myself. Yet, I'm certain it was one silently shared by everyone in that room. We all savored the camaraderie as much, if not more so, than the cooking of that Thanksgiving Day.

The morning after my Thanksgiving in Pakistan, mindful of the 11-hour time difference, I phoned home to check in on my family's Thanksgiving in Colorado. I was just getting up and they were just going to bed. Amy and Alexa had celebrated at the home of some neighbors up the street who, void of out of town family guests, had hosted a houseful of local friends. Their menu had been a little more traditional than mine, with ham instead of lamb, mashed potatoes and gravy instead of lentil stew, and glazed carrots and cranberry sauce replacing the yogurt salads. I was gearing up as they were winding down, too, which made for a short conversation. They did reassure me that I'd been a topic of conversation at dinner. "How was I doing? What was I doing? When would I be coming home?" I thought it a nice gesture on their part, if maybe a little bit embellished. I'd been gone for so long, and "out of sight is out of mind." Perhaps my family and friends were getting a little *too* used to life without me.

The first week of December arrived, which meant my two-month tour was up and I would soon be replaced. I could have requested the opportunity to stay longer and follow the story farther. The story was not diminishing; it was ramping up. The hunt for Osama bin Laden was full speed ahead. A fierce two-week battle had just started in the mountain cave complex known as Tora Bora. Mike Taibbi, with whom I'd worked in Quetta, had accompanied a crew on a harrowing journey through the Khyber Pass to cover the battle.

There'd been numerous other stories where I'd stayed well past my initial commitment. The war in Lebanon, the "People Power" revolution in the Philippines, and the collapse of Communism in Prague were some of the stories I followed in locations where I lingered long beyond my initial obligation. They and others represented stories with which I became enthralled, stories that "got under my skin"—stories in which I felt invested. I did not feel that connection in Pakistan, even though 9/11 was the biggest story of my life. As a younger and possibly more optimistic cameraman, I'd seen hope with those earlier stories to which I'd become attached. I'd seen promise in Lebanon that the warring sides could eventually coexist. I'd seen promise that a housewife turned president could lead the Philippine people with less tyranny than they had known, and I'd seen promise that democratic elections would someday replace Communist oppression in Czechoslovakia. Older and perhaps more jaded, I did not see the same uplifting promise in Pakistan and Afghanistan. The beliefs and customs in this part of the world had been forged and hardened over centuries, and I did not see change (for the good) coming anytime soon. And so, I was content to move on. I would continue to follow the story, but from afar.

Kabul had been liberated, but, in reality, the Taliban were never defeated (not to this day, at least). The military presence was growing as thousands of U.S. and other armed services began arriving in Afghanistan. My two-month tour seemed almost inconsequential when I thought about the troops and compared my time to theirs. A military deployment can last a year or more, with a hostile enemy threatening to kill you every day of that deployment. For those of us outside of the military, that's the kind of commitment and dedication we can never truly fathom.

We received word in Islamabad that, after two grueling months covering the fighting in Afghanistan, veteran correspondent Tom Aspell would be making his way out of Kabul to Islamabad and then home. We would fly together to Dubai, where we would each catch our connecting flights home; his to the island of Cypress and mine to the U.S. I'd first met Tom in Beirut, when I'd been based in Europe. He was a living legend already back then. He began his career as a cameraman in Vietnam. Then he moved to Lebanon and became a producer before taking on the role of correspondent. During his career, he covered pretty much everything. Besides Vietnam and Beirut, he covered conflicts in Bosnia, Chechnya, Baghdad, Romania, and now Afghanistan. His cameraman roots weren't the only thing we shared, either; we had something else in common. We had both loved the same woman.

He and the renowned photographer Francoise Demulder were a longstanding couple. I met her in Beirut shortly after their break-up. And, as I mentioned earlier in this book, she and I proceeded to have a torrid, three-year relationship that had a somewhat devastating effect on my marriage to Amy... the first time. But during the handful of assignments I had covered with Tom, our respective love for Francoise was never discussed. Not that she was an inconsequential figure in either of our lives. Quite the contrary. She was an epic figure. But, on those assignments, we were bound together by news stories rather than girlfriend stories. And, neither of us had had much of a stomach for gossipy kiss and tell stories.

I was sipping coffee with some coworkers in the expansive Marriott restaurant when Tom walked through the hotel's large glass doors. He spotted us from across the lobby and made his way to our table. He looked as if he had just escaped a war zone... because he had. He was disheveled but composed, gaunt and emaciated without being sickly or complaining. My bout with gastrointestinal issues had been a week-long affair. His had lasted for the entire two-month assignment, which explained the 30 lbs. he had left behind in Afghanistan.

We all stood to embrace and greet him.

Charlie began the welcome with, "What brings you to town? Things beginning to get boring up there in Kabul?"

Another followed with, "What took you so long? I thought Afghanistan was just next door—a hop, skip, and a jump away?"

I chimed in with, "Good to see ya. But you have looked better."

"Yeah, well, I guess the local Afghan cuisine doesn't agree with me." He was selfless. It was never about him, always about the story, which should be RULE #1 for all reporters. He turned the attention back to Afghanistan and continued, "It really is an incredible story up there. Yes, it's a bit... rough. I mean, after all the shit with the Russian invasion and occupation, and then five years of Taliban rule. Now, there's this quiet anticipation of 'What's next?' Nobody really knows. What is for sure is that you Americans aren't going anywhere. It looks like you'll be there for a while." He was right, although even he had no idea at the time that it would become America's longest war.

"Rough" was an understatement when referring to the conditions he and the team had endured. There was nothing remotely close to our Marriott accommodations in all of Afghanistan. He headed up to a hotel room to take full advantage of a Marriott shower—something he hadn't seen the likes of in over two months.

Since we were on the same flight that evening to Dubai, we shared a car to the airport, which gave us a little more time to get caught up. We spent it taking inventory of long-lost, mutual friends.

Referring to a cameraman with whom we were both close, I asked, "Have you seen Riggings lately?"

"He moved, or NBC moved him to Tel Aviv. He's got a place by the beach. It's almost like he's back in California. I ran into him in Bosnia. He shot some great stuff on the refugees there. Very moving. Where are you based these days?"

"Denver," I replied.

"Do you ever get to LA?"

"Occasionally for projects. I was there last summer covering the Democratic National Convention. It was good to see some old NBC colleagues."

"Do you remember George Moll?"

George was a super-creative and talented editor for ABC News. I had met him in Beirut while we'd both been covering the war there. Camaraderie crosses or spans network boundaries, and we'd hung out and socialized in the same multi-network group. But I had long since lost track of George's whereabouts since returning to the States.

"Of course, but I haven't seen him for ten years, maybe more. Where is he these days?"

"Hollywood. He's an executive with MTV or VH-1. He's producing some very interesting programs. He's quite successful. You should look him up the next time you're out that way."

"Wow. I had no idea. Thanks for letting me know, and I absolutely will give him a shout."

Shortly thereafter, we arrived at the airport and made our way through the Islamabad maze of check-in, security, and customs. We were seated in different rows in the business class cabin, so I said my goodbye and wished him well, knowing we would head in different directions once we landed in Dubai. I nestled into my large, comfortable leather seat, full of anticipation for the next 24 hours of air travel that would take me through Dubai and New York to deliver me home.

I would have plenty of time to reflect on my last assignment. What an assignment it had been. I was glad to have been a part of it, glad to have seen and witnessed it, and glad to be done with it. There was still a great deal of uncertainty in the world. I didn't know exactly what I'd be returning to. What would the news world look like back home in a post-9/11 era? What kind of projects awaited me? I would have little difficulty transitioning back to my dual role as producer/cameraman. It was a transition I was hoping to once again embrace, should the demand allow me. I wondered what effect my time away would have on my marriage. Would Amy and I simply pick up where we'd left off? It had not been a warm and fuzzy world in which I'd lived in the past few months. It would be difficult for me to flip a switch and pretend to be warm and fuzzy, even in charming Evergreen.

Tom's update on George and counsel to contact him in LA stayed with me. Perhaps the time was right to look beyond Denver, Chicago, and New York, and investigate other possibilities. It seemed ironic, perhaps incongruent, to have Pakistan in my rearview mirror while contemplating Hollywood on the horizon. Incongruency was just another challenge to be met and enjoyed.

18

A Weary Bond

The return home was a relief, but a resumption of normal domestic life wasn't automatic. My last assignment lingered with me. It was evident in our relationship that Amy and I had spent an extended period apart, living vastly different lives in wildly different settings. Even though I was physically back in Colorado, I remained partially removed. I attempted to share with Amy my observations of the last assignment, but found it difficult to articulate the assignment's effect on me. I'd asked to be involved in the coverage of that story. I'd wanted to see the how, what, where, and who of those being held responsible for the 9/11 attacks. I'd seen all of that and much more.

I was well aware of the resentment and hatred for America harbored by many around the world. I'd seen it all before. When I first encountered it in the youthful exuberance of my twenties, I thought it could be resolved, or maybe negotiated and dealt with. After Pakistan, I realized it was such a deep-rooted anger that it would never be eradicated. Like some incurable virus, it would only multiply and grow stronger.

I could have come to a similar conclusion if I, like most others, had read about that region in *The New York Times* or seen stories on *Nightly News*. But my impressions were made more vivid because of personal experiences and my proximity to the truth. That firsthand experience had hardened me. I wondered if, after so many years of proximity, perhaps a long break from even domestic news coverage might be a healthy option. As I transitioned from post-9/11 2001 to 2002, I looked in a new direction... one that might place less emphasis on the journalistic search for answers. While I contemplated breathing fresh air into my career, I also sensed my personal life needed a similar invigoration.

Outwardly, the veneer of Colorado life was bright and shiny, highly polished by the success of our two careers. Amy had climbed the corporate ladder, and very deservedly resided in the upper echelon of the Denver legal community. As a woman, she had successfully dealt with the ongoing sexism prevalent in the corporate world and law firms. Given her legal mastery and disdain for male chauvinism, she'd cut through the bullshit posthaste to establish herself as a legal force with which to be reckoned. However, it's impossible to fight that fight on a daily basis without it exacting a personal price. I could see an external, protective layer hardening her, and it was accompanied by a growing internal cynicism.

I was proud of what she'd accomplished and knew her success was a product of her intellect and tenacity. Success comes with a price, though, and what was that price? I had not attended law school, but had frequently seen the practice of law as a fight to the finish—a cerebral fight, but a fight nonetheless. In that regard, it was Amy's job to go into battle, in a legal sense, and she was good at it. I didn't care about other lawyers, but I was concerned that the personal scars produced by her professional battles would have a lasting negative impact on my wife... and us.

I could have placed the same examination on myself, but, fearful of the inevitable conclusions, I avoided doing so. Working in the trenches of network news had extracted a toll on me, but I didn't want to confront the results of self-psychoanalysis. We were both responsible for a tiny fissure beginning to form, and it was threatening our revived relationship. These were difficult observations to articulate. So, I kept them to myself and remained mostly silent on the subject.

Silence can sometimes be a prudent path to follow, but with personal relationships, it is rarely a wise option. Instead of focusing on and investing in us, we focused on and plowed into our careers. Working at a Denver law firm reminded Amy of her disdain for law firms. That disdain had been the driving motivation for her joining Boston Market six years earlier. Because of her impressive resume and extensive knowledge of franchise law, she'd been sought after by another Denver-based restaurant chain, Quiznos Subs. She was offered and accepted the position of General Counsel, the company's top lawyer. Gaining understanding of her new employer and its culture was time-consuming, and demanded she spent long hours at the office.

I looked to do more non-news projects that would require more producing and writing while utilizing my company's expanded production and post-production services. Prior to 9/11, I had added two editing suites to my office; the final pieces of my master plan. Slowly, the world was moving beyond the fear and uncertainty of 9/11. Corporate clients like First Data were returning and investing in video projects, from which I was once again benefitting.

On some projects, I would hire freelance editors, but I, too, had learned the software that powered the new wave of non-linear editing and enjoyed doing my own editing. Owning my editing facilities was a creative luxury in which I indulged. Sitting for hours in a dark, windowless room—glued to computer screens—may sound monotonous or even torturous to many. But for me, it was a magical part of the artistic process. Editing was where all of the miscellaneous elements were assembled into a meaningful and moving message. But the late nights and weekends I spent editing were time I spent away from home. I still made sure to attend Alexa's recitals, school plays, soccer games, and swim meets. It was my relationship with Amy that was paying the price.

Fortuitously, I heard from the former Applebee's president, Julia Stewart. Because of her leadership style, management experience, and the results she delivered, there'd been numerous restaurant companies that had courted her. She'd wisely and methodically evaluated her many options before choosing to lead an iconic restaurant chain that had lost its way. She had taken charge at IHOP and begun reenergizing their tired brand. As part of that reboot, she had big plans for employing video production as a communications tool. The 43-year-old company and its 1,000 restaurants had mostly been stuck in the 70s with stagnant sales and an uncertain future, and she meant to change that.

I was very pleasantly surprised to hear from her.

"Tim, it's Julia Stewart. I hope you remember me."

"Of course I remember you! I think when we last spoke, you were embarking on a brand-new executive career in the restaurant business. How goes the search?"

"The search was enjoyable. Invigorating. I talked to a number of companies."

"Was? So, you're once again gainfully employed? Congratulations. What did you decide upon?"

"Thank you. I took the job as Chief Operating Officer at IHOP. It's a great opportunity with a lot of upside. It's such a rich, iconic brand. But there is a fair amount of work to do. Which is the reason for my call. I think you were working for *60 Minutes* when we met. But in addition to the work you do for the news networks, I recall that you also produce corporate video projects, right?"

"Good memory. Yes, I do. I began working on corporate communications in Chicago and expanded that with my move to Denver. I have a full-service production company with the resources to do whatever you might need."

"Excellent. Would you please send me your reel so I can share it with my new team here at IHOP?"

By "reel," she was referring to a demo-reel or demonstration reel. It's a common tool that acts as a video resume or portfolio highlighting work done for past clients. To make the biggest and best impression for prospective clients, you edit together splashy highlights from a variety of examples that best show your capabilities and accomplishments. I had created different reels for different purposes—some that showcased my skill as a cameraman and others that did the same for my project or executive producer expertise. The fact that she knew what a reel was already demonstrated that she had a better understanding of television production than your average COO.

"Certainly, and thanks for the opportunity to present my work to IHOP. What is it you're looking to accomplish with video production?"

"Eventually a lot, but let's start with communication. There's a significant need for clearer, more impactful communication between the company, the franchisor, and the franchisees who own and operate the restaurants. In a few months, we are having our National Franchisee Conference (NFC). We'll have everyone together in Washington, D.C. for four days. I see it as a golden opportunity to employ corporate video as a powerful communication vehicle. We need a production company to help us with that. Once we've viewed your reel, you may get a call from our event planning company who handles the NFC for us, asking for an RFP (request for proposal)."

"Sounds like you're working on a short timeline. I'll send you a copy of my reel and a list of my corporate clients today. And thanks again for staying in touch and giving me this opportunity."

I soon heard back from the event planning company. My reel had been well-received and I was asked to submit a creative proposal and budget. To do so, I needed to know more about the project. The event company provided some basic standard guidelines. But to better understand what I was bidding on and attempting to create, I decided a follow-up call with Julia would be helpful. On that call, she was happy and almost excited to go into greater detail. What she had envisioned was a series of six videos of five to seven minutes in length that would play throughout the four-day conference. The aim was to remind the attendees of IHOP's rich history. A generation had grown up with IHOP. It was a piece of the American fabric. She wanted everyone to be reminded of that—to be moved by that, to once again be proud of that—and to instill that pride back into every restaurant. Some of the videos would convey additional operational or marketing messages, but pride was a central theme.

Armed with this detailed knowledge, I submitted an impressive proposal and comprehensive budget, and shortly thereafter, I was thrilled to learn I'd won the business. I was summoned to Glendale, California for a pre-production brainstorming session with the key team members of my new client. I soon learned Julia was a hands-on executive who had hit the ground running at IHOP. She was personally involved in several initiatives at her new company, and the NFC was a top priority. I was somewhat surprised at her level of interaction with this video series, given her COO title, but this was a project to which she felt closely attached.

It was an ambitious project with numerous interviews and elements to be shot in IHOP's headquarters and around LA, the birthplace of the first IHOP. As the executive producer, I oversaw every aspect of the project. The production schedule required me to travel to LA repeatedly, where I hired an army of freelancers, most of whom had become friends through my NBC connections. Critical components like talented crews, extensive lighting, teleprompters, and make-up artists were in abundance in the LA market. I then assembled a talented team to edit the series back in my Denver office. Julia and the IHOP team were impressed with the final cuts, or finished videos. Once everything was approved, I traveled to Washington, D.C. for the NFC.

Like most conferences, the IHOP NFC took place in a hotel, throughout a series of ballrooms and conference rooms. The first video was used to "open" or kick off the four-day meeting. It was shown to a crowd of 700 in a massive grand ballroom on a 20-foot video projection screen. The lights dimmed and the video began with Ray Charles' "America The Beautiful" playing as the soundtrack. The crowd sat hushed, glued to the massive screen, and not knowing what to expect. Images of Americana like majestic purple mountains and waving fields of grain were intercut with vintage images from IHOP's nostalgic past, all of it splashed across the big screen. I was backstage and peering through a curtain, watching the crowd and waiting for their reaction, which would determine my effectiveness as an EP for IHOP.

The video concluded, and the crowd... remained silent. My heart sank. I was overcome with an immediate sense of failure. I'd thought I'd nailed it, but the stillness of the crowd told me otherwise. After five seconds, which felt like five hours of silence, the crowd erupted. They all leaped to their feet for a standing ovation. They cupped their hands around their mouths and yelled in universal approval. Tears were visible on some of the franchisees' cheeks.

I was relieved by the applause, but still struggling to make sense of the initial silence. Video was a new tool introduced by the new COO, Julia. As the crowd continued to applaud and pump their fists in the air, I saw her backstage. She approached me with an applauding gesture in my direction and said, "I think they like your work."

"It appears so. I had my doubts right after the video finished. The silence was deafening. What was that all about?"

"This is a change for them. They're not used to seeing this. It just needed to sink in."

"Let's hope the other videos are well-received and sink in like this first one."

She smiled the smile of a wise corporate exec and said, "I'm confident we'll achieve what we set out to accomplish. Nice work."

"Thank you."

As the conference progressed, the other videos were equally well-received. That reception and the motivational impact they had on those franchisees in attendance justified the not-so-modest cost of producing the video series. The project was universally viewed as a success. While I was the executive producer of the series of videos, the project had been created (paid for) *by* the IHOP corporation *for* the IHOP franchisees.

In her first few months with the company, Julia had begun to install a lost pride throughout the IHOP franchisees, in part by using slickly produced moving videos. It was a familiar tool for her, but it was new and eye-opening for the franchisees. The same could be said of the handful of IHOP corporate employees who had worked at organizing the NFC and witnessed the impact of the video series. During the conference, a murmur percolated through the hotel, asking, "Who's the video guy?" That murmur grew louder as word made way back to the headquarters in Glendale, California. After the conference ended, several IHOP executives, directors, and managers were eager to capitalize on the initial bond Julia had so quickly forged with the franchisees. They saw the production of similar videos as a way to build on the communication between the company and franchisees while also helping to achieve their corporate objectives. I was soon fielding requests from the marketing department, which wanted to utilize videos to demonstrate the new ad campaigns and marketing strategies throughout the system. Research and Development wanted to energize the tired menu and excite the franchisees with new items. The training department wanted to ensure that the over 1,000 restaurants' employees were properly trained on how to flawlessly prepare those new items. And they all turned to me to help transform their ideas into video.

Julia had inadvertently opened up a floodgate of interest for my services. Anything that would bring new-age technology to bear on a stone-age brand, she was overwhelmingly supportive of. My popularity was quickly growing within the ranks of this newfound client. This popularity would require repeated trips to Los Angeles; it was the film and television capital of the world, but a town about which I knew very little. My most extensive visit had been as a cameraman freelancing for NBC during the 2000 Democratic Convention. That had happened with the support of a network, and I felt as though I'd only scratched the surface. I was fortunate to have a client who had delivered me to California. Beyond IHOP, breaking into the LA market looked daunting and intimidating. But then, so had Chicago not so many years before.

I remembered Tom Aspell's sage advice from Pakistan, to look up our mutual friend George Moll who was living and working in LA. That advice made particular sense now that I was regularly traveling to LA for work. I had lost track of George, but when I began to search for news of his career, I didn't have to search far. He'd left ABC News, where he'd been working as an editor, and applied that experience to a different genre of television. He'd gone to work for VH-1, becoming executive producer of a revolutionary television series. *Behind the Music* premiered in 1997 to immediate critical acclaim, eventually becoming the network's top-rated show. It was not the eye candy music video fare airing on MTV, and it wasn't the kind of idol worship so often used to promote musical artists. *Behind the Music* was (and is) a documentary-like look into the lives and careers of popular musical groups and musicians. It's an honest, in-depth report that examines the rise and fall, the successes and failures and struggles, of the lives of musicians. The news discipline George learned while at ABC provided the perfect foundation for running (an EP is known as a show-runner) *Behind the Music*. What made it different and popular was its insistence on sticking to the truth while avoiding the sleazy tabloid gossip that so often permeates reporting on artists and celebrities.

So many years had passed since I'd last seen him in Lebanon, I was hesitant to call George. And, with him being a bigtime Hollywood executive producer of a hit show, I didn't know what to expect even if I did succeed in reaching him. When I finally phoned him, he was incredibly accessible, asking about me and downplaying his major success. The conversation soon meandered its way back to Beirut; the many colorful characters and coworkers we'd worked with there as well as the excitement, danger, and general craziness of covering that war.

He could empathize with and was supportive of my move from shooting to doing more producing. He was in the envious position of still working as an executive producer for *Behind the Music* while also creating content on his own through his production company, County Line Productions. His VH-1 work provided security while he developed and pitched other concepts and show ideas. With his resume and talent, I was certain he'd succeed with numerous other series. But, I also thought it brazen to hit him up for work on my first "out of the blue" call. We assured each other we'd stay in touch and promised to get together on one of my trips to California.

As I networked with other network friends, I found out I had additional former coworkers who had transplanted to LA from all over the country and world. I was reminded of a former *TODAY* show field producer, Peter Johansen, who had left New York and news altogether to write comedy screenplays in Hollywood. I'd heard he, too, had become an executive producer. We had worked closely on the many *TODAY* international broadcasts while I'd been based oversees. At some point, I would need to reconnect with him. His understanding of the television business beyond news could prove valuable.

And should I ever want to navigate the news business in LA, I'd heard that Audrey Kolina was working there as well—or, more accurately, Burbank. The former Hong Kong bureau chief with whom I'd worked on the *Where in the World is Matt Lauer?* from Nepal had returned home. She was now the West Coast Senior Producer for *TODAY*. More than a lofty title, it was a big job that came with both a hefty amount of opportunity and responsibility. One of those responsibilities for news coverage was hiring freelance producers. Should they have added experience as an NBC cameraman... even better.

With a few contacts, colleagues, and clients, the LA market began to look less impenetrable. And, my one LA client was soon occupying all of my time.

It's always nice to feel as though you're contributing, providing value through collaboration, and feel wanted or needed. That had been the positive reinforcement I'd felt when working for my many network clients and those non-network clients I'd had in Chicago and Denver. And because of the expanding work at IHOP, I was again experiencing that feeling from my new corporate client.

The repeated West Coast trips were wonderful for my business, but my absence at home had contributed to my marriage's downward spiral. The positive reinforcement Amy and I were feeling through our work was nonexistent in our relationship.

Amy and I had grown up together. The roots of our relationship stretched back to high school. Our 25-year journey had provided us with deep and lasting friendships and unforgettable memories. It was a relationship whose core was strengthened by our having overcome the failure of our first marriage (to each other), a subsequent emotionally charged reunion that had led to a second marriage (to each other), and most importantly, the addition of a perfect and confident adolescent daughter. We had one of those lives that appeared to lack nothing.

But you can't judge a book by its cover.

That exterior could no longer conceal the true emptiness within; an emptiness of which we were both painfully aware and whose pain was worsening each day. Between our careers and our kid, time just seemed to... run out. And while we cherished what little free time we did have, Amy and I weren't cherishing one another. We could have tried to continue the concealment, pretending that a relationship devoid of passion for one another was normal, or even livable. But eventually, we decided to be honest with one another. The truth was that growing up together had just been the beginning. Over the many years that had followed, we'd grown distant, grown apart, and outgrown what we'd once shared. In the end, the only things growing in our relationship were the time apart and the distance between us.

A failed attempt at marriage counseling brought us both to the conclusion that separation was a better option than doing nothing. And after that, divorce would likely be the next option. It was a sad and painful conclusion, but so, too, had been the last year or so of our marriage. Once we realized the end was in sight, we were able to calmly and rationally discuss the next steps... like adults. We both agreed that to criticize, demoralize, and generally "trash" one another would only serve to deepen the pain experienced by our daughter Alexa. She was a young teenager who wondered what had happened to her idyllic world. We could only try to minimize her struggle by giving her all of our loving support while not ridiculing and disparaging each other.

And so, without the hatred of some break-ups, we sadly and quietly moved on and went in different directions.

I moved out, and for almost a year, I commuted to California to handle the constant workload being generated by a resurgent IHOP. The company's longtime CEO and Chairman had retired and Julia was promoted from COO to CEO, the top job. Her promotion, unsurprisingly, coincided with an even more fast-paced change and even more demand for my services. Over time, the airfare and hotel expenses increased to the point where I needed to establish a more stable LA presence. It was only a two-hour flight from Denver, but those two hours would make it impossible for me to be available for Alexa every day, all the time. It was another painful decision with which I wrestled. I talked at length with Alexa and Amy. We agreed my move to LA would only work if I returned "home" to Denver on a weekly or every-other-week basis.

I wanted to leave the house, our former home, intact. When I packed up for the move to LA, my personal belongings were minimal. Most of everything I owned was business-related. I had purchased a great deal of professional production and post-production video equipment. These were tools of the trade that enabled me to provide full-service video solutions. And, in the process, that equipment had generated a sizable source of income.

I had closed my office space in Denver after I'd uninstalled all of the equipment. It amounted to a mountain of cameras, lenses, lights, tripods, computers, hard drives, flat-screen monitors, and miles of cable to pack up and load out. That was a somber experience, but nothing compared to the journey from Evergreen to LA. I hugged and kissed Alexa goodbye with the promise of returning the following weekend, once I was settled in LA. We both maintained a brave face and focused on my many upcoming returns to Denver.

As I slowly drove away, in my rearview mirror, I could see her standing in the driveway and waving goodbye. My brave face didn't last long. As soon as she was out of sight, I began to cry, longing for a time that was long gone.

19

RESTART

Throughout the two-day drive from Denver to LA, I was only able to partially dry my eyes. Winding my way through the dramatic and still snowcapped Rocky Mountains provided a fleeting distraction from my constant reflection. I knew Amy and I would continue to shower Alexa with love. I also knew I'd be back to see her soon and again and again, but I worried how that would affect our tight relationship. As I drove through the wind-swept landscape of Utah's Canyon Country, I tried to focus on the many happy memories we'd created together. I vowed to work hard so that those memories would never be swept away and forgotten.

I had found and rented an expansive loft space that would double as both my residence and office. Once again, I was uncertain of my future, just as I had been 12 years prior in Chicago. I was extremely hesitant to duplicate the full-service office space I'd built up in Denver. I didn't understand the sprawling area that is Los Angeles. I only knew that LA housing costs and office space were expensive. Paying rent for both a loft and an office was more than I wanted to invest. The huge loft offered more than enough space for me to set up my sophisticated editing facility and have my separate and private living quarters. The good news was that, unlike Chicago, LA offered me a built-in, well-paying client.

At times, I felt like an in-house agency working solely for IHOP. The successful NFC in Washington, which had introduced me to IHOP, was followed by another the following year at the famed Broadmoor in Colorado Springs, and another after that. Each NFC required a new and flashier series of videos. New menu items continued to be launched and promotions rolled out, and I was hired to create the supporting videos. Julia and her team were continually introducing new ad campaigns, and I was hired to help communicate and explain that messaging internally to the IHOP franchisee community.

And with each new project, the hard-working new CEO seemed to be more involved. I had never seen a corporate executive who was so accessible and engaged with her team. She possessed a rare combination of vision and precise sense of detail. She would delegate to her team and still follow through on the progress. On my many production shoots, she became a regular subject in front of my camera—not because she was an egotistical boss who monopolized the bright light, but because she was so good. On camera, her poise, confidence, and experience were undeniable. And she was beautiful. She was a leader who brought out the best in her employees and franchisees. People seemed to genuinely enjoy following her. Even Wall Street liked her. And, for a vendor like me, she was a dream with whom to work.

As the shoots and edits increased in frequency, so also did the meetings. Increasingly, the conference rooms were replaced with restaurant settings where strategy and pre-production talk would take place over a working lunch or dinner. It was in these situations, and the "road trips" during the NFCs, where I became better acquainted with my client, Julia… and she with me. She had climbed to the top of the ladder in the world of corporate restaurants as an executive at Burger King, Taco Bell, Applebee's, and IHOP. She was equally knowledgeable and comfortable in the world of fine dining and fine wine, as was I.

We had met ever so briefly on a plane and knew little of each other personally. She was impressed with the work my team and I had produced for IHOP, which was ordering more and more projects, creating more and more work for us. She was also inquisitive about my prior life, and similarly impressed with my life and times overseas. In the world of news, I'd often worked with female field producers, senior producers, editors, and bosses. Julia was a rare breed in the corporate world—a female chief executive. The more I learned about her, the more I liked her.

I reconnected with former *TODAY* field producer Peter Johansen. He'd last known me as a staff cameraman, and so I updated him on my change of course. He had made a name for himself as executive producer of talks shows with big-name talent like Martin Short. He'd been working in Hollywood for a decade now, and had made acquaintances and forged alliances in a town where connections meant the difference between success and failure.

Hollywood speaks with its own language, and at first, that lingo was a foreign language to me. Peter told me there was something "in the pipeline" waiting to be "greenlit." I translated that to mean, "There is a program about to be approved." In the meantime, we got caught up and relived old times at NBC dinners.

In the early part of this century, "reality competition" programming was in full frenzy mode. *Survivor* debuted in 1997 and was an instant hit. Suddenly, everyone wanted to cash in and copy the format. Even kids were getting into the game. In 2003, Peter had worked as executive producer on a television series called *America's Most Talented Kid*—a talent competition for kids. The project in the "pipeline" was a proposed 2nd season. If that came to fruition, the revived series would need to hire producers. He asked if I was interested.

For better or worse, my intellectual curiosity has always been a motivating factor for me. The world of reality competition was a genre about which I was ignorant, but that was a fact that only heightened my curiosity. I was enjoying my post-Pakistan break from the news. I was busy with the world of IHOP, but could always make time to pursue another interesting endeavor. Reality TV was taking TV by storm, and so I wanted to know more. *Hell, yes*, I was interested in producing reality television.

I'd become far more knowledgeable and comfortable with the practice of networking than when I'd first returned to the states from Italy. In the 13 years since, I'd continued to make friends in network circles. Many of the staffers and freelancers who worked out of the extensive and productive Burbank Bureau were friends of mine. Some of those friendships dated back to my overseas days. I might have been taking a self-imposed exile from the demands of news coverage, but I was still both a veteran and student of broadcast journalism. I watched the news religiously (both then and now), and at the very least, I wanted to stay in touch with those who were responsible for those broadcasts.

Over the years, I'd briefly visited the complex a couple of times, but I was more familiar with the people than the place. I contacted Audrey, who immediately invited me over to say hi and take a "VIP" tour of the facilities and its inner workings.

With each networking opportunity, I made certain to stress my transition from cameraman to producer. I guess I expected more resistance to the change, as it wasn't that common of a move, but each mention was met with complete understanding and support, as if it was a natural and almost expected development.

Audrey greeted me with a sincere welcome and escorted me up to the third floor and the news desk. There, I saw a number of former acquaintances. The bureau chief, Polly Powell, I'd met years back when she'd been a magazine show producer for NBC. As Burbank bureau chief, she was responsible for considerably more news coverage and under much more pressure— none of which showed through her even-tempered demeanor.

The bustling newsroom was humming with activity. New York was the true mothership, but Burbank was a major supporting player. *TODAY* and *Nightly News* originate out of 30 Rock in New York and Burbank had its studio where live inserts into both shows were shot. I could see a cameraman and soundman team, both friends of mine, who were tweaking their gear and lights for an upcoming live shot. Producers and correspondents were busy going over scripts for stories on which they were working. On the first or main floor were located the eight edit rooms where those stories were assembled. Graphic artists were working at digital terminals to create Computer Generated Imagery (CGI) that would support the editing process and finish stories. The intake room resembled a high-tech NASA control room, where satellite feeds from all over the world were received and recorded. The lot itself was old and a bit dated, but the equipment and technology used to make television there was state of the art.

As I proceeded on my VIP tour, I ran into the oldest of friends, dating back to my first tour of Beirut in 1983. Mike Mosher started his NBC career as a soundman in the Cairo bureau. He was one of those rare exceptions who made the leap from crew to producer. Covering just about every news story in Europe, the Middle East, Africa, and Asia, he quickly rose within the ranks of NBC. From Beirut to Manila, we'd covered a lot of ground and stories together. He'd been Bureau Chief in Tokyo when NBC had decided to close that bureau (along with many others), after which they'd relocated him to LA. He was Audrey's equivalent on *Nightly News*—West Coast Senior Producer. He was surprised and somewhat startled to see me, as I hadn't told him about my move west.

"Wow, Tim Ortman! What are you doing here? Are you working for us… again?"

Audrey saw an opportunity to get back to work and excused herself from my tour. "I'll let you boys get caught up and relive your war stories. I'll be in my office. Tim, don't leave without saying goodbye."

"Mike! Good to see you. It's been a while; I can't even remember the last time. No, not in the employ of NBC News at the moment. I just stopped by to say hi and get an in-depth look at the nerve center you guys have here."

"Are you living out here? When I last heard, I think you were in Chicago, or Denver maybe."

"That's right. But now I'm an Angelino. And I'm following in your footsteps. I've set down my camera and am doing some producing."

"That's great. Did you see Polly? Does she know you're living here now and producing? She and Audrey hire tons of freelancers around here. I'm sure they'll put your ass to work."

"I did, and yes, they both know I'm producing and not shooting these days. I'm easing into things and in no hurry to go back into battle."

Mike burst out laughing. "You and me both. These days, I'm more likely to trip over a cable and break my neck than get shot."

It was good for me to see the Burbank operation up-close and from a different perspective other than as cameraman. It was also good to reconnect with friends. Network news coverage had and would always be such a big part of me. I wasn't ready to "jump back into the fire" quite yet, but it was reassuring to know they'd have me if I so desired.

Working in and better understanding the lay of the land in La-La Land was expanding my life. But a big portion of my life still resided back in Denver. The concern I'd had over moving to California and away from Alexa made for weekly or semi-weekly return trips to Denver. Just living in a different city, any other city, was a tortuous adjustment. But the frequency with which I returned somewhat eased the pain for both of us. I found I was still able to attend many of her swim meets and school events.

Because Amy and I had insisted on and followed through with an amicable divorce, my trips to Evergreen allowed for an unusual and even unorthodox living arrangement. The large house in Evergreen had a separate guest suite in the basement. It had been Steve Azzato's temporary residence during the McVeigh and Nichols trials, but rarely used since. Staying there allowed me to spend more time with my daughter and also allowed my ex-wife to get away or socialize with peace of mind. My being able to kiss my daughter goodnight and then travel two floors below her allowed both of us to sleep soundly.

California is a nice place to live... and visit. Soon, Alexa was spending her spring and summer breaks from school with me. She enjoyed attending beach camp and making new friends. An NBC editor and dear friend, Judy Lieber was able to score tickets to *The TONIGHT Show*. Judy accompanied her daughter Annie and Alexa (they became friends) to see Jack Johnson perform live. At that time, he was Alexa's favorite pop artist, and that evening created a favorite memory, too. It was impossible to shrink the physical distance that separated us, but over time, the pain we both felt dissipated and we were able to get back to simply being dad and daughter. We both saw that any space between us caused by my post-divorce relocation could be filled by the closeness we'd always had.

As a dad, knowing that Alexa would be alright and that our relationship would continue to flourish was enormously fulfilling. My post-divorce personal life was not nearly as full. I was unfamiliar and even leery of the online dating scene. I'd at first found the LA work scene to be intimidating; the dating scene was far scarier. I had a handful of male friends I would hang with, and I was busy, not lonely. But there was no rebound personal relationship in which I had invested.

At that time, it was fairly common knowledge at IHOP that the CEO was going through a divorce of her own. What I was contemplating made very little sense, but what I had sensed was a slight mutual attraction that resided just under the surface of our working relationship. She was never flirtatious, but sometimes engaging with me, beyond the work we shared. Perhaps she would be open to joining me for dinner.

Ridiculous, I thought. Julia wasn't my coworker. She was *the client*; my boss. I had enjoyed many client dinners, and yet what I envisioned with her was something different. I wanted to get to know her better outside of work. And, while she often

366

expressed interest in my background and life, there was never any time for that. I began to rationalize the unthinkable. This would be an opportunity for both of us to explore each other and see if there was, in fact, a mutual interest. Unless, of course, she declined my invitation, which would be embarrassing at best. Being "declined" at a college party was demoralizing. Having my hopes dashed by a CEO would be understandable, but every bit as ruinous to my self-esteem. And, there were business repercussions to consider.

One afternoon, an extensive video crew and I had again "overtaken" her executive office. She was always accessible to give interviews and on-camera appearances for the many projects we were producing. After the lighting was disassembled and the camera equipment packed up, the crew slowly departed. It was just Julia and me in a large office. I asked if I could have a moment with her. Thinking I was going to go over the video project with her, she said, "Of course."

I had decided to pursue something completely different from the video project. I was going entirely off-script.

Always wanting to give her best effort, she asked, "So, how did I do?"

"You nailed it, and I'm not just saying that to suck up to the client. We've talked about this before. You're just so comfortable on camera, which is no small task."

"Well, I guess that has something to do with the fact that I've worked in the restaurant industry for 30 years and it's a business I'm very comfortable talking about."

"That might have something to do with it. May I change the topic?"

"Sure."

"I don't mean to pry into your personal life, but I understand you're going through a divorce. I can empathize. I'm recently divorced myself, and hope yours goes as smoothly and painlessly as possible."

"Thank you. It seems like it is a common practice anymore. Things don't always work out as we first envisioned."

"Getting back to being comfortable, in front of the camera or otherwise... how would you be if... you and I had .... well, I mean that, should you... comfort, could I comfort you over... I MEAN, would you be comfortable joining me for dinner sometime?"

There, *I'd said it*. Perhaps not so eloquently or practiced, but I'd just asked the boss to dinner! Normally, I would have needed a few glasses of wine to help muster that kind of courage. But I was totally sober... in her office, which now looked like the edge of a cliff that I'd just leaped off.

She struggled to respond. "Uh, well..."

Uh Oh.

I immediately feared the worst. "Look, I don't want you to read too much into this. We've been to countless dinners together. I just thought it might be nice to dine and talk without the communications, marketing, and/or training departments at the table."

"Tim, I am flattered. It's just that..."

Uh oh, again.

I sensed a disaster. "I may have overstepped my bounds here. Let's maybe step back and..."

"No, that's not it at all. I would very much like to go to dinner with you."

"You would?"

"Yes. You're an interesting guy; a talented guy. It sounds like you've led a very exciting life, and I would very much enjoy having dinner with you."

Minor salvation, but confusion was governing my racing brain. "But...?"

"But, I'm CEO of a publicly-traded company. I have to answer to shareholders and follow corporate guidelines. I can't date vendor partners or other employees, even if I want to."

I had not thought about the bothersome details like pesky shareholders and guidelines.

"Well, it's all in the name. It's not a date, really. It's a get-to-know-you-better dinner and a movie."

"Get-to-know-you better?"

"That's right. And, once you get to know me better, it's highly unlikely you'll want to date me."

"You make a convincing argument, but still..." She paused and, out of character for her, struggled with what to say next. "Okay. So... let's you and me do this 'dinner and a movie.' But it's a good news and bad news scenario."

"What's that?"

"The good news is, if we enjoy each other's company, then we go out to dinner again, and maybe again."

"I don't see a problem so far."

"Well, the bad news is, at that point, I may like you enough that I have to fire your ass."

"I'll take my chances with those odds. Dinner and a movie, it is."

* * * * *

Julia and I had each spent so much time dining in restaurants that, as a change of pace, I chose Bistro Ortman, my loft, as the setting for our first date... I mean "dinner." Thanks in part to my seven years based in Europe, I'd learned my way around a kitchen and even mastered a handful of dishes. I had a wine selection that rivaled the wine lists at most casual restaurants, and as a television professional, owned the latest and greatest, big-screen, high-def TV for movie watching. Underneath that superficially confident appearance, I was nervous as hell hosting my CEO dinner companion. As an anxiety-reducing measure for me, I'd pitched the evening as an informal, low-stress dinner... with even lower expectations.

I welcomed her into my apartment, poured her a glass of champagne, and showed her around the wide-opened floor plan. She seemed particularly impressed with the portion of the loft where I had installed all of the high-tech editing equipment that I had brought from Colorado.

I'd decided to cook rack of lamb for dinner—something simple and yet elegant sounding. Its simplicity is that it begins on the stovetop and then slowly and effortlessly finishes over time in the oven. I'd cooked it dozens of times before, but this was my first attempt in my new loft... on my new electric stove. For twenty years, I had only cooked on gas stoves.

After the tour, we shared some appetizers over conversation, which revolved mostly around our kids. She joined me in the kitchen as I started dinner. The side dishes were already prepped. I just needed a few minutes to focus on the main dish, the lamb. I poured some oil into a preheated sauté pan and then placed the rack of lamb into the pan to sear, just as I'd done so many times before.

WOOSH. An enormous, nuclear mushroom cloud exploded from the pan and immediately engulfed my entire kitchen in smoke. Julia ran through the loft, taking cover behind a couch. Stunned and blinded by the smoke and splattering oil, I struggled to find the control knob for the electric burner. My lack of familiarity with electric stovetops had allowed the pan to become radio-active hot. Within seconds, a high-pitched and deafening fire alarm sounded.

The alarm was not just in my unit. Because I lived in a large, modern building, I had triggered the central alarm for the entire building. I called the leasing office to explain that it was just smoke, not fire. And they explained that because I had tripped the central alarm, the Pasadena Fire Department had to be dispatched. They were already on their way. Once they arrived, they could silence the alarm. Until then, it would loudly serenade my abruptly interrupted evening.

Waving a towel through the thick smoke, I found Julia across the loft. I asked if she was alright. Once she realized the kitchen was not on fire, she took a sip of champagne and tried in vain to control her laughter.

I heard a siren outside and worked my way through the smoke-filled loft and out into the also smoked-filled hallway. It was amazing how much smoke one fatty rack of lamb was capable of producing. I could see a squad of firefighters walking down the hallway. They were in full gear, wearing helmets and yellow flame-retardant clothing, and carrying axes as they made their way toward the scene of the crime. I greeted them in the hallway.

Trying to ease the situation and get back to what was left of my dinner, I offered, "Sorry, fellas. There's no need for alarm... eh, I mean worry. I was just cooking some dinner and—"

The lead fireman responded, "I kinda figured that. I can smell it. What are ya making?"

"Rack of lamb."

"Smells good."

"Thanks. I feel like an idiot. It's just smoke. A bunch of smoke, but it looks worse than it is."

These veterans had seen it all before. "I know. I'm sure, like you said, it's nothing. But we've got to come inside and check it out. Hope you're okay with that."

"Sure, of course. Come on in."

Julia had taken the lead and opened windows to help dissipate some of the smoke. Now that my intimate dinner party had expanded to include four first responders, I made the introductions all around. Jerry, the lead fireman, took a quick mandatory stroll through my smokey loft to make sure there weren't any hidden, smoldering embers. Seeing an absence of raging flames, he radioed to the team at the firetruck, "All's clear." Someone then accessed the building's main alarm panel and switched off the fire alarm. As Jerry was surveying my apartment, he suddenly fixated on the corner of my loft dedicated to editing. With my two Emmys and hundreds of videocassettes stacked on bookcases, he turned to me and enthusiastically said, "You're in the business!"

"In the business," as I quickly learned, was an LA phrase referring to the television and movie industries. Hollywood was a company town. All of the many industries that were a part of television and film production comprised "the business."

"Yes, I am."

Jerry's interest only heightened. "What are you, like a producer or director? I probably seen some of your work."

"Producer... well, actually, I started out as a cameraman and then transitioned to doing more producer work. If you watch the network news then you've probably seen some of my work. But I really don't do, like, television series or films that you would've seen..."

Undeterred, Jerry continued, "You know, I have my SAG card." SAG is the acronym for Screen Actors Guild. It denotes someone who works "in the business." The guy standing in my living room wearing a helmet and clutching an ax did not look like an actor to me. Yet, he began to enumerate his unsolicited resume while simultaneously pulling his business card from his wallet.

All of a sudden, I saw myself conducting an impromptu audition for a struggling actor who played a firefighter in real life… for a role that I neither had nor could offer. Julia and the other firefighters were all silently perplexed at the direction this fire rescue mission had taken. And, I desperately wanted to move on from both the kitchen fire and the casting call to resume my dinner with the CEO.

I thanked Jerry for both his business card and for volunteering his onscreen credits.

"Jerry, that sounds like an interesting list of credits there. Thanks for sharing. But, at the moment, I don't think I have anything that is right for you. I'll hang onto your card and, in the meantime, I'll have my people call your people. And if you guys have seen enough here and you're comfortable the smoke is under control, I'd like to get back to ruining dinner for Julia."

Julia and I thanked them profusely for their efforts. Satisfied that I'd only burnt dinner and not the apartment building, they headed out of my loft and back to their truck.

Julia could not resist offering her observations. "Who knew, when you lit the building on fire, you'd end up conducting a job interview."

"Hollywood. I guess you just never know where or when your big break is going to happen. One minute, you're putting out a fire, and the next, you're George Clooney."

Well, so much for a laid-back, stress-free dinner. I was able to salvage enough semi-burnt lamb and sides to assemble our meal. We transitioned into easy conversation that focused on our past careers before IHOP. She had lived all over the country and traveled extensively while working for giants like Burger King and Taco Bell, both having identified her potential early on. She keenly articulated some of the difficulty faced by women executives, but without sounding angry or resentful. She was well-read and an avid news consumer, which was evident through her sincere interest in the many stories of travels from my overseas past. Maybe it was the wine, a genuine attraction, or a combination of both, but Julia and I shared plenty of laughter over dinner.

After we shared dinner, we sat on side by side recliners to share a movie. One of my favorite films is the 1995 epic *Braveheart*, which won Oscars for both best picture and best director. Eight years after its release, Julia had still never seen the movie. I convinced her she would love it and she begrudgingly settled in for a not-your-typical date movie, even though we were not on an officially sanctioned date.

It is one of my favorite films, I can quote most of the dialogue from the film, which I did freely that evening. To add dramatic impact, I paused the film to provide additional, historical background for many of the gruesome battle scenes. This made the three-hour movie even longer and prompted my dinner companion to make a request.

"If Mel Gibson won the Oscar for Best Director as you said, maybe you should let him tell his story instead of telling it for him?"

She made a valid point, and after that, I resisted adding more play-by-play. As the hero's life came to an end, so too did our evening. It was getting late and she needed to get home to her babysitter and kids. I phoned for a taxi to take her the short ride home and walked her to the lobby of my building.

I had pitched it as a "get to know you better" dinner. The more I knew, the more I liked her. I wasn't sure that feeling was reciprocal. "Well, that was an eventful evening," I told her. "I hope you liked that whole fire and smoke thing I planned before dinner."

"That was an unexpected touch. You just don't see that level of... excitement at dinner parties that often."

"Well, there's plenty more to see."

"Actually, I think I've seen enough."

Uh oh, again.

I wasn't sure how to read that response, but I was leaning towards a negative interpretation. "Seen enough as in, enough is enough... like, never again?"

"More like I've seen enough to make an executive decision... and I'd like to see more. How about you?"

"More is good. More is great. I think more is... a must."

"Sounds like we're on the same page."

Just then, her cab arrived. As we walked outside, she said "Okay, I'll let you plan our next date, perhaps in a restaurant somewhere."

I opened the door for her and, as she sat in the back seat, she said, "Tim, I can't wait to see you again. Oh, one more thing. You're fired."

20

REPELLED BY REALITY

Julia was principled and highly ethical in her corporate leadership. Seeing things from her perspective, it was inappropriate and a clear conflict of interest to date the boss of IHOP while working for IHOP. But I wasn't forced to drop everything and escorted out of the building. I had five or six projects in various stages of completion with different departments. The stakeholders of those projects were shocked to hear that I would be resigning their business to date their CEO. I would, however, finish those commitments before moving on to a more serious and personal IHOP focus.

Meanwhile, I hoped some of my other opportunities "in the pipeline" would materialize into work.

Peter called at the perfect time to inform me that the proposed 2nd season of the talent competition *America's Most Talented Kids* (AMTK) had officially received the green light. While the first season had aired on NBC in 2003, the second season would air the following year on an NBC-owned cable network, PAX. Things moved quickly to get the show up to speed. I was hired as a field producer. The show's musical contestants ranged from eight to thirteen years old. Once they were selected, I worked with Peter and the other show producers to identify interesting and compelling backstories about their talents, lives, or both. Freelance crews were hired to shoot the stories with me. I then wrote and edited that material into 2:00 pieces that aired throughout the program.

Peter shared the executive producer title with two other EPs, Mark Cronin and James Rowley. It was through Cronin's production company Mindless Entertainment that the show was produced. Mindless Entertainment was based out of the historic Raleigh Studios, whose Hollywood history reached back to the days of Charlie Chaplin and Douglas Fairbanks. Raleigh sat across the street from the legendary Paramount Pictures lot. I was working in the heart of Hollywood.

The excitement I felt while working on AMTK was generated by working in a new location in a different kind of television, which posed new challenges. While I knew Peter from my NBC News days, this was an entirely new and different team with whom I was meshing. It was exhilarating, at first.

AMTK was a complicated show with many moving parts to orchestrate. There were many weeks of pre-production, shooting, and rehearsals that preceded every show. Each episode was then taped in a large television studio in front of a live studio audience, and featured seven musical performers who, one by one, performed their act before three celebrity judges. During the actual show taping or the talent competition, there was a great deal of excitement and anticipation felt by the contestants, their families, and supporters. That feeling was somewhat contagious, and felt to a lesser degree by those of us on the crew.

The tenets of storytelling I'd learned from working in news served me well while working on AMTK. Those basic principles applied whether the story was news or entertainment. But that was where any similarity between news and reality or talent competition ended.

The second season of AMTK was well-received and seen by enough viewers to merit a third season in 2005. Much of the same crew stayed intact and returned for season three. Peter shared his EP role and Mark Cronin's Mindless Entertainment was again the production company. Through Mindless, Cronin seemed to have a "Midas Touch" when it came to creating popular, whimsical reality or competition series. He had produced a number shows like *The Surreal Life*, *The X Show, Strange Love*, and many, many others (he is still at it and highly successful today). His connections were extensive at many entertainment cable networks. In between the two seasons of AMTK, Mindless Entertainment had negotiated a series with Game Show Network (GSN). *Extreme Dodgeball* was a gameshow competition of themed teams playing against one another in an elimination format. I was hired to produce the same kind of background stories that I'd done for AMTK.

The work was plentiful. One show led to another and another. The American television audience demanded the kind of mindless programming at which Cronin excelled. He had cracked the code, delivering hit after hit after hit to American viewers. I was employed as a small part of this hit-producing team, and as such, I was grateful. But that wasn't a fulfilling or lasting feeling.

Everyone on the crew of AMTK, *Extreme Dodgeball*, and other shows felt as though they were working on something special; something important. Sure, at the same time, they realized it was all from Mindless Entertainment, but they took the production aspect seriously. Yet, increasingly, putting on my serious face to produce for a game show or talent competition became a forced exercise. I no longer saw these programs as special. The break from news to focus on my new corporate client, IHOP, had been refreshing. Given my news background and experience, though, I began to struggle with my new reality direction. I no longer saw my work as meaningful, but trivial.

I simply could not bring myself to drink the Kool-Aid. I was becoming terrible at pretending that this form of television meant anything to me other than a steady paycheck. I had not entirely abandoned the news business while dipping my toe into the reality pool. I was still an avid watcher and reader of news. I still socialized in news circles within my network of network friends. Now I needed more than friendship. I needed to once again feel a news connection and enjoy my work.

In 2003, after years of inspections to verify the destruction and absence of Saddam Hussein's chemical, biological, and nuclear weapons, the Bush administration increasingly believed Iraq was stockpiling weapons of mass destruction (WMDs). This belief, and a desire to bring Democratic rule to the people of Iraq, was responsible for the U.S.-led invasion of Iraq. Like the previous U.S.-Iraqi war 12 years earlier, this war was big news. Unlike the previous war, this war would turn into a protracted war that is still being fought today.

Given that I'd just embarked on a new path in LA in 2003, I did not volunteer to cover the war in Iraq. Now, that path had me reevaluating my direction. Looking for more real and less reality work, I phoned George Moll. It was 2005, two years after the initial invasion, and I was intrigued to hear him mention Iraq.

His production company was off to a productive start. He had created, developed, and successfully pitched a series on the war in Iraq entitled *American Soldier*. More so than any previous war, the war in Iraq relied heavily on units from the Army National Guard, Army Reserve, and Marine Corps Reserve. George had come up with the idea to follow soldiers of the National Guard, who hailed from small towns in America, as they deployed and fought in Iraq while simultaneously following their families back home. He'd then worked with the U.S. Department of Defense to enlist the Army's support for the idea. At the same time, he'd pitched the execs at Country Music Television (CMT), who loved the idea. When I phoned him, he was in the early stages of staffing the series, which had just been greenlit. He asked if I was interested and, of course, I was. We then scheduled a meeting at his offices.

Unlike Raleigh Studios, George's Countyline Productions was housed in a lengthy and modern three-story office complex near Santa Monica (not far from his former MTV and VH-1 offices). The neighboring offices showcased nameplates of A-list producers and directors. His large, hi-tech office was busy, but offered room for expansion. The perimeter of the office featured a series of sophisticated, glassed-in edit rooms that encircled an open and central workspace. People were working in most of the editing rooms, which I found odd for a show that had yet to begin production. I was shown to George's office for what would feel more like a creative discussion than a job interview.

From the get-go, the conversation was easy-going.

"George, good to see you. This is impressive, and you've got people busy editing already."

"Oh, we've got a number of projects going on. But the one I wanted to talk to you about... the big one is *American Soldier*."

As the creator and executive producer, he knew this concept inside and out. It was a show near and dear to his heart, and one about which he spoke passionately. They had identified the National Guard unit the series would follow—a close-knit group of friends who'd enlisted together and who hailed from a small town in rural Georgia. They were headed for Camp Stryker, a logistical and life support base within the much larger Victory Base Complex, which occupied the area surrounding Baghdad International Airport. George was both eloquent and direct, fond of getting to the point.

"So, Camp Stryker. What do you think?"

"I think it's in the middle of Baghdad, which is in the middle of a war in Iraq."

"Well, that is an important point since we're doing a show about soldiers in Iraq. What I was referring to, given all of your international travel, your many trips to Beirut, and having covered armed conflicts before, is that you'd be perfect as our producer in Iraq."

The more I'd learned about the show, the more I'd sensed that was the direction in which he was headed, I'd almost been able to feel that question coming. And yet, I was unprepared to respond.

"That's quite the recognition. I appreciate it. You know, neither of us are 25 anymore, and I'm not ready to say yes or no. I need to give this some more thought." Because of our shared news backgrounds, I knew I could be irreverent with George when talking about war... or maybe *especially* when talking about war. "So, how about you? You were in Beirut, too. Are you going to Baghdad, too?"

He burst into laughter. "That's a fair question. But, no, I'm not headed to Baghdad. I have to admit it will be something to see. But I need to stay right here and keep an eye on the show, the whole show, and not just the part from Baghdad. Look, take some time to think about this. Just get back to me within a week."

Professionally, this was the kind of assignment I could sink my teeth into. It was the flipside of the reality and corporate work I was doing. It was international news coverage, again. The reason I hesitated to commit to an extended tour in Iraq was entirely personal. My relationship with Julia had grown on many fronts. Six months after her divorce was finalized, John (her ex-husband and the father to her small children) had been killed in a tragic motorcycle accident. I had grown very tight with Julia and particularly close to her kids, seven-year-old Alec and five-year-old Aubrey. I'd moved out of my loft and in with her, Alec, and Aubrey. It also would have been difficult to, once again, pack up and leave Alexa behind as I hit the ground in a tumultuous foreign land. I had three additional, very important people in my life to consider, all of whom weighed heavily on my decision.

I wanted to be honest with Julia regarding the new opportunity offered me. I briefly described George, our mutual experiences in Beirut, and *American Soldier*.

She was surprised, almost startled. "Baghdad?! I know... you've been very honest and candid about sharing your past experiences, all the years covering international news. It's all very... interesting and fascinating. I don't know anyone with similar experiences. But that was your past, I thought. Are you still interested in chasing those kinds of stories... today? Now?"

"I will always be interested in international news. At first, I didn't ask to be involved in the network coverage of the Iraq war. But this is something different. It's an opportunity that just recently came up and I thought I'd discuss it with you and see what you thought."

I could see something was brewing inside. The direct, unbridled, demanding CEO side of her took control as she answered, "My thoughts. I think it's a fucking war, Tim! A dangerous fucking war where people die. That's what I think. I'm not sure what... even *how* I'll tell the kids. They lost their dad, and in the two short years they've known you, they've grown close, really close, to you. What about Alexa? And, you and I are just starting this... thing. I can't, I would never try to determine your career path for you, but I wish you would give this some serious thought. Baghdad, seriously?"

"No decision's been made. I told George I'd get back to him. You make a very compelling argument and this is not something I have to do."

Her argument was irrefutable. Accepting the job would be entirely one-sided and selfish. I could not go cover a war and leave behind all of the people who mattered to me. I mattered to them, too. Unlike the National Guardsmen from Georgia, I had the luxury of saying no. I would not be going to Camp Stryker.

I phoned George to thank him and respectfully decline his job offer. "George, look, thank you for the offer. *American Soldier* sounds like an exciting project. I was looking forward to working with you, but I can't go to Baghdad. I do appreciate it. There are just too many personal considerations I need to think about these days."

"I knew it! I didn't really expect you to take the job. You're right, we're not 25 anymore. There are other roles you could do on the show."

"Ones that don't involve being based out of Camp Stryker?"

"We'll have crews and producers following the families back in Georgia, but those jobs are already filled. We do still need story editors back here to edit the various episodes together. If that interests you, come by and we'll discuss what it entails."

"Story editing sounds more my speed right now. I'd love that."
We set up a meeting that week to go over my new role. I had
never worked specifically as a story editor, but knew the job
title was self-explanatory. A story editor edits the story. I met
with George and his senior producer, who performed a more
nuts-and-bolts, detailed oversight of the show's many collabo-
rators.

Like many television series, *American Soldier* would consist
of 13 episodes. Each episode would have its own story editor. I
was assigned my dedicated editor, who'd mastered the editing
software and controlled the computer's buttons, keyboard, and
mouse to digitally assemble the thirty-minute program.

Because this was not a two minute news story, but rather a
thirty-minute show, I would have months to complete my episode. Each episode was given its own "theme" and chronological
order in the overall 13-episode series. Episode one dealt with
the group of friends/soldiers arriving in a war zone. Subsequent
episodes showed their longing for home, interactions with their
new chain of command, life in Camp Stryker, being part of a
convoy, and going on patrol "outside the wire" into Iraqi neighborhoods and among the locals, and the life of sustaining casualties and living with the omnipresent threat of attack. Each
story editor/editor team worked independently and yet collectively with the other teams cranking out the other episodes.

My first task was to go through and view the hours and hours
of video relevant to my episode, which would play towards the
end of the show's 13-episode run. There were camera crews with
field producers shooting tape of the men in Baghdad, and crews
simultaneously shooting tape of their families back home. This
created an enormous amount of material, all of which had to be

viewed and logged before I could start telling a story.

Editing these two separate but related elements together was a powerful tool to show what war was like for both the soldier and his family. This was made even more impactful with the videos taken of cell phone calls home. To have video from two different sides of the call, from two different parts of the world, was emotional and real. Once I'd viewed and taken notes on all of the various and relevant video segments from both sides of the world, it would be my job to write a script that would assemble those different pieces into a compelling story.

It was an incredibly collaborative process. In addition to his mastery of the nuances of editing, the editor with whom I worked was a wonderful sounding board. I bounced script ideas off of him, like, "Does this soundbite make sense here? Should we hear from the wife and family at this point or later in the show? Do we need to show more camaraderie among the soldiers?" His responses were always helpful. The senior producer was attentive, always offering her input to make the episode stronger. The other story editors broke from constructing their episodes to drop by our edit room (as would I to theirs) to weigh in on our progress. Once we made substantial progress, George scheduled a one-on-one viewing, adding his input and making the show stronger and better.

The show and the entire process proved to be one of the more rewarding projects I'd done since arriving in LA. I felt like I was covering something important. It was not for a major network, and I was able to do it from the comfort of a Santa Monica office while living at home in Pasadena. We had a small viewing party at home when it was time for my segment to air. It's the nature of the television beast to work on something for six months, and the final product flies by one evening in thirty minutes. Nevertheless, I felt a sense of accomplishment and was happy to be back to working on at least the periphery of news.

It was a worthwhile project and one that went beyond the exploding bombs from airstrikes and Humvee convoys to show the personal lives of those who serve and fight in our armed services. The viewers, network, and Army thought otherwise. The war would go on for years, which was a great reason for *American Soldier* to go on, too. It did not. Unlike *America's Most Talented Kids, Extreme Dodgeball*, and countless other similar programs, *American Soldier* was not renewed for a second season, which was a decision those of us on the team struggled to understand. I found it ironic that the American public, while waving their flags and pounding their chests in patriotic gestures, was more interested in watching contrived game shows and competitions than the real lives of their genuine heroes.

Julia continued to excel at her CEO position. Alexa still resided with Amy while finishing school in Colorado, but spent more and more time in California. Our blended family with Alexa, Alec, and Aubrey gelled, all of us spending more and more time together. Not long after *American Soldier*, Julia and I married in 2007. About that time and with Julia at the helm, IHOP acquired her former employer, Applebee's, in a multibillion-dollar takeover (that is a book in and of itself). With their combined annual sales of over 8 billion dollars, Julia became the Chief Executive Officer and Chairman of the largest casual restaurant chain in America. I thus had the luxury of being selective regarding which projects and assignments I pursued and accepted.

Not all of those projects were news-related. I once again enjoyed a diverse mix of journalistic and corporate endeavors intended for broadcast, cable, online, and internal distribution.

However, I did continue my long-running affiliation with NBC News. I enjoyed producing occasional general assignment stories. Each morning that I drove through the gates of the famed Burbank lot brought a smile to my face and reminded me of the rich history established there by over a half-century of news coverage.

My network of friends suggested I reach out and contact another former *TODAY* show producer, Roland Woerner. He was working at Current TV at that time. Between our mutual friends in the business and my resume, which I'd emailed to him, he was familiar with my work. I, however, knew little about Current TV and what he was up to. After a visit to their offices in Culver City, and with Roland's tutelage, I was soon well-informed about all things Current TV. It was the brainchild and product of former Vice President Al Gore and Joel Hyatt. Hyatt had made his name (and fortune) in the 70s and 80s by forming Hyatt Legal Services and presenting it as a low-cost legal alterative to high-priced law firms. His many television commercials had made his company (and himself) a nation-wide phenomenon. He had also become a well-connected politician. He and Gore had formed Current TV in 2005, in part to create an independent news network focusing on politics.

In 2013, Gore and Hyatt sold Current TV to the Qatar-based Al Jazeera Network. Al Jazeera had plans to launch Al Jazeera America and create a news channel to compete with MSNBC, CNN, HLN, FOX News, and BBC America. Al Jazeera planned to scrap the existing programming on Current TV, but maintain their distribution network and most of the staff, like Roland. He and his co-EP Steve Lange had pitched some programing ideas for news shows to their new bosses at Al Jazeera America. Those ideas had been well-received, and Roland and Steve were beginning to assemble a possible staff, to be ready in case those ideas should get green-lit and turned into actual shows. I was at the former Current TV (now Al Jazeera America) offices to assess my interest in possibly working for the brand new and exciting launch of Al Jazeera America.

I knew as little about the Al Jazeera Network as I had Current TV. What I had heard about Al Jazeera was that they had a penchant for playing beheading videos from Al Qaeda and ISIS terrorists, and broadcasting those hideous images throughout the Arab world. And now Roland, a network broadcast journalist, was contemplating going to work for them? I wanted nothing to do with it, and said so during that meeting.

"Al Gore selling to Al Jazeera. I had not heard that. And what kind of programming are you guys going to be doing? Putting English subtitles on videos of beheaded prisoners?"

"Not exactly. Al Gore would not have sold his company to them if that was the plan. I think you have a flawed image of Al Jazeera America. They intend to be a legitimate, unbiased, broadcast news source in the image of the BBC, but here in America. To accomplish that, they've hired veteran newsmen and women from all of the major U.S. news networks."

Roland went on to list the many veteran news executives who had left NBC, ABC, CBS, the BBC, and other networks to join and launch Al Jazeera America. I recognized most of the names, and it was an extremely impressive list. Furthermore, to ensure journalistic independence, Al Jazeera America was based in New York, free from any censorship or interference possibly coming from the home office in Doha, Qatar. They had my attention.

Roland and Steve proceeded to talk in vague, big-picture terms about one show in particular which they had pitched and believed would soon be green-lit. *TechKnow* was the name they'd given to a news and information series which would focus on the development and implementation of all sorts of new technology with lifesaving implications, as well as how that technology would impact and improve lives around the world.

They not only had my attention; in the span of one meeting, I was a convert.

"Where do I sign up? That sounds amazing. So, you guys see this as a 30-minute news show, like a magazine show, with different reporters traveling around the U.S. shooting and then editing stories focused on life-saving technology?"

"Exactly. But because this type of news is based in science, our reporters are going to be young scientists and PhDs with knowledge and a greater understanding of technology. They may lack TV experience, which is why we're looking for experienced producers who can help teach them those television nuances."

I left the meeting impressed with Roland and Steve, hoping their program idea would materialize and that I'd be a part of it when it did.

Six months later, in October of 2013, I did hear back from Roland. *TechKnow* was a 'thing' and would soon begin production. I was asked to join the team as a producer. No one knew how long the show would run, so the length of my commitment was somewhat tenuous. That did not damper the excitement I felt over being part of an exciting news series. True to their word, Roland and Steve assembled quite the ensemble team for *TechKnow*. There were eight to ten seasoned segment producers hired. Many of us had network credentials and all of us knew the ins and outs of production and storytelling; some of us shared work experiences and friends at NBC.

As planned, a small group of roughly six young scientists from all walks of technology was hired as our on-camera reporters. They were all brilliant in their disciplines and all glaringly inexperienced in news coverage and television production. No one pretended otherwise. Every scientist/correspondent was eager to learn, hungry for knowledge beyond their already impressive degrees. It was a fulfilling working relationship for everyone involved.

Qatar has the highest per capita income in the world, and owns the third-largest share of natural gas reserves and oil reserves on Earth. As a result, the state-owned television network, Al Jazeera, is extremely solvent. Yet, *TechKnow* was still a first-run show on a start-up network. As producers, we were all required to wear numerous producing hats. We were tasked with identifying and developing story ideas that met the show's guidelines. Once those ideas were approved, it was up to us to find the relevant tech experts to interview and the elements to shoot, arrange travel, and coordinate those arrangements with the local freelance crew, communicate the story with the reporter/scientists, oversee the shooting in the field, log that field material back in the *TechKnow* office, write the script, revise the script with Roland and Steve, work with an extremely talented staff of editors to edit the story, have Computer Generated Graphics created, revise and finesse the story, and have a final viewing before going on-air. This was similar to the way the process worked at the networks, except in that our *TechKnow* staff was a fraction of the size.

Everything fell on the producer's shoulders... and that was the most rewarding aspect of the job. The stressful demands of the work schedule paled in comparison to the rewards of such an unrestrained, creative process. And, it was all done within the professional framework of a network news structure. Al Jazeera America had established news bureaus in New York, Washington, D.C., Chicago, Detroit, Seattle, Nashville, New Orleans, Dallas, Miami, San Francisco, and Los Angeles. We were but one show on the new news network. There were weekly video calls with the upper news management in New York, complete with live Q&A sessions meant to keep everyone apprised of the progress and direction of the network.

I immediately began digging for stories about the technology of national interest with lifesaving implications. I phoned an acquaintance I'd recently met at a wine dinner. He also happened to be a senior astrophysicist at NASA's Jet Propulsion Laboratories (JPL), located in California. I briefed him on *Tech-Know* and set up a lunch date on which to pick his enormous brain for any possible story ideas.

"Is there anything you guys at JPL are working on that might fit the criteria for this television show? Something not proprietary that won't jeopardize national security?"

"There might be. You see, we were looking into the origin of the universe. In that search, we sent microwaves into outer space, and—"

"Okay, I'm sorry to interrupt. Did I mention this is a *television* show? Origins of the universe? I fear that may be a tad bit beyond the comprehension of most TV viewers... and news producers. Can we rewind our conversation and bring it back down to Earth?"

He looked at me with a dismissive gaze that acknowledged the vast chasm between our respective IQs, and persevered. "Yes, please permit me to elaborate and I believe you will comprehend the elucidation."

I felt so far out of my league, and realized it was going to be a long lunch. As lunch progressed, my guest proceeded to explain a fascinating technology. Probing deep space and looking for evidence of the "Big Bang," JPL used special microwave signals sent into the far reaches of outer space. They'd discovered the signals offered an interesting correlation between outer space and Earth.

Those signals can penetrate almost any material, like concrete, metal, and wood. At the same time, they can detect even the slightest movement—like, say, a beating heart or an expanding lung. JPL partnered with FEMA and Homeland Security to create a program called FINDER (Finding Individuals for Disaster and Emergency Response). They packaged this microwave technology in a portable, suitcase-like device. When natural disasters like earthquakes and tornados strike, FINDER can detect survivors, conscience or unconscious, who've been buried under rubble or even entombed in concrete.

We flew to Virginia to a governmental test facility. There, VA TASK FORCE ONE, an elite search and rescue team, demonstrated the amazing capabilities of FINDER. We carefully hid our willing correspondent in a gigantic pile of rubble that had been meticulously constructed by the government as a practice site to resemble the real aftermath of a natural disaster. Without fail, FINDER repeatedly found our correspondent. It truly was lifesaving technology on display.

There were many other similar stories.

I took Al Jazeera America to the East Coast and visited the U.S. Marine Corps at Camp Lejeune. The Naval hospital there was experimenting with cutting-edge technology used to treat Post Traumatic Stress Disorder (PTSD) and Traumatic Brain Injury (TBI). Doctors were using a hyperbaric oxygen chamber, the kind used to treat deep-sea divers, to deliver 100% pure oxygen to the brains of afflicted soldiers in the hopes of expediting the healing process.

In the same story, I returned to the West Coast, where an entirely different technology had shown promising results for treating PTSD and TBI. A partnership between the Department of Defense and a research institute at the University of Southern California created a Fully Immersive Virtual Reality therapy tool called BRAVEMIND. Amazingly realistic combat scenarios in Afghanistan and Iraq were digitally recreated in 3D. Wearing VR headsets and with the supervision of highly trained psychologists, stricken soldiers relived the harrowing moments that had triggered their PTSD in the hopes of confronting and overcoming their fears.

Researchers at the University of California, Riverside discovered a complex recipe of everyday household, non-toxic ingredients to create a chemical compound that makes humans invisible to mosquitos. A private company took the compound to the next step, advancing the molecular formula and creating a wearable adhesive path. At the time of our story, the product was undergoing millions of hours of extensive testing in Africa, where 500,000 people die each year from mosquito-transmitted malaria, most of whom are children under five.

A pioneering archeologist at the University of Alabama at Birmingham employed the latest satellite imaging technology in her study of the ancient past. Expanded bandwidth coupled with advanced infrared technology allowed satellites, from 380 miles above the globe, to look down and peer below the earth's surface. She used outer space tech to detect previously undiscovered archeological sites of ancient civilizations. In doing so, she also discovered that thousands of sites had been looted. ISIS combatants had excavated priceless antiquities and sold them on a multibillion-dollar black market, as a means to fund their ongoing terrorist activities.

These are just a few of the stories I discovered and covered while working on *TechKnow*. And, I was just one member of a larger team doing the same. However, Al Jazeera America failed to make a lasting connection with the American television audience. The cable news landscape was already well-served by MSNBC, CNN, and Fox News. After three years and hundreds of millions of dollars, Al Jazeera closed their Al Jazeera America news operation.

My initial fear of Arab interference from Qatar into our independent journalism on *TechKnow* proved to be unfounded. Not once did I witness any censorship or interference from anyone. There was only genuine support for ongoing, insightful, and factual storytelling. While working there, I realized the Al Jazeera Network had impressive credentials as a global news network, having won Emmy and Peabody Awards in the past. It was ironic for me that the surprising and interesting news coverage of *TechKnow* was the result of working for an employer of whom I'd been so suspicious, initially. It was a lesson that sometimes our preconceived notions can betray us.

TechKnow and *American Soldier* are two examples of what I considered fascinating programming that went beyond entertainment to inform viewers on developments important to the lives of us Americans. Regardless of the audience size, I'm proud to have been a part of those series. Roland Woerner and George Moll, those responsible for the creation of such programming, had journalistic roots in the network news business. In their search for potential programming that might interest an American audience, that news experience was a subtle but constant presence. Producers like them and many others have proven the television we watch and stream need not be entirely frivolous. There is an abundance of that. There is also a need for captivating news and information. It need not always be packaged to resemble *Nightly News* or the *TODAY* show. And, it is a refreshing and enlightening break from the countless panels of argumentative "opinionators" who are too often mistaken as newsmakers. We, as viewers, simply need to seek out more of the real and less reality in our TV.

* * * * *

In the Spring of 2014, after 52 years, NBC News moved its entire West Coast news operation from the Burbank lot to the NBC/Universal Studios complex down the road in Universal City. The Brokaw News Center was named after the network's most famous and respected journalist, a friend and colleague of mine. It was a deserving and lasting tribute to the face of the network, the man who'd joined NBC News in 1966 and anchored *Nightly News* for 22 years. The brand new, state-of-the-art, modern structure combined NBC News, MSNBC, CNBC, and Telemundo all under one roof. It was and is a futuristic, scalable structure able to adapt to and utilize the newest and most advanced broadcast, cable, and streaming TV technology.

Reading about it in *Variety* would not suffice for me. I was anxious to get my firsthand look at the new Brokaw News Center. Fortunately, my first visit would not be a leisurely tour. Audrey Grady had remarried a prominent obstetrician-gynecologist and changed her name from Kolina to Grady. She had a new last name and a happy new life, but the same important job—West Coast Senior Producer for *TODAY*. She called with a freelance producer opportunity. Multiple *TODAY* producers had given birth around the same time and were all enjoying maternity leave... around the same time. She was shorthanded and there was no exact date set for the producers' return to work from maternity leave. She asked if I was available for the foreseeable future. I was, and happily signed on as a freelance *TODAY* producer for the last half of 2014.

I was welcomed with open arms, and wide-eyed as I toured the new news facility. Everything was brand new, and by comparison, made the old Burbank facility look even more dated than it had been. Many of the familiar faces were seated at modern new desks and inside shiny new glass offices and conference rooms. Bureau Chief Polly Powel sat at the long white "assignment desk" in the center of the newsroom. Seated next to her was Zoya Taylor, a hardworking producer I'd met while covering the McVeigh and Nichols trials. Because of her always valuable contributions and genial personality, she'd been promoted to Deputy Bureau Chief and Polly's right hand. They were joined by several staffers at the same desk, all of whom concentrated on computer and video monitors while simultaneously working the phones. It was a streamlined, updated news nerve center reminiscent of the Starship Enterprise. The many editing suites, graphic stations, and satellite intake and transmission rooms had all gotten complete, top-to-bottom make-overs.

Mike Mosher was still Audrey's peer at *Nightly News* as Senior West Coast Producer and was happy to see a familiar face. I would not be working with him, however. Even though *Nightly* and *TODAY* covered the same assignments, they did so with separate staffs and I was dedicated to *TODAY*.

With the new facility came entirely new security measures and computer interfaces. Just getting on the NBC Universal property required a different routine. All of the old IDs, badges, and access cards were useless, and so I was issued new everything. There were new logins and updates to the updated, intra-NBC computer system. Things like accessing the vast network of bureaus' "Who's Where," or viewing *Nightly* or *TODAY*'s daily rundown, or even just communicating with coworkers was a new and different online exercise in comparison to the bygone days of the Burbank lot.

In addition to the many recognizable faces I'd seen, there were even younger and more energetic employees who were busy at work. Initially, I struggled with the many new computer skills required by the updated operating systems. But then I looked around me and realized I was surrounded by solutions to my computer problems. I quickly befriended some of my new, twenty-something coworkers. They were all extremely smart and uber-impressive. The intense competition they'd endured to get accepted to top universities was nothing compared to the competition to work for a major news network. For each job to be filled, NBC (and its competitors) had the luxury of being highly selective in choosing new employees from a pool of exceedingly skilled candidates. It was clear that everyone hired at the networks was the best and the brightest. They were eager and young, with largely uncomplicated lives that allowed them to drop everything at a moment's notice and charge off to cover a breaking news story... just as I'd done when I'd been their age. They admired my experience and I their energetic enthusiasm. I will always be enthusiastic about news, yet devoid of the energy from my twenties and thirties.

A developing news story at that time was the investigation into Bill Cosby's past. It was a seedy and sordid story of sexual battery, drug-induced sexual assault, and rape. The incidents were alleged to have occurred over more than forty years, between 1965 and 2008. Stand-up comedian Hannibal Buress had included Cosby's alleged sexual misconduct in his routine, video of which went viral. The viral video brought renewed focus to Cosby and his many accusers. It was certainly a newsworthy story, but one that demanded an adherence to the facts... the accusations, denials, and charges. Given the ugliness of those accusations, it was tempting to jump to conclusions and opine. Many did. That's never the role of independent network news.

My four-month freelance gig with *TODAY* began to feel more like a comfortably permanent or perma-lance gig instead. There were other stories to cover, some of them even being breaking news and requiring last-minute travel. But the Cosby story had staying power, and it was one with which I stayed, albeit not to the bitter end (four years later, he would be found guilty of three counts of aggravated indecent assault and sentenced to three to ten years in state prison). Eventually, those female producers did return to work from their maternity leaves. I had enjoyed every moment of working in the Brokaw News Center, though, and those in charge felt the same way about me. I continued to receive calls from Audrey, Mike, and the assignment desk looking to employ me. But unlike the previous, steady and mostly predictable four-month-long gig, I was asked to cover breaking news of wildfires and other devastating disasters. My busy personal and family life made me unavailable to cover that kind of news, though it was the kind I'd covered for more than thirty years.

I was flattered by the interest, but no longer had the energy or inclination to chase news. I'd indeed grown tired of the arduous and demanding nature of news coverage, but I have still never tired of the news.

I will forever watch, read, and listen to news reports, but it's no comparison to being on the ground when news occurs. I must confess that I am, at times, desirous to exchange my television viewing recliner for the front row seat I so frequently occupied during newsworthy events. But while I may sometimes miss news coverage, it doesn't miss me. It's exciting to see the scores of enthusiastic and energetic young producers, camerawomen, and cameramen rushing to fill the void created when people like me move on to other pursuits. I admire the next wave of journalists and photojournalists. The fierce competition for the top jobs has intensified, meaning that only the best and the brightest, the most driven and dedicated candidates, will be offered the rare and valuable opportunity to cover the news.

But will they have the same kind of robust audience we enjoyed? To be certain, audiences for all forms of news have shrunk and shifted as our lifestyles have changed. Our society has become more polarized, and so, too, have some news outlets, causing audiences to fragment and splinter. But through it all, there have always been viewers, listeners, and readers on the other end, consuming and using what we've reported.

Yet, there is concern for the future that the audience is not only changing, but disappearing.

21

NEXT-GEN

Television ratings are almost as old as television itself. In 1950, the AC Nielson Company applied the methodology it had used to gauge radio audiences to the new frontier of television. For years, this was the most trusted science for measuring the size of viewing audiences. The networks would utilize the data to set advertising rates. The number of eyeballs watching a show would determine how much to charge advertisers for a commercial spot within that show. It would also help to determine which programs were popular and which weren't—which programs to renew and which would get axed.

As the ratings' popularity grew, so did the data. Audiences were more closely scrutinized—beyond simply size. Broadcasters (and advertisers) wanted to know more about their viewers. Age, gender, location, income, viewing habits, and other personal data were entered into the equation. When the digital age hit, that data collection went from a "best guesstimate" scenario to a highly sophisticated science.

What that science tells us today is revealing. If you are one of the millions of Americans who sit back and tune into a television network for your news and information... you are a dying breed. Most of us so-called Baby Boomers, who came of age watching Tom Brokaw or Dan Rather, prefer to watch live, linear, scheduled news programs. That is our norm. But it is not the way millennials or Gen Y get their news... if they are getting news at all.

To be certain, television and television news are still important and major mediums. However, since the 80s, television news viewership has been slowly but steadily declining (akin to the readership of newspapers). Viewers of Fox News, MSNBC, and CNN can differ wildly. There is one common denominator across all three cable networks—the average viewer for all three is in their 50s. As older viewers die off (and fail to be replaced by younger ones) and the ratings for both broadcast and cable news networks decline, so also do the advertising revenues, which means fewer financial resources dedicated to news coverage and reduced budgets for this same coverage.

The ratings skew between older and younger viewers presents another, even more worrisome problem. Older, loyal viewers are bolstering the declining ratings as younger viewers tune out. But in viewing the changes in this fashion, we may be inadvertently concealing the very real and alarming fact that television news is rapidly losing touch with an important segment of the population—our youth and our future.

As file compression formats improve and connectivity increases, streaming and online video "beyond the box" options have thrived. More people are watching video on more devices than ever before. Billions of dollars are being poured into content created by companies like Amazon, Google, Apple, Netflix, Hulu, and others. These online giants are cranking out original, critically acclaimed and highly successful movies, dramas, comedies, and documentaries... one after another. We are experiencing a renaissance of television, but not television news. All of the content being created is for entertainment purposes. None of it is for news coverage. The new companies ordering all of the new content have shown an utter lack of interest here, a total aversion to getting into the news business.

For their part, the networks have reworked and retooled their newscasts in the hopes of appealing to a younger audience. Younger and younger reporters are appearing onscreen in an attempt to make the news appear more relative to younger viewers. To keep pace with the seemingly minuscule millennial attention span, stories are shrinking in length. What used to be a two-minute story now runs less than a minute. It is difficult to maintain the same journalistic principles in such an abbreviated format. Often, the "who, what, where, when, and why" of a report must be sacrificed and shortened to simply the "what" and the "where."

Traditional news judgment has been "augmented," borrowing from social media. A topic that is "trending" on social media can become a news story. This may widen the appeal of news for the next generation, but those in charge of news coverage were given that responsibility because they understand what constitutes news. Journalism, whether televised or not, should always judge a story on the merit of its newsworthiness and not its attractiveness for the masses. Seeing news coverage as a popularity contest is a slippery slope down which to embark.

Push versus pull strategy is a means to describe the fundamental difference between the way the older generation gets their news and the way the younger generation gets their news… and most everything else. For example, as a member of the older generation, I watch the *Nightly News* with Lester Holt. That 30-minute news program is produced, written, reported, assembled, and then broadcast to me. I choose to watch the program, but have no choice or say in the information contained within that program. That decision is made by a higher authority, the team of newsmen and women responsible for the show every night. They build together the news from that day and then send or "push" it to me.

It's the same with *The New York Times*. I choose to subscribe to it, but the publisher, editors, reporters, and writers determine what is newsworthy and then assemble that information into a comprehensive form and email or "push" the entire publication to me each day.

The younger generation, which includes my kids, tends toward searching individual topics of interest, clicking on links, and then downloading or "pulling" the selected information to their devices for consumption. Their preconceived notions or preferences dictate where they visit, and what they read and view.

We all seek out topics of personal interest. I am more likely to search out the results of sporting competitions and league standings than women's skincare and moisturizing products, unless it's the week of my wife's birthday or our anniversary. But when it comes to news, a major difference between "push" and "pull" is that the news being pushed to me has been vetted, verified, fact-checked for accuracy, and organized by large, professional staffs of independent journalists—producers at, say, NBC News, or editors at *The New York Times*.

Searching for or pulling links to information in which I'm interested or which only confirms or agrees with my thinking can be problematic. There a number of trusted, journalistic online sites like the Associated Press, Reuters, and *Politico*. But because the internet is so vast, there are also countless crackpots and anonymous sources spewing tons of unverifiable nonsense under the guise of news. The internet can be a deafening echo chamber, a cacophony of misinformation. And if we only "pull" or seek out news that agrees with us, our intellectual curiosity as a society will eventually atrophy and die.

Only a portion of the broadcast and cable television spectrum is dedicated to news coverage. A much smaller fraction of the internet is dedicated to news coverage and viewing. The internet is a powerful and mostly unregulated medium whose presence and influence in our lives will only increase. But its inability to keep us informed and engaged in global events is frightening. Content providers and software creators are diving in and thriving as more and more users log on... but to what means and for what real benefit? In 2014, Amazon paid almost a billion dollars to acquire Twitch TV, which is a live, online gaming site. Today, Twitch has 15 million active users daily. That's more than the total daily viewers of Fox News, MSNBC, and CNN... combined.

With almost three billion users, social media rules the internet; Facebook, Twitter, and Instagram are the kings. But while they have created huge networks of loyal users, they are not *news sources*. Think of the term "source." Look at your water bottle, and it likely states some form of "Bottled at the Source." A source is the origin of something. These sites do not cover, break, or originate news. They disseminate the opinions of their users (and often trolls and bots); they reuse or recirculate news from other legitimate sources. But they do not originate news. To my recollection, I have never seen a reporter from Facebook, Twitter, or Instagram receive recognition for excellence in journalism. They are a source of thoughts, opinions, and banter—a regurgitator of news. But they are not a news source.

There are many studies conducted by knowledgeable researchers that substantiate the claim that "old media" is still a far better and more utilized way of delivering and receiving news than "new media." Television news viewing is habitual. It is an appointment or date we make with the news. It is ritualistic, reoccurring, and constant, all of which means that those of us who tune into our preferred network or newscast choose to be informed regularly. This leads to a bond forming between those covering the news and those consuming the news. It stands to reason, and those same studies confirm, that people who view or read something habitually spend far more time doing so than those who don't. Internet news users spend far fewer minutes per day on news than those who receive it from traditional sources. Sadly, consuming news regularly is not an important part of the lives of most young adults today.

It is absurd to think that, as the younger generation ages, they will drop their phones and tablets and revert to the sort of regular viewing of live linear network news that their parents enjoyed. Meanwhile, the dominant online players have demonstrated that news is not their priority... or even an interest. If the legacy news networks (or anyone for that matter) wish to be relevant for the next generation, they will need to experiment, on many fronts, to appeal to and meet the demands of the next generation. The challenges facing television news are more about news delivery than news coverage. Executives and producers need to embrace, through trial and error, digital platforms, on-demand and mobile distribution, and even interactive news vehicles. This transformation will require agility, a data-driven and analytical mindset, and a true willingness to break from the past in an all-out endeavor to better understand their future consumers and transform them into interested and loyal viewers.

The broadcast and cable news networks have spent decades and decades strengthening their brands, developing talent that has given us journalistic superstars and curating vast archives of historical footage. It is imperative that they keep it up and do the same for the next in line.

I know some people might ask, "Why?"

Watching network television news programs helps people become more knowledgeable and politically aware. Regardless of one's side of the political spectrum, awareness is far better than ignorance. That awareness naturally leads to involvement and activity, which is far better than inactivity. A knowledgeable and aware society tends to be more civically engaged. If our society is going to continue to advance and improve, that can only be accomplished through personal involvement. The previous generation benefitted from it; our generation benefitted from it. And, it's imperative that the next generation uses the news to stay aware and involved. That may be a lot of responsibility to heft upon the broad shoulders of network news, but it's true.

All of journalism, but in particular broadcast and cable journalism, has come under increasing scrutiny and attack from both the left and the right. I don't want to argue the merits of CNN or Fox news. That's a debate better suited for cocktail parties and Thanksgiving dinners. I am a self-proclaimed news junkie—a lover of TV news and an enthusiastic participant. And, throughout the pages of this book, I have repeatedly aimed my criticism (deserved, of course) at our many errors and excesses.

Yet, we cannot let "what's wrong with the process" obstruct the value of that same process. The news media is a rare tool, an asset gifted to us and protected by some visionaries a long time ago. There are millions of people from countries around the world who have no idea what it is like to watch an independent, uncensored, and truthful news report of their choosing. Those living under oppressive dictators or Communist regimes would so value what we take for granted... if they only had the chance.

Fortunately, our freedom of speech, and our freedom of the press, are here to stay. Those who would try to restrain or limit it are but the lunatic fringe. It is not threatened by censorship. Rather, the real threat to our freedom of the press comes through complacency and ambivalence. The power of the press is in its embrace. Broadcasting to an audience or society that simply doesn't care about the news is tantamount to producing a lost treasure. Which is another reason to urgently get the next generation involved in the news.

The renowned journalist from the last century Walter Lipman described the news as our window onto the world of public affairs. If we fail to look through that window, we will know little of the world that lies beyond our personal experience.

22

TAINTED TRUST

The term "watchdog journalism" refers to one of the key functions of the news media, to monitor those in power and hold them accountable for their actions and how they wield their power. In their book, *The Elements of Journalism*, authors Bill Kovach and Tom Rosenstiel refer to this as, "watching over the powerful few in society on behalf of the many to guard against tyranny."

That is an enormous responsibility, and one not to be taken lightly, or exploited or corrupted by bias. The increased opining dressed up as news, so prevalent in today's broadcast journalism, has weakened the intent of this oversight capacity. Because it's such an important pillar of true journalism, the watching or oversight needs to be conducted in the most straightforward and honest manner possible. Yet, even then, those in power don't always welcome the scrutiny from the press. The mainstream news media is in the business of reporting the truth, and sometimes that truth hurts.

To ease that pain, many choose to discredit such reporting or any given story and dismiss it as being fake, even when the facts related to the story are proven to be true. The ostrich burying its head in the sand is an appropriate comparison that comes to mind.

It has also gone far beyond denying a story's validity or truthfulness. The denials from those in power have become more vehement, driving personal attacks on the responsible journalists, their employer, and eventually the entire news media industry. If you don't like what you hear or read, blame the press. As a result, the mainstream news media has increasingly worn a bullseye on their back.

According to a recent Gallup Poll, trust in the news media has been in decline since its pinnacle of 72%, right after Watergate and Richard Nixon's resignation. That trust hit an all-time low point in 2016, with just 32% of Americans expressing trust in the media. However, in recent years, that number has rebounded; 41% of Americans (69% of Democrats vs. 15% of Republicans) have expressed trust and confidence in the news media.[10]

This increasing polarization between the right and the left, and their vastly different perceptions of the news media, reflects the divide so prevalent in our society. A healthy differing of opinions has always been interwoven through the fabric of America. Long ago, cable news viewership had already become entrenched. Mirroring the divide in our society, right-wing viewers and voters religiously turned to Fox News for their "fair and balanced" coverage. And, similarly, left-wing viewers and voters turned to anything but Fox News. This American news division existed long before Donald Trump threw his hat in the ring, but that chasm has widened ever since.

So much has been written about the 2016 presidential race,

10 Brenan, M. (2019). "Americans' Trust in Mass Media Edges Down to 41%." Retrieved May 5, 2020 from https://news.gallup.com/poll/267047/americans-trust-mass-media-edges-down.aspx

which was an election like no other. While Donald Trump recklessly steamrolled over 16 competing Republican candidates, the juggernaut that was Hilary Clinton appeared unstoppable. Presidential campaigns are usually slugfests, and 2016 was a particularly bloody one. From her vanishing emails to the size of his manhood, there was always plenty to report. The '16 campaign was not one I worked on. Pursuing other non-news endeavors, I had chosen to step back entirely from the world of network news. However, I still maintained contact with close friends from NBC who were front-and-center on politics when it came to covering the rallies, campaign stops, and interviews for both candidates. Their firsthand accounts provided me with a value-added sense of "being there" while I watched from afar like most everyone else. I will always possess a sharp interest in American politics, and was fixated on the process—savoring each debate, rally, and soundbite.

We all know how that election turned out. Almost immediately, President Trump's disdain for the non-Fox news media became one of his primary and most-pervasive themes. With so many news divisions reporting on the President, the President had many targets for his anti-press vitriol, with *The New York Times*, *The Washington Post*, CNN, and MSNBC topping his list of those most reviled. At rallies, both before and after the election, he continually voiced his contempt for journalists by pointing directly at the national news media and decrying, "There they are... the fake news media," then continuing with adjectives like *disgusting*, *crooked*, and *dangerous*.

And the attacks on the mainstream press aren't only coming from the right. As a crowded and, at times, contentious field of 27 Democrats seeking their party's 2020 nomination, they also took aim at the news media. Some complained their plans were misrepresented. Some complained their opponents were getting preferential treatment from the same media. And some even complained that the media wasn't tough enough on the President. As I have tried to point out throughout this book, the news media has made mistakes and deserves the embarrassing black eyes it has inflicted upon itself. But far too often, it's simply an easy target of disgruntled politicians, being blamed for their doings or misdoings.

When politicians become "former" politicians, many of them have a change of heart and hence form a different interpretation of the role of the news media. After leaving office, during an interview on *TODAY*, George W. Bush said, "Power can be very addictive. And it can be corrosive. And it's important for the media to call to account people who abuse their power."[11] Bush is not alone. At his final press conference, just two days before leaving office, President Obama told reporters, "...you're supposed to be skeptics; you're supposed to ask me tough questions."[12] And, other presidents have championed the need for an independent and free press... once their administrations were no longer the subjects of journalistic examination.

The crucial need for our news media is not going away. The principles of journalism remain an unshakable cornerstone to our and any democracy, resilient to the jealous attacks from those who are fearful of the informative power of the news. The more the news media gets targeted, the more valuable it becomes. In the face of media criticism, the unintended consequences have been that people are increasingly turning *on* and tuning *in* to the news.

---

11 Bush, George W. (2017, February 27). Interview with Matt Lauer on *TODAY*.

12 Obama, Barack. (2017, January 18). Final White House Press Conference.

While viewership of local television news, generally viewed by older audiences, has steadily declined since 2016, cable news has enjoyed a steady increase in ratings. MSNBC has experienced a record increase in viewers since President Trump took office, at times even eclipsing Fox News in total prime-time viewers. Fox continues to be the most-watched cable news network while CNN's ratings vacillate at times, but for the most part, remain steady.

And cable news isn't the only journalistic industry to enjoy an increase in popularity. *The New York Times* continues to add online subscribers and readjust their subscriber projections... *upward*. In 2018, at a time when many newspapers experienced continued layoffs, *The New York Times* added 120 employees to its newsroom, which brought the total number of journalists employed by the paper to 1,600—the largest in its storied history.

The Washington Post has experienced similar growth. The deep pockets of owner Jeff Bezos have allowed the *Post* to lead the charge into online subscriptions, recruiting not only top journalists, but also top engineers to help drive the digital transformation.

The fact of the matter is that whether you're right-leaning or left, whether you're one of the president's followers or fact-checking foes, the dreaded news media, in one form or another, via new platform or old, continues to provide a valuable service. That should be good news for anyone who wants to be informed, but it comes with an important caveat. As referenced above, an important function of the news media is to hold accountable those in power. Add to that the fact that the news media itself, and its journalists' reporting, must also be held accountable. This should apply to the right, left, and everyone in the middle.

As a veteran of the broadcast news biz, I understand that conservative Republicans are more likely to turn on Fox News while liberal Democrats are more likely to turn on MSNBC. A difference of political and or socio-economic beliefs helps define who we are, with whom we socialize, and what we do. The adage "different strokes for different folks" is true. Only a fool or masochist (or a foolish masochist) would try to convert a liberal Democrat to becoming a habitual Sean Hannity viewer or persuade a conservative Republican to tune in regularly to Rachel Maddow. That ain't going to happen. But, whomever you tune into, we should always be looking for information rather than confirmation. We become lazy if we're only looking for "our" news. And we allow our networks to become lazy if we only expect them to feed us "their" news. We should be demanding "the" news. If we only ask our journalists to give us what we want, manipulating the facts to fit our preconceived notions, then we are asking too little of our journalists. Journalism should challenge our view, not conform to it.

The late U.S. Senator (D-NY) Daniel Patrick Moynihan once said, "Everyone is entitled to his own opinion, but not to his own facts."[13] In today's news world, we must be attentive and diligent in deciphering the difference between differing opinions and alternative facts. Most of us are savvy enough to know the difference when we see or hear it.

In demanding the news, in our quest for information, it's okay for us to question what we're told from time to time. We didn't used to do that. Back in the day, what the big three news networks reported was beyond question. That seems like a long time ago. That is part of our societal News Division—a divide

---

13 Quoted in "An American Original." *Vanity Fair. October 2010.* Retrieved May 19, 2020 from https://www.vanityfair.com/news/2010/11/moynihan-letters-201011

between where we once were and where we are with today's news. In questioning a story or even an entire broadcast, it is important to seek out second opinions. If those second and third opinions validate the story, then it's likely the story was real and not fake. And that also reflects how our news consumption has changed. If you want to be informed in today's world, it's helpful and sometimes necessary to watch, listen, *and* read—to rely upon a variety of news outlets to get the whole picture.

On most evenings, I sit down and watch Lester Holt on NBC's *Nightly News*. I know I am not getting his opinion. I am getting the cold hard facts, which is exactly and only what I'm looking for from that broadcast. I say that not as an endorsement of Lester Holt or the *Nightly News*, but to point out that the delivery of unbiased news, void of opinion, is very much alive and well, and not only via NBC. Yet, even as a devoted viewer of NBC, from time to time, I do question some of their reporting and look to other sources to confirm the occasional story. I may even look to an opinion for another angle. I am a news junkie, but not a news purist, and in addition to unbiased news, I also enjoy hearing analysis. The important thing is to identify it as such. And, to discover whether it is self-serving and extreme, or rooted in fact and credible?

I realize CNN has become a lightning rod for some conservative Republican viewers, and in many instances, their ire is justified. But I often find the political coverage on CNN to be some of the best in the business because it is not offering a singular, homogenized perspective. Whether on a primary or presidential election night, CNN regularly seats Republicans and Democrats side-by-side at the same desk on the same program to provide their different interpretations of an election's nuances. I get opinions from both the right and the left, Democratic and

Republican. For instance, I'll hear from former Senior Advisor to Obama, David Axelrod, followed by former U.S. Senator (R-PA) Rick Santorum. Even if you don't recognize the names, it's safe to say they don't always agree (in fact, it's rare that they do). I am not endorsing CNN here. I'm just applauding the way they present political dialogue. It's healthier to hear multiple opinions than just one, and their political coverage illustrates that diversity need not always be polarizing. There can be common ground, and even in analysis, the news media sometimes helps us to find it.

I know there are disciplined journalists at Fox News who take great pride in their profession (because I've worked with some of them). In 2019 and 2020, there were 11 debates held during the primary process that determined Joe Biden as the Democratic nominee for president. Several news outlets participated in hosting those 11 debates. Fox News was barred by the Democratic National Committee (DNC) from hosting a debate because, as DNC Chairman Tom Perez put it, Fox News "is not in a position to host a fair and neutral debate for our candidates."[14] From a news perspective, I saw that as a bad decision. It was a missed opportunity for those candidates to reach Fox viewers, some of whom are persuadable voters. Additionally, it silenced reporters, Fox reporters, from asking tough questions of those who wanted to be president. Journalism only works if we all get to ask the tough questions.

The bias from the far-right news and the far-left news has only fueled and expanded the news division between us, and as a result, made us an even more divided nation. The differ-

---

14 Grynbaumo.i., M.M., & Herndon, A. V. (2019, March 6). "Democrats Reject Fox News as 2020 Debate Host, Citing Ties to Trump." *The New York Times*. Retrieved from https://www.nytimes.com/2019/03/06/business/media/democrats-fox-news-debate-host.html

ence between the simpler news time of the past and the current complex news world in which we reside can appear confusing to most of us. We may disagree with the perceived angle of a story or the motivation behind an opinion or program. We may long for the halcyon days of Walter Cronkite; I know I do. But those are not reasons to jettison or malign the entire system, or to throw in the towel or tap out on the news.

As viewers and readers, we are all stakeholders in this business of news. We have a stake, an interest, in just how well or misinformed we are. The more we know about both the world and the news, the better off we are. Extremes are dangerous for both our society and our news. The more extreme the viewpoints, the less reliable they become. The competition for our news attention will continue to increase. And there will always be special interests on the fringe trying to meddle in our news and peddle their agenda.

It is the mainstream news media that I'm familiar with. I've attempted to chronicle some of the growing pains it's endured (which I witnessed) over the last thirty years, at times agreeing that much of the added scrutiny was deserved, even constructive. Yet, the same media that's been battered, bruised, attacked, dissected, analyzed, repurposed, and repackaged... continues to survive. We love to hate it, but mostly we need it.

My journey through the world of news has been a rich and somewhat rare learning experience. It is a ride that spans four decades. It took me two books spilling over 700 pages to attempt to describe an often thrilling, exhausting, distressing, dangerous, engaging, gratifying, and always enlightening ride. I needed to sift, sort, assemble, contemplate, edit, and reflect upon both monumental and inconsequential events before I could begin to describe my experiences and share my observations.

As I traveled back through a sometimes hazy maze of memories and emotions, I remained guided by a steadfast belief that an informed society is much better than an ignorant one. A strong and independent news media is the transformational tool that can make the difference between the two. Information is empowering, and we should all yearn for empowerment.

The news, our news, is imperfect at best, but it's the best we have, and I'm thankful we do.

SELECTED BIBLIOGRAPHY

Alderman, Derek H. "TV News Hyper-Coverage and the Representation of Place: Observations on the O. J. Simpson Case." **Geografiska Annaler. Series B, Human Geography**, vol. 79, no. 2, 1997, pp. 83-95. **JSTOR**, www.jstor.org/stable/490620. Accessed 5 May 2020.

Brenan, M. (2019). "Americans' Trust in Mass Media Edges Down to 41%." Gallup. Retrieved May 5, 2020, from https://news.gallup.com/poll/267047/americans-trust-mass-media-edges-down.aspx

Brenner, M. (1997, February). "American Nightmare: The Ballad of Richard Jewell." **Vanity Fair**.

Browne, D. (2014, March 23). "How Pakistan Succumbed to a Hard-drug Epidemic." **The Telegraph**.

"Convention on the Rights of the Child." UNICEF. Retrieved from https://www.unicef.org/child-rights-convention 5/15/2020.

"Five Principles of Ethical Journalism." (n.d.). Ethical Journalism Network. Retrieved May 05, 2020, from https://ethicaljournalismnetwork.org/who-we-are/5-principles-of-journalism

Gramlich, J. (2020). "How We Evaluated Americans' Trust in 30 News Sources." Pew Research Center. Retrieved May 5, 2020, from https://www.pewresearch.org/fact-tank/2020/01/24/qa-how-pew-research-center-evaluated-americans-trust-in-30-news-sources/

Griffin, M. (2017). "How News Has Changed." Macalester College. Retrieved May 5, 2020, from https://www.macalester.edu/news/2017/04/how-news-has-changed/

Katzman, Kenneth & Thomas, Clayton. "Afghanistan: Post-Taliban Governance, Security, and U.S. Policy," report, November 7, 2017; Washington D.C.. (https://digital.library.unt.edu/ark:/67531/metadc1043173/: accessed May 5, 2020), University of North Texas Libraries, UNT Digital Library, https://digital.library.unt.edu; crediting UNT Libraries Government Documents Department.

Konner, J., Risser, J., & Wattenberg, B. (2001). **Television's Performance on Election Night 2000: A Report for CNN** (Rep.). Atlanta, GA: CNN.

Newman, N., Richard Fletcher, Levy, D. A. L., & Nielsen, R. K. (2016). "Reuters Institute Digital News Report 2016." Reuters Institute for the Study of Journalism.

Nielsen, R. K. and Sambrook, R. 2016. "What is Happening to Television News?" Oxford: Reuters Institute for the Study of Journalism.

Ostrow, R. J. (2000). "Richard Jewell Case Study." Columbia University. Retrieved May 5, 2020, from http://www.columbia.edu/itc/journalism/j6075/edit/readings/jewell.html

Patterson, T. E. (2008). "Young People Flee from the News, Whatever the Source." **Television Quarterly**, **38**, 32-35.

Robert D. Richards & Clay Calvert. (2002). "**Press Coverage of the JonBenét Ramsey Murder and its Legal Implications: A Dialogue with John and Patsy Ramsey and Their Attorney, L. Lin Wood.**" 10 COMMLAW CONSPECTUS 227. Available at: https://scholarship.law.edu/commlaw/vol10/iss2/5

Rosenberg, H., & Feldman, C. S. (2009). **No Time to Think: The Menace of Media Speed and the 24-hour News Cycle**. New York, NY: Continuum International Publishing Group.

Shepard, A. C. (2000). "The Columbine Shooting: Live Television Coverage." Retrieved May 05, 2020, from http://www.columbia.edu/itc/journalism/j6075/edit/readings/columbine.html

Wonneberger, Anke & Kim, Su Jung. (2017). "TV News Exposure of Young People in Changing Viewing Environments: A Longitudinal, Cross-national Comparison Using People-meter Data." **International Journal of Communication Systems**. 11.

Zuckerman, E. (2008). "International News: Bringing About the Golden Age." Media Re:public. Harvard University. Retrieved May 5, 2020, from https://cyber.harvard.edu/sites/cyber.law.harvard.edu/files/International%20News_MR.pdf

ABOUT THE AUTHOR

Photo by Sam Sewell

Tim Ortman has spent 35 years - a lifetime, working in television news. He's worked for all major U.S television news networks (NBC, ABC, CBS, CNN, FOX) and the BBC. As an Emmy Award winning cameraman and producer, his understanding of the overall television production process is comprehensive with extensive experience shooting, lighting, story editing, writing and producing.

Over the span of four decades, his globe-trotting travels have taken him on assignments in five continents, covering everything from war, revolution, famine, terrorist attacks, Cold War Summits, and the fall of Communism to presidential elections, Papal visits, Olympiads and Olympic Park bombings and the occasional press conference. He has been fortunate to have occupied a front row seat on numerous historically significant happenings.

His view of the network news world was formed early on. As an impressionable 20-something staff cameraman for NBC News, Tim was based in Europe during the 1980's, when the news biz was at its most trustworthy zenith. After seven years of international news coverage, he returned home to focus on the domestic side of world news. He formed an independent production company which enabled him to build upon his NBC reputation while fostering working relationships with the other news networks which expanded his news resume.

His stateside return intersected with the explosion of 24-hour news. He worked, watched and witnessed as a transformational change overtook the business of network news. As a network veteran, he possess a rich perspective from the inside looking out which was formed over a tumultuous time in news. *News Division* is his insightful reflection throughout that period.

After a long time of uninterrupted bliss in the television world, Tim hit the ‹pause› button to pursue another, yet completely different passion. While living and working overseas, Tim became a fan of wine and followed that fascination to produce his own brand of wine. He eventually become a Sommelier with the Court of Master Sommeliers and joined the esteemed wine organizations the Commanderie de Bordeaux and La Confrerie des Chevaliers du Tastevin.

Acknowledgements

Working in the news media for any length of time can simultaneously open your eyes and toughen your skin. You quickly learn to insulate yourself from the hardship, sadness, tragedy, and death so inextricably linked to the coverage of news. Compared to that weight, the cacophony of criticism hurled at the mainstream news media is barely audible to the members of the "working press". Yet, I must acknowledge I did take note when I heard a sitting President refer to the news media as the "enemy of the American people." It was a retaliatory statement, the product of unflattering news coverage of candidate and subsequently, President Trump. It was also one of many reasons I decided to embark on a literary journey writing *News Real* followed by *News Division*. In doing so, my motivation was not to retaliate against the President and his supporters, but rather to provide a very real and accurate picture of the news media in which I lived and worked; a picture of an informative ally not an enemy.

What I know about the news business has been enriched by who I know in the news business...the bonds I formed and the friendships I made. I'm fortunate to have so many to call upon for valuable dialogue and keen insight. I'm indebted to many for aid in my reflection on stories from many years ago. The facts of those stories are easily verifiable. But the nuances and aftereffects from those stories were made more impactful by reliving those events with those who lived them as they unfold-
˙· Steve Azzato, Gordy McLean, Jack Chesnutt, Mike Mosher,

Audrey Beles-Grady, Stacy Brady, Heather Allan, Phil Alongi, Mike Taibbi, Sandy Gleysteen, Conan Nolan, James Crumley, and the unparalleled one-two punch of husband and wife news team, Sam Sewell and Judy Lieber. They all added clarity and depth to so many memories. Thanks for letting me tap into your cerebral news archives. It was rewarding working with you then, and reliving those many rewards now. That collective reflection made this book a more gratifying and worthwhile endeavor.

A network news veteran, colleague, and longtime friend, Derwin Johnson, also contributed to that contemplative process of looking back. And, as I buried myself in this book, his perspective helped to reiterated and reinforce some of the salient points of network news. His not so gentle media coaching added much needed practice to a very unpracticed author.

I had the good fortune of working with Martin Fletcher, one of the best writers in broadcast journalism. He continues that excellence with his post network literary career. When I completed my first book he urged, "...get on with the next one, you have loads to share!" Martin, your advice like your writing is inspiring.

A huge note of thanks is due the team at Incorgnito Publishing Press. Publisher Michael Conant's initial insight allowed for the launch of my first book. That same enduring and valuable insight paved the way for this second book and allowed for me to grow as an author. Most writers rely heavily on their editors. I've relied more heavily than most on mine. What began two books ago as an enlightening relationship has grown into a full-blown creative collaboration. I wouldn't want to write without the editing and input of Jennifer Collins, editor extraordinaire.

To Julia, Alexa, Alec, Aubrey, Jeff and John; your sincere interest and unwavering support were an enormous boost and confidence builder. Any and all achievements are made more special when shared among a loving family.

CREDITS

This book is a work of art produced by
Incorgnito Publishing Press.

Jennifer Collins - Editor

Monica Baker - Proof Editor

Star Foos - Artist/Designer

Daria Lacy - Graphic Production

Janice Bini - Chief Reader

Michael Conant - Publisher

October 2020

Incorgnito Publishing Press

Direct inquiries to mconant@incorgnitobooks.com